AUSTRALIA'S CENTRAL AND WESTERN OUTBACK

THE DRIVING GUIDE

AUSTRALIA'S CENTRAL AND WESTERN OUTBACK

THE DRIVING GUIDE

Ian Read

LITTLE HILLS PRESS

Little Hills Press Pty Ltd
Regent House, 37-43 Alexander Street,
Crows Nest, NSW, 2065, Australia

ISBN 1 86315 061 7

Printed in Australia

DISCLAIMER

While every effort has been made to check the accuracy of the information contained herein, no responsibility is accepted by the author or publisher for inaccuracies or changes which may have occurred during the writing, publication or sale of this work. If things have changed please notify the publisher so that following editions can be updated. All used contributions will be acknowledged.

CONTENTS

ACKNOWLEDGEMENTS

I wish to thank the following people and organisations who helped make this work a reality: the Department of Road Transport, South Australia; the Department of Transport and Works, Northern Territory; Department of Conservation and Land Management (WA); Main Roads Western Australia; Charles Burfitt of Little Hills Press; Central Lands Council; Hamersley Iron Pty Ltd; Ian Smith of Carnegie Station, WA; Ray Rainford of Rainford Motors, Nowra, his son Jeff and son-in-law Steve for keeping my vehicle going; Graham Spetere, Noel Clegg, Warwick Gamble, Ian Pepper, Alison Treasure and Jim Sears for accompanying me on my journeys; and Coralyn Treasure, my number one travelling companion, for her uncritical and financial support. Most of the routes described herein were undertaken in one of the following vehicles: Morris Marina, Holden Kingswood, Ford Laser or Nissan Pulsar.

PREFACE

This is a book about outback Australia. Not all of outback Australia, but a portion of it centred around, and spreading out from, that part of the country where South Australia, Western Australia and the Northern Territory meet and share common borders: the Central and Western Outback.

Lying immediately north of the settled agricultural lands of South Australia, north and east of the Western Australian wheat belt, and arbitrarily limited by the tropical desert plains of the Northern Territory, the Great Sandy Desert of Western Australia, and the dry arid plains of the Lake Eyre Basin, the Central and Western Outback occupies that portion of Australia commonly referred to by geographers as the Western Plateau. Its moderately elevated tracts of level to slightly undulating country lies between the Central Lowlands (which includes the Lake Eyre Basin) to the east and the coastal plains and cliffs of the Indian and Southern Oceans to the west and south. Whilst mostly a land of level skylines, the Central and Western Outback does contain some of the grandest upland country of the continent, namely the Flinders, MacDonnell and Hamersley Ranges and their outlying lesser ranges.

The countryside of the Central and Western Outback is predominantly arid, fringed on its southern and south-western margins by semi-arid lands. Being outback country it is sparsely populated, but like other sparsely populated areas elsewhere, the resonance of the people it houses fills the landscape. The principal activities of these people are the extensive grazing on natural pastures of beef cattle and sheep, and in specific regions and localities, mining and tourism.

The undertaking of journeys to this part of Australia is increasing in popularity. There are a number of reasons for this. Firstly, the Central Outback is in relatively easy reach of the populated south-east corner of the continent; similarly the Western Outback is in easy reach for those people living in the settled south-west corner; people can travel there and back along the sealed highways from their respective 'corners' within two weeks (the length of the non-summer school holidays). Secondly, many Australians are realising that they do not know their own country. Television programmes, especially documentaries, have gone a long way in showing people what there is to be seen and experienced in the outback. Thirdly, the mining boom and 'beef road' programme, initiated in the 1960s, has opened up much of the Central and Western Outback with the construction of new and upgraded roads; the sealing of major outback highways has increased accessibility as well. Fourthly, publicity associated with mining ventures and related environmental problems has drawn further attention to previously 'unknown' areas. In other words, more information has become available to the potential travelling public. Coupled with increased affluence, and supplemented by massive increased sales of four-wheel drive (4WD) vehicles and, to a lesser extent, campervans, many people have turned their travelling attention inwards, to the outback. These vehicles, through rarely necessary, have given an added confidence to travel to remote places.

Anyone with a normal amount of common sense can safely complete a journey along any of the routes described in this book. Nonetheless, travellers contemplating such a journey should be well prepared. People still occasionally perish out there, primarily through ignorance. Vehicles should be in top condition and, if of conventional drive, have a good ground clearance. Bush driving experience on remote roads and tracks is an advantage, as is a rudimentary mechanical knowledge. Maps should be sought and studied. In remote regions, or off the beaten track, a reliable person should know where you are going. A breakdown or accident on an isolated road could see you stranded or suffering from injury. Thought must be given to the time available, food and water requirements for all the people present, and necessary items for the vehicle. Information about the road ahead, especially in remote country, should be continually sought.

Travel with a purpose. It might be to visit old mining sites and to do some fossicking, to experience the wild, arid coastlines and do some fishing, to travel through wild and remote places, or to simply appreciate the variety of outback landscapes. Learn everything there is to know about the country one plans to visit: its climate, its extremes, its economic pursuits, its Aboriginal heritage, the nature of its bush, its landscapes and its non-Aboriginal history. Much of this information is contained herein, but more information is always available.

Do not just talk to other travellers and roadhouse operators (though they are the people to ask about the road ahead), seek out the locals. If they see you are interested in them and 'their country' (they live there after all) then more than likely you will be treated as a guest rather than just another tourist.

Nobody likes tourists.

They are people who drive too fast, cut up wet unsealed roads leaving huge ruts that dry with razor-sharp edges, camp near stock watering places, leave litter (which includes cigarette butts, orange peel, tissues and toilet paper), take photographs secretively, demand immediate attention, and complain. This is still frontier country in many ways, and is not like your local neighbourhood. Respect the people who live there. After all, if you are taking the effort to travel outback, why not put some effort into the journey's preparation and advancement. Whatever happens, it is sure to be one of those once-in-a-lifetime experiences. Become a traveller. As a traveller you will be introduced to things that as a tourist you would never see.

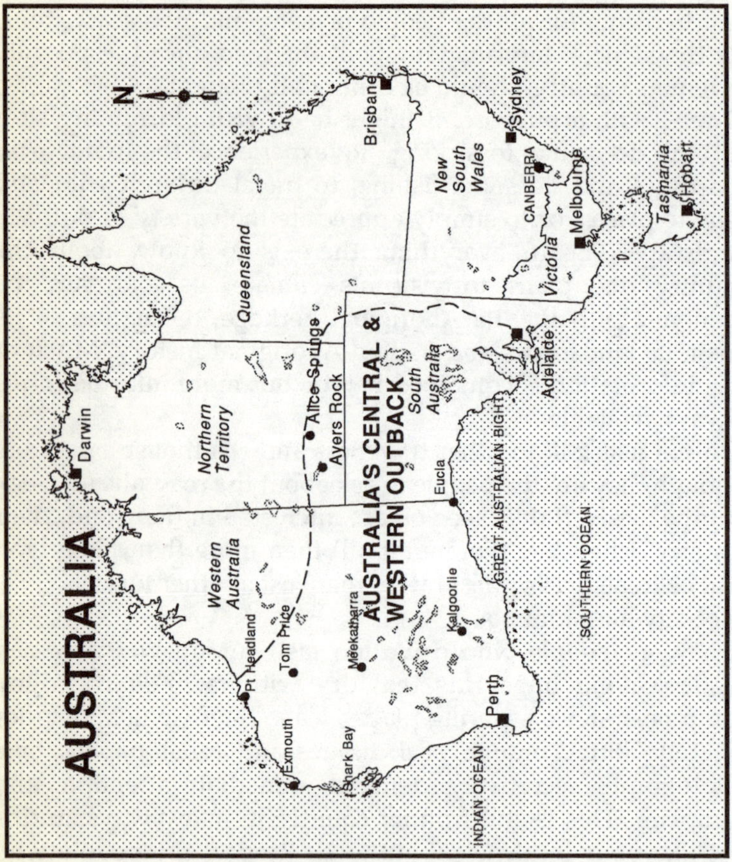
AUSTRALIA
N
Darwin
Northern Territory
Queensland
Western Australia
Pt Headland
Tom Price
Exmouth
Shark Bay
Meekatharra
Kalgoorlie
Perth
INDIAN OCEAN
Alice Springs
Ayers Rock
AUSTRALIA'S CENTRAL & WESTERN OUTBACK
South Australia
Eucla
GREAT AUSTRALIAN BIGHT
SOUTHERN OCEAN
Brisbane
New South Wales
Sydney
CANBERRA
Melbourne
Victoria
Adelaide
Tasmania
Hobart

PART ONE

CHAPTER ONE

INTRODUCTION

THE CENTRAL AND WESTERN OUTBACK

Curtin Springs is a working cattle station and roadhouse located east of the Ayers Rock Resort in the Northern Territory. It is a popular stopover for tourists heading for 'the Rock'. Aborigines use Curtin Springs too, as a refuelling point as they move between Alice Springs, the Pitjantjatjara Lands to the south, and the Western Desert communities out Docker River way. They often make their camp a short distance away from the roadhouse. Sometimes they approach tourists in the roadhouse camping ground, as often as not asking for food. This is not so unusual amongst Pitjantjatjara and other traditional clan groups. If someone has something they want they will (usually shyly) ask for it. Refusal does not offend, it simply states that your need was greater than theirs. If their request is satisfied, the provider may ask for something in return, as the spirit of reciprocity is strong. I once exchanged food for knowledge.

He was a young grandfather; not yet an elder. He told me that he was recently divorced. His former wife lived at Tennant Creek while he and his new wife lived at Indulkana, a Pitjantjatjara settlement north-west of Marla, South Australia.

"You're a slow learner", I suggested, "having two wives."

He laughed. With the ice broken I felt I could ask him about his relationship to the country. He told me his mother's country was Uluru (Ayers Rock) and his father's country was Pukatja (Ernabella). This reference to 'country' told initiated

Pitjantjatjara people more than where his mother or father was born. It also told them what stories from the *tjukurpa* (Dreamtime is a very rough translation) they knew and were entitled to know (knowledge of the *tjukurpa* stories and their relationship with other stories being a source of prestige and power); and what group within the clan that person belonged to (influencing who he could talk to, who he must avoid, and who he might marry: there are practical reasons for this, avoiding incestuous relationships being one).

I asked him if he knew the stories connected with his mother's and father's country. "Yes", he replied.

"A little or a lot?"

"Mm, just this much", he replied, using his fingers to explain.

"Do you know the stories from beyond Uluru to beyond Ernabella?" I enquired. The stories from the *tjukurpa* are handed down from generation to generation, from initiate to initiate. Familiar with the stories from their own parents' country, the details of which increase with age and further initiations, the Pitjantjatjara also know that the stories extend beyond their parents' country into neighbouring groups and clans, the details of which may only become known if a person travels, or has some connections with groups and clans further away. Many of these stories are known to extend long distances; some, such as the Wanambi (rainbow serpent) story, crossed the continent. The stories were, and still are over much of the Central and Western Outback, made visual by features in the landscape: certain rocks, groups of trees, waterholes, creek beds etc; and aural by chants and songs, the beat and timbre of the songs being common along the length of the story. For this reason sometimes the stories are known as songlines. My informant told me he did know the stories from beyond his parents' country, but "only a little bit".

We continued to speak of country and places. Oodnadatta ("I don't like there, I get homesick for my country; it's too open, no trees"); Marree ("I spent a month there"); Nepabunna, Port Augusta, Whyalla, all in South Australia. Then we headed north to Papunya, Ti-Tree, Tennant Creek ("I often go there to see my daughters"). Moving out of the Northern Territory, our minds took us to Western Australia: Kununurra, Broome, Wiluna, Meekatharra ("Yes, yes, I've been there. That's all my country [the songlines again?] all one country. All around I've been, all over"). The man got up. He had eaten, he had spoken, and now finished, he left. End of business.

I sat and thought about what I had been told. The grandfather was certainly well travelled, but I did not have the opportunity to ask if he had been following the stories, the songlines, thus proclaiming all this land to be one country, his country. Elsewhere I had read that, during the early days of European occupation, some Aborigines travelled far and wide, beyond their parents' country, either trading, or tracing the stories. Perhaps this man was maintaining the tradition.

Unlike the settled south-east and south-west corners of the continent, the Central and Western Outback regions along with the country to the north, still have a strong Aboriginal presence, where some traditions are still maintained and where the Aboriginal Law is still strong. If one were to start in the midst of Pitjantjatjara country where Curtin Springs is located, for instance, and move towards the south-eastern or western corners of Australia, one would, generally speaking, move from country where Aboriginal Law and traditions were strong to country where they were virtually non-existent, there being significant declines in its influence as one moves from the deserts to the cattle country, from the cattle country to the sheep country (a major decline here), from the sheep country to the closely settled agricultural country, and from the agricultural country to the cities. This decline is related to a number of factors, the most significant perhaps being the duration and intensity of European occupation. The agricultural lands and outback sheep country were either cleared or fenced into paddocks; here there were conflicts over land and water resources, with the Aborigines being either displaced, dispersed or exterminated. With this obliteration of the Aboriginal landscape went the stories, the language, the culture and the understanding of the Law. In cattle country, with its less dense occupation, vestiges of the traditional ways remained, albeit in a corrupted form. In the desert lands beyond the cattle country the traditions remained alive up until at least the 1950s and 60s, when a superficial blanket of European occupation was thrown over much of the Western Outback in the form of the Woomera Rocket Range and the atomic testing facilities at Emu and Maralinga. With it came tracks, trucks, European Law, and the coercive removal of the indigenous population to the fringes of the cattle country. Not all Aborigines were collected in this final round-up; as late as the 1970s two traditional Mandildjara people of the Gibson Desert were brought into Wiluna, while in the 1980s a group was found living in the Great Sandy Desert.

The European occupation and settlement of the Central and Western Outback advanced on two fronts: the Central Outback from the then settled districts of South Australia; the Western Outback from the settled districts of Western Australia. The first wave of occupation, the explorers, occurred during the middle years of the 19th Century. Edward Eyre, in 1841, after having explored the Flinders and Gawlers Ranges crossed from east to west via the southern Nullarbor Plain. Between 1858-62 John McDouall Stuart explored the Flinders Ranges, the Gairdner Plain area of South Australia's Far North, and parts of Central Australia, finally crossing the continent and reaching the northern coastline at a point near present-day Darwin. In Western Australia, F.T. Gregory made a number of explorations over a twenty year period. Between 1840 and 1861 he ventured across the sandplains north-east of Perth, made his way over the Murchison, Gascoyne and Fortescue River Basins, and crossed the plains, hills and ranges of the Pilbara. Other lesser known explorers followed, filling in the gaps. Between these two major areas of exploration lay a vast tract of unknown country. This was explored by perhaps the greatest unsung hero of Australian exploration, Ernest Giles, who during 1872-76 traversed the Gibson and Great Victoria Deserts between the then established overland telegraph line in the east and the sparsely occupied pastoral country in the west. Though great were his travels, his name is barely remembered for he unfortunately discovered land that was then deemed to be of no economic use. Explorers achieved fame either by finding lands capable of exploitation, be it grazing country, future stock routes or mineral deposits, or by dying in this cause.

Following the explorers, though not necessarily immediately, came the pastoralists. In the Western Outback pastoral expansion was somewhat slower than in the east of the country, as distances from markets were enormous and the population base was low. Gold had been discovered in the 1850s in eastern Australia and its population and settlements grew at a rapid rate. In the west the local population had to be supplemented by convict labour. Transportation did not begin until 1850, but following its introduction the pastoral occupation began to expand beyond the few isolated stations then in existence. The increasing availability of ticket-of-leave and expiree labour enabled the sheep grazing industry to move into the near coastal areas of the Murchison, Gascoyne and Pilbara regions by the 1870s. Mostly, grazing was restricted to the major drainage lines and their adjacent floodplains. These areas were developed first, for not only did they provide adequate feed and water, they were relatively accessible to the coast. Ports were established at Geraldton, Cossack and later at Carnarvon. Commercial wool production was based on shepherds tending flocks on outstations up to 120km from a permanently occupied home station.

With the introduction of corrugated iron water tanks and roof catchments, and the drilling of bores in the 1880s, the drier country beyond the rivers was infilled so that by the 1900s most of the above regions, as well as the Goldfields (apart from the sandplain country) and parts of the Nullarbor, were under pastoral occupation. Only on the desert fringes in the east did further occupation occur early in the 20th century. Though the mainstay of this pastoral occupation was sheep over the past few decades beef cattle have become the dominant livestock in many areas, particularly in the eastern areas of the Pilbara, Gascoyne and Goldfields regions.

The Central Outback underwent a similar expansion. Shepherds and their flocks occupied the Flinders Ranges and the saltbush plains of the Lake Eyre district by the 1870s. In the 1880s the drilling of bores into the Great Artesian Basin allowed the drier tracts of country to be infilled. By the turn of the century the sheep frontier had enclosed the mulga and saltbush plains of northern South Australia, while further north the cattlemen (sheep having already been tried and found wanting) occupied the northernmost plains of northern South Australia and the rangelands of Central Australia. Unlike their western counterparts who could use coastal shipping to transport their produce to market, the pastoralists of the Central Outback used the original Ghan railway to transport their produce. The railway ran northward through the Flinders Ranges out onto the arid saltbush plains via Marree, terminating firstly at Oodnadatta, then later at Alice Springs. To reach these distant railheads the settlers, like their Western counterparts, often used camel trains to transport supplies and produce.

The pastoral occupation of these regions of the Central and Western Outback had a devastating effect on the Aboriginal population. The earliest settlers had to live and run their stock near sources of permanent water; this obviously put them in conflict with the local Aborigines. If attempts to absorb the newcomers into Aboriginal clans failed (it mostly did though many shepherds took Aboriginal 'wives'), or if they occupied ceremonial grounds, or threatened water supplies, the Aborigines retaliated, usually by killing stock, for which they themselves became victims of retaliation either by intentional killings or by displacement.

In some areas the Aborigines, after pacification, became absorbed into the growing pastoral industry. As many of the grown males became stockmen, the old, the young and most of the women, having lost a major determinant of their economic and social livelihood, gravitated to the isolated homesteads and infant townships. For some, this was a reasonable alternative to having their traditional lives disrupted because, if still living on their own 'country' they could continue to practise aspects of their ceremonies and maintain contact with their sacred sites. The governments of the time though did not rest; originally denying their existence through the concept of *Terra nullius* (roughly translated as unpeopled land, a concept only officially dismissed by the High Court in 1992) they moved the Aborigines, often forcibly, onto reserves. By so doing they separated families, even to the point of removing half-caste children from their mothers. Some of these they trained as servants for wealthy European families. Many of these separated people are still alive today.

The results were tragic. As kinship ties were broken and most became alienated from their own 'country', the spirit of the people departed leaving behind those degraded people that many non-Aborigines see as 'the typical Aborigine'. Whilst they offer a visible presence in many outback towns today, it is not the full story. Trapped in a cycle of poverty and unemployment, with a high incidence of disease and alcoholism, they are but a microcosm of Aboriginal society. Australian Aborigines, like all invaded people, have been hated, despised and patronised, but most commonly, misunderstood.

The environmental impact of the pastoral occupation of the Central and Western Outback was severe, although the severity varied from place to place. The greatest impact was, obviously enough, that of stock. By the end of the 19th century, millions of hooves had trampled and compacted the soil, while millions of mouths had eaten the edible grasses and shrubs. As older members of the plant community died or disappeared, the new generations were instantly devoured. In the dry times the stock ate the mulga and ring-barked other trees and shrubs over wide areas. Even today mulga is cut down for animals unable to get any other herbage during times of drought. The cutting of mulga thins its stands in the shrubland country with the result that understorey grasses replace the lower stature shrubs. Although grasses are welcome food they are short-lived plants and quickly die off during prolonged droughts, a time when palatable shrubs are needed. Ultimately the introduction of stock has changed the floristic structure of the vegetation.

The problem was exacerbated by overstocking, which during times of drought has seen vast tracts of country partially or totally eaten out, particularly on the saltbush plains of South Australia. As the plant life was browsed and cropped and their roots destroyed, the top soil was no longer bound together. Strong winds then lifted the soil and transported it elsewhere, often as far as the south-east coastline. In the Western Outback significant tracts of mulga country have been degraded by overstocking in the northern Murchison and eastern Gascoyne regions, particularly on the stony country. Where once there was a relatively dense mulga shrubland, today the stands of mulga are sparse and in some places dead, their passing marked by the gaunt, dried sticks that were once living shrubs. Underneath, the ground cover has altered too with just the occasional squat shrub breaking through the rocky ground.

Rabbits also changed the character of the land. Starting from a small population released near Geelong in 1859 they spread across south-eastern Australia, reaching southern Queensland by 1886. The rabbit frontier moved out across the continent south of the tropics, all but devastating the then pastoral industry. By the end of the 19th Century it had reached Western Australia. The government of the day, realising it was going to be a major pest, built a succession of 'rabbit-proof fences' (including one that was over 1,700km long) but these proved to be inadequate as some rabbits had already passed beyond the line of the fences. Eradication of rabbits was expensive and ineffective. Myxomatosis, a viral disease, was introduced in the 1950s; this partially reduced the population but the virulence of the virus decreased with successive generations. Rabbits are still a problem today.

Other introduced animals have reeked havoc on the landscape too: goats are voracious eaters, stripping virtually any edible plants in their path; foxes are cunning killers which do not require surface waters for survival - they have survived by eating small marsupials, often to the point of extinction; while cats have bred to become lethal hunters.

Station developments have also had an impact on the landscape. The erection of fences around boundaries and paddocks required millions of fence posts. Though steel wire was used from early on, the posts were of wood. Obtained locally each post was hewn from standing timber. Given the small stature of the local trees, each plant only provided one or two fence posts, hence millions of trees were removed. Local timber was also used for the construction of yards and buildings, further depleting this resource.

The impact of stocking varied from place to place depending on the prevailing vegetation, topography, remoteness of country, density of settlement and the attitude of the pastoralist, consequently the land suffered varying degrees of degradation. Nonetheless, it is still possible to find relatively pristine country within these rangelands, country that has been only lightly or never grazed. Fortunately, attitudes change and the dry country environments are becoming better understood and many problems and mistakes of the past can be avoided with careful management practices.

Not all of the Central and Western Outback has been occupied by pastoralists. Between the main grazing areas of South Australia/Northern Territory and Western Australia lie two of Australia's great deserts: the Gibson and Great Victoria. Though not subjected to grazing, the depopulating of Aborigines following the establishment of the Woomera Rocket Range has altered the nature of these predominantly wilderness environments. Up until very recently in Aboriginal history all of this land was occupied, albeit at low population densities. In order to encourage the growth of grasses for game animals, the Pitjantjatjara and other desert clans utilised a practice called firestick farming. This involved burning off patches of spinifex country during the cooler season when fires were easier to control so promoting the growth of grasses and forming a patchwork pattern across the landscape with the unburnt spinifex. Not only did the patchwork pattern reduce the likelihood of a massive lightning-induced hot season fire, it also produced a mosaic of different animal habitats resulting in a diversity of animal species.

Mammals such as the rufous hare-wallaby need vegetation of differing ages to survive. They nibble on the young, soft green shoots of spinifex and other shrubs and herbs that appear after fire, while they shelter in mature, unburnt spinifex; a safe, relatively cool hide that offers shade but no nourishment. With the absence of regular cool season burns, the country assumed a widespread uniformity as spinifex dominated the landscape. With the loss of diversity of plant species, some animal populations declined. Furthermore, the spinifex became prone to hot season wildfires that completely burned the country over wide areas. The burrowing bettong, virtually extinct on the mainland (but surviving on some off-shore islands) may well have succumbed to this altered fire regime. Although it could have survived hot season fires by retreating underground, the widespread burns of these fires temporarily removed the vegetation, leaving the animal hungry and easy prey for predators.

This situation is changing on two fronts: firstly by Aboriginal clans reoccupying what they call their 'grandparents' country' and living semi-traditionally by utilising some of the old practices with modern technological ways; and secondly by the declaration of nature reserves which are managed in accordance with past Aboriginal practices, such as firestick farming, again using modern techniques. This reoccupation has a number of benefits: not only does it help restore the area's ecology to pre-contact conditions, but it utilises Aboriginal knowledge which can only help in land management practices.

Coupled with the pastoralists moving into what was then

Aboriginal country were the miners. The earliest miners generally arrived as parts of a rush. As the explorers and pioneering pastoralists moved about the Central and Western Outback any mineral-rich outcrop or deposit could set off a rush as outsiders moved in to seek their fortunes. This happened at Coolgardie, Western Australia, in that region that was to become known as the Eastern Goldfields. Although other mineral deposits, including gold, had been discovered before 1892, the first year of the Coolgardie rush, it was the finds in that vicinity that set off one of the greatest gold rushes in Australia. Within hours of news being received of the discoveries many would-be prospectors were heading east across the waterless sandplains. Over the remaining years of that decade there were further finds, and by 1900 there were over 50 towns and townships in the Coolgardie-Kalgoorlie-Leonora districts. This gold rush had the effect of raising Western Australia's population nearly three and a half times in a ten year period, climbing from just over 53,000 in 1891 to over 184,000 in 1901.

Further rushes in the region, as well as in the Yilgarn region to the west (some finds in the Yilgarn pre-dated the Coolgardie rush) and the Murchison Goldfields to the north-west, created more mines, townships and towns, raising the state's population to over 282,000 by 1911. This population increase provided the impetus for the European occupation of the mining country: tracks became roads; railways expanded; tramways ran through the bush to extract timber for the mines; tents and hessian dwellings became corrugated iron houses; and brick homes clustered around imposing government buildings and hotels. These became the towns which continued to thrive as long as payable gold was found. Many towns had a fairly short life, for instance Bulong near Kalgoorlie or Day Dawn near Cue; others hung on becoming service centres for surrounding stations or passing travellers, eg Menzies; some were revitalised with new mining activity and/or tourism, eg Coolgardie; while one, Kalgoorlie, became a major regional centre.

While gold was the main impetus for rushes in the Western Outback (Marble Bar and Nullagine in the Pilbara were also founded on this metal) it was the discovery of other minerals which lead to the establishment of mines, towns and related infrastructure; in fact, virtually all the settlements of the Western Outback, except for the coastal ports, seaside settlements and highway roadhouses have a mining rather than a pastoral history, for instance: Northampton (lead); Wittenoom (asbestos); Newman, Tom Price, Paraburdoo, Pannawonica (iron ore); and Kambalda (nickel). The establishment of these mines has led to the construction of roads, railways, powerlines, pipelines, etc, thus populating the countryside (albeit somewhat sparsely) and entrenching European occupation.

In the Central Outback the impetus of mining was far less dramatic. Arltunga, east of Alice Springs, was the source of a minor rush which led to the creation of the first township in Central Australia; a short time later the township of Stuart was laid out near the telegraph repeater station of Alice Springs in order to service the Arltunga field. Further south opal was discovered at Coober Pedy, and later at Andamooka and Mintabie, each of which have grown into very idiosyncratic towns and townships peopled by a variety of characters. Elsewhere, mining in the Central Outback has been a large-scale affair developed by corporations, for instance: Leigh Creek (brown coal), Iron Knob (iron ore) and Roxby Downs (gold, copper and uranium).

While mining played a part in the occupation of the Central Outback, it was the Overland Telegraph Line and the original Ghan railway that opened up this country to exploitation. Completed in 1872, the Overland Telegraph Line was considered to be a major engineering achievement of its time. It ran from Adelaide to Darwin connecting up with a telegraph line that ran across Asia (and under the sea) from Europe and London. Its construction enabled the Australian colonies to be in quick contact with Great Britain. The OT Line, as it became known, followed an old Aboriginal pathway that connected a series of mound springs (natural outlets of the Great Artesian Basin) across the dry, arid plains of northern South Australia. At intervals telegraph repeater stations were built as the telegraphed signal weakened over long distances; these stations became the first European settlements in the area, while the OT Line itself became the route of travellers. Following this same route over much of its length was the Ghan Railway, a narrow gauge line which, due to the use of steam locomotion, was dependent on the reliable water supplies of the mound springs. The Ghan railway and its attendant telegraph line eventually superseded the OT Line; the repeater stations declined in importance while railway townships became the area's focal and supply points, places like Marree, Oodnadatta and Alice Springs.

Other settlements in the Central Outback, of which there are few, developed as combined pastoral and highway service centres (eg Kingoonya, Glendambo); tourist centres (eg Ayers Rock Resort); defence establishments (eg Woomera); Aboriginal communities (eg Docker River) or highway roadhouses (eg Nullarbor).

CHAPTER TWO

BEFORE YOU GO

Potential travellers planning to undertake journeys to the Central and Western Outback need to give some thought to their forthcoming adventure. While more people than ever before are venturing into this region, and traffic, at least during the cooler months, is as busy as it has ever been, this is still remote and isolated country where you may have to depend on yourself to get out of trouble. Below are some tips based on personal experience which you may find helpful, either as a first-time outback traveller, or one with a few journeys under the belt.

Transport: How to Go

Although this book is primarily aimed at people travelling by self-drive vehicles, this is not the only way to get outback. Those who do not wish to sit for hours behind the wheel might like to consider the *fly-drive* option, flying from home to a large outback centre, then hiring a vehicle to tour the local district. This is an expensive way of travelling, but does at least save the tedium of getting to the outback. One disadvantage of this option is that you have little chance to acclimatise to the new environment.

Joining a *coach tour* is another option; this can be either very expensive, if staying in overnight accommodation and having all meals bought or prepared for you; or moderately expensive if on a camping tour where you are expected to contribute to meal preparation, setting up camp, etc. Advantages with these options is that most of the work is done for you; disadvantages include not having the flexibility to linger in places which appeal to you, and to being stuck with the same group of people, some of which you may not like - it also limits your interaction with the local population. These types of tours come into their own when they are of short duration or when visiting relatively inaccessible areas.

Non-driving independent-minded people might like to consider using ground-based *public transport*. For instance, bus lines operate along the following routes described in this book:
Port Augusta-Coober Pedy-Kulgera-Alice Springs;
Port Augusta-Leigh Creek-Lyndhurst-Marree;
Alice Springs-Erldunda-Ayers Rock Village;
Port Augusta-Ceduna-Norseman-Southern Cross;
Kalgoorlie-Kambalda-Norseman-Esperance;
Southern Cross-Kalgoorlie;
Dalwallinu-Meekatharra-Newman-Port Hedland;
Geraldton-Mt Magnet-Meekatharra;
Geraldton-Carnarvon-Karratha-Port Hedland;
Overlander Roadhouse-Denham;
Carnarvon-Minilya-Coral Bay-Exmouth;
Nanutarra-Tom Price-Paraburdoo;
Karratha-Wittenoom-Tom Price (April-September only);

In addition a mail truck conveys travellers to Oodnadatta and William Creek from Coober Pedy. Unfortunately no passenger trains directly follow the routes covered in this book although it is possible to travel on the following lines:
Port Augusta-Tarcoola-Alice Springs;
Port Augusta-Tarcoola-Kalgoorlie-Southern Cross.

As most services originate from the state capitals or regional centres, getting to these destinations is not a problem. The advantage of this means of travel is that one is free to move, within the constraints of the timetable, from any one point to another at will. A disadvantage is that you will travel from settlement to settlement; to visit the country in between you would have to hire a vehicle or join a tour, either of which is not always possible.

Flying is another option, but negates the purpose of this book inasmuch as one flies over the country and does not pass through it. It is also very expensive. Not as ridiculous as it sounds is travelling, during the cooler months, by *touring* or *mountain bike*, especially along the sealed roads. Although basically for the fit, bike travel is very cheap and fair distances can be covered each day. Thought must be given to food, water and camping requirements, for these services may not always be available at the end of a cycling day. Likewise *motor bikes* are another alternative, especially on the sealed roads.

The principal means of reaching and travelling the Central and Western Outback is by *motor vehicle*, whether conventional vehicle or four-wheel drive (4WD). Contrary to popular opinion, a 4WD is not necessary to visit the outback; **I have travelled over many of the routes described in this book in a Holden Kingswood or Leyland Marina!**
It seems ironic that as outback roads have been upgraded, even sealed, that a 4WD is even considered necessary (there are exceptions). Bear in mind that many outback people themselves drive conventional vehicles but, it must be said, they have experience in the conditions that outback roads present to them. For the inexperienced outback traveller contemplating lengthy trips on unsealed roads, the 4WD option must certainly be considered. It is worth mentioning here that each of the route maps has been graded (see Part Two: The Route Gradings Explained) indicating which unsealed roads are okay for conventional vehicles, which are suitable for experienced drivers of conventional vehicles, and which are purely 4WD routes.

The advantages of *conventional vehicles* are:

*you probably already own one;

*they are usually cheaper to run;
*they cause less damage to the roads (being of lighter weight, and from being driven more carefully);
*and they limit the amount of things you can carry (most people travel with far too much stuff).

The disadvantages are

*they have low clearances (which can be modified);
*they are not of such robust construction (1970 models and earlier often are);
*they cannot get you out of a bog as readily as a 4WD (usually easily avoidable except for that fatal statement, "I'll just give it a go");
*and they cannot travel places a 4WD can.

For those of you who have contemplated travelling outback in a conventional vehicle, by all means do so but if inexperiensed be aware of your, and your vehicle's limitations.

The advantages of *four-wheel drives* are :

*they can go places that conventional vehicles cannot go;
*they do have excellent ground clearance (except for sedan models);
*they are mostly of more robust construction
*they are ideal for towing caravans on long stretches of unsealed road;
*they do come into their own in wet conditions on unsealed roads (even though driving on these roads at that time is considered bad form by the locals unless it is absolutely necessary);
*and they do provide a sense of security to the inexperienced traveller.

A compromise between conventional vehicles and 4WDs is the *campervan.*

These high clearance vehicles also offer comfortable accommodation. A disadvantage is that you have to pack everything up even if just travelling down the road to pick up some supplies.

To overcome their lack of confidence, or in order to travel with like-minded people, many self-drive travellers elect to travel in *convoy* with other vehicles, be it on a pay-and-join basis led by an experienced person, perhaps someone with a knowledge of bird or plant life for instance, or on a more informal basis with friends, 4WD club members, etc.
This has a number of advantages such as ,
*the pooling of camping and food resources,
*helping each other with mechanical problems,
*sharing ideas and information, etc.
Disadvantages include
*restrictions on free time and travel outside the group;
*being stuck with people you do not like;
*and limited interaction with the local population.

In a few instances, like crossing the Gibson Desert or travelling the remote areas in mid-summer, convoys are the only sensible way to travel.

Popular are *bush bashes* organised by community groups with often good intentions. Whilst some are little more than high speed vehicle rallies, others are large convoys of up to 50 vehicles travelling en masse. After meeting up at a pre-determined location the group travels together across the outback, usually for a period of ten or so days during the cool season school holidays. Whilst the gregarious often enjoy this type of activity (there is usually a large contingent of beer drinkers aboard) and the timid may find some like-minded travelling companions in the group, any advantages of convoy travel are negated by the sheer numbers involved:

travelling in other vehicles' dust clouds; never having any time alone to enjoy the countryside or campsites; having minimal contact with the local population; and the feeling that the group of which you are part is rapidly diminishing local supplies and intruding on the space of solitary and small group travellers.

If concerned about costs or the environmental impact caused by vehicle usage, some options are available, for instance: travelling with friends (four of us regularly venture outback in the Kingswood) - choose your potential travelling companions carefully, though, they might not be your friends by the time you get home; travelling slowly, thus increasing fuel economy and safety and reducing wear and tear on the vehicle and the roads; keeping the vehicle tuned for maximum fuel economy; reducing your load to a safe minimum to also improve fuel economy; and consider shortening the length of your journey (most people attempt to travel too far in a limited amount of time).

A word of warning: if travelling the outback in a modern vehicle, keep in mind their vulnerability.

Although wonders of technological advancement and fuel efficiency they are about as useful as a pogo-stick if the on-board computer/fuel delivery system breaks down (they do!) in the middle of nowhere. They are then just a pile of expensive junk, and you will look longingly as a beat-up older model vehicle held together with fencing wire rattles ever onwards. If you cannot fix an immobile vehicle stranded in a remote place you will be up for a lot of expense. Perhaps you should consider *hiring* a vehicle, a not altogether cheap option.

Preparing your Vehicle

The most important thing you can do for your peace of mind if taking your own vehicle outback is to make the vehicle mechanically sound. Attend to all those nagging doubts, squeaks, rattles and leaks before you depart.

Have the vehicle thoroughly inspected beforehand by your mechanic.

*Tell him or her where you are going and have them check the vehicle's suspension, tyres, fuel system, cooling system, brakes, etc.
*Replace the wheel bearings and universals (if still okay keep the old ones for spares).
*Replace any dodgy items and those due for renewal (some replaced items might do for spares), have a tune-up, change the oil, the filters, and grease the nipples.
*Add coolant to the cooling system, and replace the battery if more than a year old.
*Pack away all the spares required (see Appendix 2); chances are you will not need any of them. Even if you do not know how to replace them yourself (it would help your self-confidence if you did), then someone will probably be able to help you.

An important point, especially for conventional vehicles, is the ground clearance.

For peace of mind an adequate ground clearance is necessary if travelling extensively on unsealed roads. One way of controlling this is not to overload the vehicle; carry only what is absolutely necessary. Height can also be gained by the fitting of helper springs or air shock absorbers (there are arguments for and against this last option).
If intending to travel on Grade 4 roads (see Part Two: The Route Gradings Explained), then fit sump and fuel tank guards, and plastic hosing (cut along one edge) over brake

If all this seems to be too much, remember that your mechanic could do this work in a day, and if you do more than one trip, or go travelling for an extended period of time, it will more than 'pay' for itself.

and fuel lines.

Another possibility of reducing costs, particularly if you have some mechanical ability, is to buy a cheap older model of a popular vehicle, a 1970s Holden or Ford for instance, and spend a few weekends making it mechanically and structurally sound. If problems do occur in the middle of nowhere, not only are parts reasonably available (there are thousands of these vehicles still out there, most of them in running order), but costs can be minimised; of course, you would still carry all the required spares. Nonetheless, if you have made adequate preparation beforehand, very little will go wrong.

Climate: When to Go

This too is crucial, if not for your peace of mind then at least for your comfort and enjoyment.

Forget about travelling in summer unless very experienced, or you do not plan to travel in the remote areas, generally considered to be anywhere beyond (as covered in this book) Marree, unsealed roads off the Stuart Highway between Port Augusta and Alice Springs, unsealed roads in Central Australia or beyond Arltunga, Laverton, Leinster, or any of the unsealed roads off the Great Northern and North West Coastal Highways. Summer travel is usually okay on the sealed roads, although many days will be very hot; at these times carry extra water in the car. Note that the Pilbara region can be extremely hot for most of summer.

In summer you can expect to suffer the effects of dehydration and heat exhaustion, as well as intense and blinding glare in arid or treeless country, even if travelling in an air-conditioned vehicle.

People who live in hot climates are acclimatised; people who only experience hot weather occasionally are at risk. More serious problems can arise from heat stroke; becoming hopelessly bogged and over-exerting yourself; breaking down on a lonely road which, though relatively busy in winter, may not see another vehicle for days in summer; or from leaving an air-conditioned vehicle only to exhaust yourself by setting up camp or clambering over sand dunes during a hot afternoon. The drinking of alcohol at these times will only hasten your potential demise. People still perish in the outback and it happens in summer. **Do not count on station folk helping you out at this time; they might well be holidaying down on the coast!**

Also note that the Pilbara and North West regions may be subjected to tropical cyclones during summer/early autumn.

The times to travel the Central and Western Outback are autumn, winter and spring.

Keep the following points in mind.

Autumn and spring days can still be hot, but the bad heat rarely lasts for more than a few days (note: in the Pilbara, Gascoyne, North-West and Central Australian regions summer should be reckoned on lasting from November to March inclusive);

Winter days are generally mild in the south to warm in the north; note that they can be quite cool in the Flinders Ranges, Central Australia and the higher country of the Goldfields region. Winter nights are cold and may be freezing in the Flinders Ranges, Central Australia and the higher country of the Goldfields region - prepare yourself for temperatures falling to -5C; it does not happen every night, but it might happen on the night you are camping out.

Autumn days are usually wind free, but daylight hours are shorter than in spring. Heavy rains are likely, once or twice a decade, at this time, dumping the average annual rainfall overnight - these can flood creeks, close roads and strand travellers on unsealed roads for weeks on end. Also note that the tail-end of the northern monsoon may bring showers at this time. This is rarely more than an inconvenience.

Winter days in the southerly regions, particularly the Flinders Ranges, Gawler Ranges, Goldfields and Murchison regions may be showery, but not necessarily every day. This may be inconvenient for unsealed road travelling and camping. Early spring days too may also be showery. Although spring days have increasing daylight hours, it is also the season of winds in the southern regions and, in some places, dust storms.

Unless you like flies, thought should be given to travelling between late autumn and early spring.

Preparing Yourself

Having decided how to go and when to go, have you thought about yourself? **Unless travelling on an all-expenses tour, you will need to think about food and water.**

Always travel with some *food* with you wherever you decide to go; being held up by floodwaters or a breakdown, even on the busiest roads, may see you stranded for a short time. These inconveniences are better handled on a full stomach. Unless staying entirely on the main sealed highways, do not count on being able to buy meals; it is cheaper and more reliable to prepare your own, be it a lunchtime picnic or three meals a day. Stock up beforehand and replenish wherever possible. If travelling in the remote country you will have to prepare most of your meals; in these cases always carry enough food to last everyone in your vehicle for at least five days.

Likewise always carry *water*, even on the busiest roads. During summer, or at any time in remote country, carry sufficient water to last for five days, roughly four litres per person per day. Remember that this amount, 20 litres per person, will be a major contributor to your load.

Be Prepared to Camp Out

Unless on a tour, do not count on getting indoor *accommodation* every night in hotels or motels, especially during the school holidays: be prepared to camp out. For this you will need either bedrolls or a light-weight tent, plus bedding or sleeping bags. Cheap accommodation can usually be found at caravan parks (on-site vans or cabins) or at backpacker lodges. The cheapest accommodation is, of course, bush camps (see Chapter Three: Bush Camping).

The more information you can assemble the more interest you

Supply yourself with a good set of road and other *maps* in order to get an overview of the country you plan to visit (this book is good for the close-up details).

will get out of your travels. Try to include everyone who is accompanying you in the pre-trip planning so that they too feel a part of the venture.

You will also need *money*. While the larger centres have automatic teller machines, most of the smaller ones do not, even if they have a bank (which may not be your brand). Also many outback establishments do not have credit card facilities. You will need to carry cash (replenish supplies in the larger centres) or travellers cheques, or perhaps open a bank account which allows you to withdraw limited amounts at post offices (Commonwealth Bank). EFTPOS facilities are nowdays quite common.

For a suggested list of things to take see Appendix 3.

Permits

There has been considerable negative comments made about the need for non-Aboriginal Australians to obtain entry permits to cross Aboriginal land over the years, ever since some Aborigines have been granted land rights. These comments have often been racist in tone and are based on ignorance. As you will see below, it is not just some Aboriginal land that require permits for entry; a number of government controlled areas also require permits.

In order to traverse the following routes on Aboriginal land **all** people, both Aboriginal and non-Aboriginal (excepting members of the clans which own that particular land) require permits:

1. Katajuta-Wa border (Map 51): contact Central Lands Council, Alice Springs.

2. Warburton area-NT border (Maps 50, 51, 53): contact either Aboriginal Affairs Planning Authority, Perth: or Ngaanyatjara Council, Alice Springs.

3. Marla-Mintabie (Map 3): contact either Pitjantjatjara

Council, Alice Springs, or apply at Marla Police Station for immediate service.

4. Mereenie Loop road (Glen Helen/Hermannsberg-Kings Canyon, Map 17); permit available of day of travel at Glen Helen, Hermannsberg or Kings Canyon. Note that two separate permits are required to visit Gosse Bluff - one is available at Mereenie Loop Road pass outlets, the other from the Aboriginal Areas Protection Authority, Alice Springs.

All other routes which cross Aboriginal land are on gazetted main roads and **do not** require permits providing the traveller stays on the road reserve (roughly 30 to 50m either side of the road).

When applying for permits allow a minimum of two weeks (do this before leaving home). It may be possible to apply in person in Alice Springs and obtain a permit in shorter time (a few days).

Note that vehicles over five years old will require a **certificate of roadworthiness** from a mechanic or motoring organisation for travel across Aboriginal land on the following routes: Laverton-Warburton (Map 50); Warburton-Katajuta (Map 51); Carnegie-Warburton (Map 53).

Travellers no longer require a permit to visit Giless Meteorological Station.

In order to camp within the desert national parks in northern South Australia, or gain legal access, you will require a **Desert Parks Pass** costing around $50 and lasting for a year. This covers all the parks and reserves in northern South Australia, including the Flinders Ranges; specifically the Witjira and Lake Eyre National Parks, as mentioned in this book. Though expensive, this permit does include an information booklet. Desert Park Passes are available from numerous outlets throughout the South Australian outback.

Note also that a **Desert Park Camping Permit** is available for one or two nights camping at Dalhousie Springs, Witjira National Park. This permit is available at Desert Parks Pass outlets.

Overnight bush walkers require permits for camping in

Watarrka National Park (Kings Canyon).

Permits are also required if you wish to deviate from the Stuart Highway between Pimba and Coober Pedy (Maps 1 and 2) as beyond the road reserves is the Woomera Prohibited Area. This also applies to the road between Tarcoola and the Stuart Highway via Bulgunnia Station (Map 2). Permits are available from the Department of Defence, Woomera. Note that restricted areas surround Woomera Airfield and the Nurrungar Base.

Permits are also required if you wish to fossick. You do not need a permit to fossick in South Australia, but you do need permission from the claim holders. If you intend to dig for opals you will need a **Precious Stones Prospecting Permit** available from the Department of Mines (Adelaide or Coober Pedy). In the Northern Territory you will require a **Miner's Right** (about $5) obtainable from the Department of Mines and Energy (Darwin or Alice Springs). Likewise in Western Australia you will need a Miner's Right (about $10) from the Department of Mines, Perth.

Loading the Vehicle

How you pack the vehicle and have access to its contents will have a major bearing on how well you enjoy your travels. While the load lists seem endless, individual items often take up surprisingly little space, and after a week on the road everything should have its place. It will surprise you, on your return, how much spare space there seems to be!

Following are some loading hints.

1. Think light, and is this thing I am holding really necessary? Appendices 2 and 3 will give you an idea, but you will probably need to make your own lists.

2. Compartmentalise things into, for instance, clothes and personal items, food, cooking utensils, camping gear, spare parts, tools, etc. Cardboard boxes are ideal for many of these 'compartments' as they flex, are light, and are replaceable.

3. Load so that each 'compartment' is relatively accessible; this saves double handling. For instance, emergency food and water can be buried deep in the vehicle; lunch-time tucker and water should be easily accessible. Let each 'compartment' have its own position. It may take a few days on the road to determine this.

4. Have one person in charge of loading: then any 'compartment' or item therein that is missing will be noticed. Insist that items are replaced immediately after use. If this habit is established early, then the ease of travelling, stopping for lunch, setting up camp, etc, is greatly enhanced.

5. Distribute the load evenly, with heavier items stored low to keep the vehicle's centre of gravity low. This is especially important on rough roads, sand dunes, etc.

6. If using a roof rack, make sure it is strong and only store lightweight gear on it.

7. Do not store jerry cans of fuel in the cabin or on the roof rack. Store safely away from cigarette smokers. Beware of static build-up; earth against bare metal on the car before opening. Jerry cans of fuel are potential bombs.

8. Pack the load tightly so that items do not become missiles in event of sudden stops or accidents.

CHAPTER THREE

ON THE ROAD

Not everyone likes the outback. It tends to be a place that you will either love or hate. There is many a story told of people heading off into the wide, open spaces only to return to the more equitable coastal climes after a few days on the road. Perhaps it was the intense dry heat, the glare, the vast empty plains, the never-ending dry scrubby bush, the rough-looking townships, the flies, or the all-pervading dust that hastened their return. Even those who love it can be affected by these attributes. While usually relishing the freedom that the wide open spaces instil, these people find that the minor discomforts and hardships heighten their sense of awe and wonderment; they realise that the rough-looking townships harbour characters who are not possessed by image or style, but take life as it comes, often with a dry wit and sense of irony; and they know that the intense glare of a midday sun which so bleaches the landscape will be replaced at dusk with a vivid beauty which can bring tears to the eyes.

In this chapter we will look at some ways of reducing these hardships so that your journey is enjoyable.

Always remember, when travelling in remote country (as indicated on the maps herein) you should always inform a reliable person of your intentions. That reliable person could be the local police (they are in radio contact with other police stations); or it might be a family member or friend back home.

Ring them telling them of your plans. On arrival, always inform them you have completed your journey. Not to do so might involve a search party and considerable expense for you.

General road conditions, warnings and notification of road closures can be obtained from the following sources:
South Australian roads - ph (08) 11 633;
Northern Territory roads - ph (089) 527 111
Western Australian roads - ph (008) 803 314.
For further information on Western Australian roads ring (099) 41 2107 for the Carnarvon district; (091) 72 1688 for the Port Hedland district; or contact local shire councils.

Travelling Etiquette

One way of enjoying your travels is to be a pleasant traveller, one who respects other travellers, road users and locals. Unfortunately, as more urban and coastal people head outback, they take their speedy ways with them.
The first step is to slow down, both physically and mentally. After all the pre-departure preparations this is not easy, but after a week or so on the road you will find yourself more relaxed. By travelling slowly (which may mean doing a shorter trip if your time is limited) you will mentally slow down, giving you more time to absorb your surroundings and to appreciate the countryside, its settlements and inhabitants.

It used to be customary to wave at fellow travellers, and in many places it still is. Though perhaps tiresome on the busiest roads, make the effort on the quieter routes. It acknowledges the presence of others as equals and denotes friendliness; it is these people who will come to your aid if required.

Likewise consider other road users on narrow-sealed and unsealed roads. Slow down. A stopped car might require assistance, perhaps a message to be carried to the next settlement. By slowing down when passing or overtaking other vehicles, you will reduce the dust hazard and likelihood of windscreen breakages. Remember that in the outback you are likely to meet up with the same travellers (even locals) time and time again.

It is generally considered bad form (even illegal) to travel on unsealed roads in wet conditions. Naturally formed unsealed roads are readily cut-up by vehicle usage, resulting in deeply gouged wheel tracks which dry to form imbedded ruts, making travel after rains uncomfortable at least. Though you may pass along a road but once, a local may have to travel the same road regularly. Stay off wet, unsealed roads unless absolutely necessary; either find an alternative all-weather route, or wait until the road dries out. This usually takes only one sunny day.

Likewise, do not camp on station properties without permission (it is okay to camp on road reserves for a night or two) and, in all cases, leave gates as you find them.

Never leave a closed gate open even if you know someone is behind you.

They might turn off, turn around, or even break down before reaching you. Stations, unless providing facilities for travellers, should not be approached except in absolute emergencies. Whilst most station people are friendly they get sick of having to pull people out of bogs, supply them with petrol, or answer silly questions. The days when station people eagerly awaited the arrival of strangers for company have long gone.

In all towns and townships, respect the locals, both sober and drunk. Drunks are best avoided at all times (which means do not camp near townships on Saturday nights, except in the company of others). If you have just spent hours behind the wheel and are feeling tired and dazed on arrival in town, stop somewhere quiet, under a shady tree if possible, and unwind for five or ten minutes. Get out of the vehicle and have a good stretch, perhaps walk around a little. Doing this will relax you and help remove the tension. By relaxing before dealing with the locals you will not come across as just another fast, grumpy tourist.

Be careful with photography in townships; not everyone likes having their picture taken, especially Aborigines or those who have moved there in order to start new lives. If you want to take photographs, of buildings or whatever, spend some time in the township, talk to a few locals and do not hide the camera. If the locals think you are really interested in the area they will relax when you start taking photographs. If you want to take photographs of people, ask first and establish a relationship. What may seem to be a small, unfriendly township on your arrival should not be by the time you depart. The locals' reservedness is probably for a good reason, based on bad past experiences. Fast travellers with flashy vehicles who complain are not well tolerated.

If you wish to talk to Aborigines, and they will certainly enrich your travels, then stand at a distance in a prominent place. Individuals may wander by and say hello, or a member of a group will eventually saunter up to see what you want. Do not expect to be invited to the next initiation ceremony, but asking questions or showing interest in their culture will elicit responses. You will be expected to pay for photographs as reciprocity is a strong cultural attribute.

The Pressure of People

An aspect of life is that we all impact on the environment, and as more people travel outback, then the outback environment is impacted as well. There are ways of reducing your impact and consequently the total environmental impact. Some of these have already been mentioned in the previous chapter.

If you do not like feeling the crush of people in your travels, avoid travelling during the school holidays, especially to the Flinders Ranges, Central Australia, or the coastal towns of the Western Outback. By travelling outside these times you can still experience the outback as though it was your own, but with the comfortable reassurance that other travellers are about the place too.

Other ways of reducing your impact is by staying on the roads and tracks at all times, including walking tracks. Vehicles leaving the road not only destroy the vegetation, but also imprint the landscape with wheel tracks and gouges; these imprints can last for up to twenty years! If looking for a bush campsite, do it in daylight by either following another person's tracks (preferably an established track) or by turning off onto hardpan surfaces (scalds, dry claypans, etc) which leave no imprint.

Do not throw litter or food scraps from a moving vehicle, and always take all your rubbish with you, including cigarette butts and tissue papers, and deposit them at approved sites. A small plastic bag in the vehicle serves well as a litter bag. With toilet deposits, dig a small hole, do your business, then either burn the toilet paper or take it, suitably wrapped, with you. There is many a roadside and tourist site marred by thoughtless people who have blown their noses, had a fag, then a crap, only to leave behind their tissues, butts and toilet paper. These items take years to rot in the dry country.

Maintaining your Sense of Humour

This is crucial if you are to enjoy your journey. Bear in mind that outback travelling is an experience and an adventure, and there will be times that it is tiring. If you suffer easily from environmental stress, or lack a sense of humour, then perhaps touring the Central and Western Outback is not for you. There are ways, though, of reducing these stresses.

Try to avoid travelling west (north-west in winter) during the late afternoon, or east in the early morning.

The incoming sun and glare will be blinding, making travel hazardous as well as tiring. If you do not hit a kangaroo then you will probably still end up with headache. Likewise, travelling in a northerly direction is more tiring than heading south as the sun, especially in winter, will strike the windscreen at an angle, increasing the glare and giving the landscape a washed-out look. This can make travelling dreary. Also, beware of the fatigue-producing and hypnotic effect of running for hours over dead-straight bitumen roads.

Tiredness

Much of the tiredness and fatigue experienced on the 'boring stretches' is due to dehydration. That lethargic feeling and slowness of thinking can be overcome by regularly sipping water. In the dry outback climate you will be losing moisture by sweating even though you do not notice it due to rapid evaporation. Always carry water in the vehicle cabin. Soft drinks and alcohol only increase the problem.

Carry an old rug, blanket or tarpaulin which can be thrown over the vehicle when you have stopped for lunch or whatever. By placing it over the roof and covering some of the windows (hold it in place with the doors) you can shade the car, making it feel cooler. It also reduces the glare.

At all times during daylight hours outside of the vehicle wear a shady hat and sunglasses. If walking, always carry drinking water. On extended walks carry some food, walk with company, and inform a reliable person of your intentions. At least leave a note on the windscreen mentioning date, time, direction or destination, and expected return.

Bush Camping

The vast majority of outback travellers will spend at least one night in the bush. To make this as comfortable as possible, refer to the items listed in Appendix 3.

Try to look for a campsite before dusk and try to camp where others have been; if not possible, look for old road alignments, gravel pits or a hardpan surface (scalds, dry claypans, etc). These surfaces are usually level, hard, clean, safe for (small) fires, and leave virtually no imprints.

Always choose your campsite on foot, not through the windscreen of a moving vehicle travelling in ever-increasing circles (I have seen people do this!). Never camp in creek beds or by flooding rivers.

Flash floods can kill (it may be dry where you are but raining upstream) and flooding rivers may rise rapidly overnight. Never camp under large trees; there may be dead limbs about to fall. Also do not camp near stock watering places, homesteads or out-stations. Remember that mosquitoes like water too.

Camping

Where possible use camping stoves for cooking. Firewood is scarce in many areas, and in popular areas it may be non-existent. If having a campfire, dig a shallow trench and use wood sparingly; the dry timber of outback trees emits considerable heat. A small stick fire is sufficient to boil a billy and a few sticks placed on a bed of coals will produce that fireside ambience considered desirable by campers.

If it is very cold, do what the Aborigines do: make a couple of small stick fires and sit between them; raging blazes waste wood and only heat a part of you. Select your wood carefully as it may harbour animal or insect life.

In popular camping sites there may be a shortage of wood; the sharing of campfires may be possible in these instances. When finished, bury the fire by filling in the trench. Remember that in this day and age the collecting of firewood by pushing over small dead trees with your vehicle, or having huge roaring blazes, is for idiots.

When camping do **all your washing and cleaning away from waterholes, creeks, etc**, as soap, shampoo and detergent will pollute or contaminate them. For your toilet dig a pit well away from the camp and any water, and bury the waste. It is preferable to burn the toilet paper on a campfire, but not whilst cooking! Also give some thought as to where to use your generator, radio or portable television. In quiet places this not only disturbs stock, but wildlife and other campers as well. Also, beware of broken bottles and glass in or near waterholes.

If no facilities are available, take all of your rubbish with you for later disposal on a town tip. Buried rubbish will soon be dug up and scattered by wildlife. If camping for a few days, or if leaving camp for a part of the day, put food well away; thieving crows have been known to wreck a campsite and to demolish a large amount of food. In many places, particularly around waterholes, there will already be a lot of litter. Though unpleasant, you can feel virtuous by cleaning up and properly disposing of other people's rubbish. Not only will your campsite be cleaner but a clean campsite generally stays clean when other travellers arrive.

Note that it is illegal to bush camp within 16km of a caravan park or camping ground in Western Australia.

Rest areas (some with toilets and water) are located on some sealed highways. While good for rests, lunch stops, etc, they are generally not the best place to camp. Often filthy from litter, they are also close to the highway.

Breakdowns

If your car breaks down, or if you have an accident, stay with the vehicle. As long as someone knows where you are, and that you have not arrived when you said you would, someone will be along eventually to help you. While you have spare food and water, you will be okay. If you must leave the vehicle, leave a note on the inside of the windscreen stating date, time, direction of destination, and expected return. If it is hot or shadeless, make shade with your spare rugs, blankets, etc, or lie under the car (you may have to dig a trench first). Do not exert yourself during the heat of the day. If the situation is desperate, light a smoky fire by day (use spinifex, engine oil, spare tyres) and a bright fire by night.

You can avoid virtually all breakdowns by thoroughly preparing your vehicle before departure, and you can avoid most accidents by travelling safely and slowly, and by being extra careful when travelling at dawn, dusk or at night.

Avoid night travelling if at all possible; if you must, then keep your speed under 60 kilometres per hour. That should be slow enough to stop a kangaroo from landing in your lap via the windscreen.

This is a real problem, as most outback roads are unfenced. Remember that during dry times animals, especially kangaroos, will use bitumen and other hard road surfaces as water catchments from which to drink.

If you have broken down in a settlement and spare parts are not available, one of the quickest ways of getting the part is to ring a friend back home, have them buy the item and post it as soon as possible to you.

NOTES

THE MAJOR REGIONS OF THE CENTRAL AND WESTERN OUTBACK

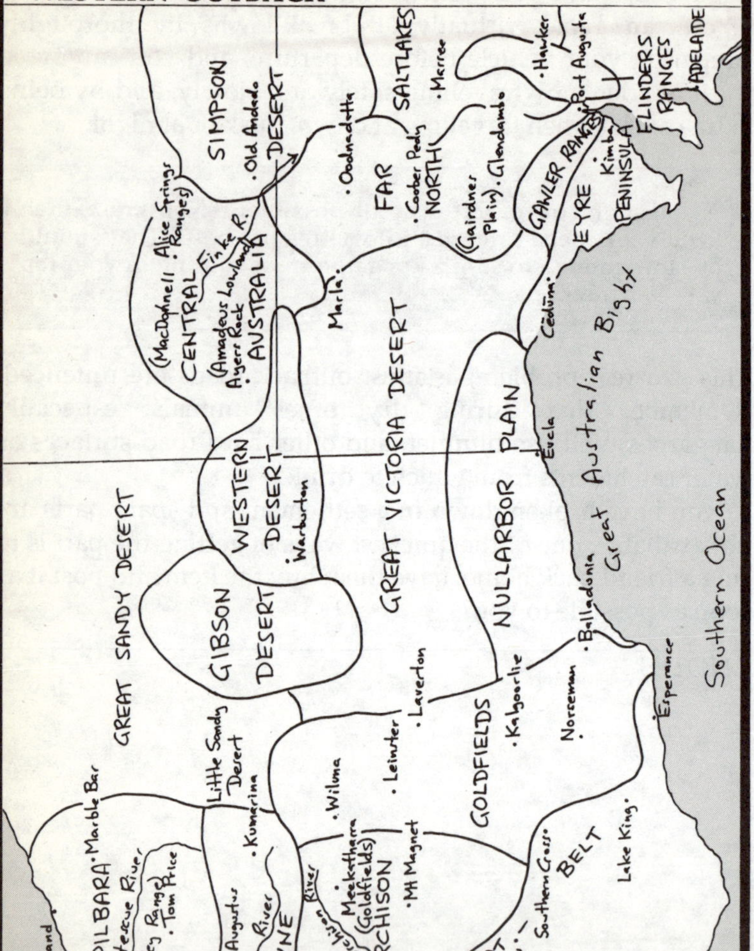

CHAPTER FOUR

THE REGIONS OF THE CENTRAL AND WESTERN OUTBACK

The regions of the Central and Western Outback are many and varied, although to the untrained eye, or to those in a hurry, they can appear monotonous and boring. The variations within regions, its differing landscapes, involve, for the most part, subtle changes in the lie of the land. The weather too influences the characteristics of its landscapes, for it has a direct effect on the nature of its habitats, the type of ecosystems, and the degree and intensity of its economic activities.

Generally these landscapes are level and dry. Consequently, like all things that possess a measure of uniformity, uncharacteristic features, however small, in the larger setting stand out. This is a secret to appreciating outback travel. If the size and uniformity get to be too much, seek out the small. You may have to get out of the vehicle to do this. For instance, mallee scrub might look dreary to travel through but take a slow look at a singular shrub: see the variety of colours on its trunk, the configuration and shape of its leaves, the patterns its leaf litter makes upon the ground, the insect life the shrub and its immediate environment harbours. Similarly if saltbush plains seem deadly dull, find a track off the road, pull up, turn off the engine, disengage the idle chat and experience the immensity of the space. At the same time allow your eyes to see the landscape: the minute undulations of the horizon, the texture of the vegetation, the traces of the watercourses. By so doing the seemingly monotonous and boring might simply be realised as a state of mind rather than something the landscape possesses.

Following in this chapter are brief descriptions of each of the regions that the described route maps traverse; they are presented to give an overview of what you might expect to see there.

CENTRAL AUSTRALIA

Central Australia is singularly the most popular tourist region of outback Australia for a very good reason: it is its most spectacular and scenically grand region. High rocky ranges cross its breadth, attractive sand plains run its length, deep canyons and gorges penetrate its depths. Given the semi-arid environment and paucity of vegetation, the geology of the Central Australian ranges is often stark, sometimes awesome; its beauty enhanced by the ever-changing colours of the rock faces as the sun moves across the sky.

Central Australia sits astride the Tropic of Capricorn. Running east and west of Alice Springs, the region's major town, a regional and tourist centre of some significance, are the **MacDonnell Ranges**, a series of parallel, linear ranges marked by high cliffs, towering bluffs, broad ridges and deep chasms set about a rocky, undulating lowland of hills and lesser ridges and ranges. The Western MacDonnells are by far the more spectacular section of the ranges, and the most visited, while the Eastern MacDonnells have a more intimate feel and some excellent geological formations.

South of the MacDonnell Ranges (the northern parts of Central Australia will be discussed in *The Northern Outback*) lies an area of mulga-clad plains and lesser sandstone ranges such as the James Range. Here too are interesting features, such as the incredible colourful eroded ridges of Rainbow Valley, the relic palm forests of Palm Valley, the Finke River gorges and in the George Gill Range, the deep and awesome King Canyon with its incredibly sheer walls and intriguing beehive domes. These southern ranges mark the northern boundary of the **Amadeus Lowland**, a vast tract of country dominated by sand plains which support a confused pattern of sand dunes and sandy flats vegetated by desert oaks, one of the outback's more graceful trees. The Amadeus Lowland reaches from the Simpson Desert to the dunefields of the Western Desert. Apart from a series of saltlakes, of which Lake Amadeus is the largest, and a number of small sandstone ranges, the district also contains two of Central Australia's most incredible attractions: Uluru (Ayers Rock) and Kata Tjuta (The Olgas). Both of these features are former mountain ranges eroded into their current configurations. What makes them amazing, apart from their sheer size, which is immense, is that they are virtually devoid of vegetation. Uluru stands like a huge pebble upon the sand plain while the Katajuta monoliths rise like giant cupolas into the sky, many of the domes being separated from each other by canyons barely a metre wide. Eastward lies another upstanding feature, Atila (Mt Conner), a flat-top mountain of similar dimensions.

The Amadeus Lowland merges with lesser hills, ranges and granite domes in the vicinity of Kulgera and Marla, and although not as spectacular as the districts further north, the distant purple ranges rising above the mulga-clad plains do give this country a Centralian appearance. It, like the lands to the north, is extensively grazed by beef cattle on large stations, although most of the scenic features are held in national parks or reserves.

Given its moderate elevation (400-700 or more metres) and remoteness from the sea, Central Australia experiences extreme temperatures ranging from blazing hot summer days to sub-freezing winter nights.

EYRE PENINSULA and Western Australian WHEATBELT

These two regions are not outback regions. They are cultural regions greatly modified by non-Aboriginal Australians for cropping and grazing purposes, predominantly wheat and sheep. This has been done by replacing the natural vegetation with introduced crops and pastures. As a result of these massive land clearances, many plants and animals have become endangered; some have become extinct. Another effect is that the country has become drier. Removal of complex mosaics of vegetation and the natural systems that occurred within these environments means that these areas today receive less rainfall than they once did, as evidenced by measurements within the cleared cropping land and adjacent uncleared land. Nonetheless, there are pockets of uncleared country within both regions contained in reserves. In addition, portions of the Eyre Peninsula, in the west around Yalata and east of Kimba, could be seen as outback country. Therein lie large tracts of land either unaltered by non-Aborigines, or only lightly grazed.

The creation of a cropping landscape has created some similarities between the two regions: small wheatbelt townships dot the main transport routes, each characterised by either silos (Eyre Peninsula) or wheat bins (Wheatbelt); paddocks are fenced and generally quite large compared to other cultivated landscapes; farm sizes, though often large, are small compared to sheep or cattle stations; and often the only place to see native vegetation is along the road reserves.

The landforms of both regions have some similarities: undulating granite plains marked at intervals by granite domes or low hills. Both have sand plains too, but there the similarities cease. In the Western Australian Wheatbelt the plains are bounded by low rises delineated by breakaway slopes; in the Eyre Peninsula the plains support either longitudinal dunes or low limestone ridges. Annual rainfall is similar in both regions, generally over 250mm, with most rain falling in winter.

FAR NORTH

Although the term Far North is often used to describe South Australia's pastoral districts, that country lying north of the settled districts or agricultural lands, in this book it refers to the landscapes that lie between the Great Victoria Desert in the west and the sandy plains to the west and north of Lake Eyre. It is a broad land of stony downs, low tablelands, multi-channelled creeks and mulga-clad plains.

The Far North can be divided into two distinct areas: sheep country and cattle country. Dividing each is the dingo fence; it very roughly coincides with the boundary between the mulga-clad plains and stony downs.

The sheep country is a fenced land of large sheep stations (including Commonwealth Hill, the largest sheep station in the world) which occupies the southern areas of the Far North. Known as the **Gairdner Plain**, its landscapes are one of mulga and saltbush shrublands (woodlands of western myall in the southernmost areas) occasionally interrupted by sand dunes and saltlakes. In a few localities, principally in the Woomera area, low tablelands with stony surfaces break the horizon. Being a low rainfall area, about 200mm per annum, windmills and bores provide water for stock. On average distances between homesteads range from 30 to 80 kilometres.

Along its northern boundary the sheep country encroaches upon the arid stony plains and low tablelands sometimes

Island Lagoon claypan, east of Woomera (Map 1)

collectively known as the **Oodnadatta Tableland.** These vast saltbush-covered plains, downs and low rocky hills, drained at intervals by broad, sandy coolabah-clad creeks resemble the landscapes of the Channel Country of Queensland, to which they are geologically related. It is here that the Great Artesian Basin reaches its westernmost extremity, a factor important in supplying the water needs in this sparsely settled cattle country where homesteads may be more than 120km from their neighbours.

FLINDERS RANGES

Standing above the arid lowlands, the Flinders Ranges is a collection of uplands characterised by proud, upstanding ranges of quartzite (a rock very resistant to erosion), lesser ranges of other rock types, and undulating but still elevated lowlands which lie between the ranges. The western escarpment of the Flinders Ranges is a long range standing up to 700 metres (occasionally higher) above a rift valley occupied by Lake Torrens and Spencer Gulf. At the base of this range is a stony, gently sloping plain upon which saltbush grows. Slicing this western rampart at intervals are creeklines which have cut deep gorges into the escarpment, resulting in a complex of deep valleys and high ridges with occasional isolated, rocky peaks. These peaks are occasionally, once every few years, covered with a very light mantle of snow, one of the very few places in the outback to receive this form of precipitation.

Behind the western range of upthrust rock are mostly gentler ranges and hilly country which occasionally form high cliffs and bluffs. South and south-west of the Hawker area are broad, almost level intermontane plains divided by long, linear ridges. Being at moderate elevation, these central hills, ranges, lowlands and plains are wetter than the surrounding lowlands and so support cypress pine woodlands, grasslands and river red gum-lined creeks.

Most of the Flinders Ranges is sheep grazing country, at least in the drier north (the wetter south, beyond the scope of this book, supports agricultural land), with typically outback stations on the lowlands and smaller pastoral properties on the uplands. Late last century though, this country was thought to be suitable for wheat cropping, farmers then thinking (after a succession of wet years) that 'the rain follows the plough'. With the return to normal rainfall the wheat crops dwindled, the farmers became bankrupt and the land reverted to sheep grazing. A legacy of these times are the numerous ruins of former homesteads and townships, a landscape feature which makes this part of the outback unique.

GASCOYNE

Lying between the major upland districts of the southern Pilbara and the vast, endless granite plains of the Murchison, is the Gascoyne region, an area that encompasses the entire Gascoyne River basin. The Gascoyne is one of Western Australia's major river systems, although it is rarely more than a riverbed of sand connecting numerous waterholes. It rises on the imperceptible divide that separates the basin from the short and uncoordinated drainage of the interior deserts and extends westward over 600km (as the crow flies) to the coast.

The Gascoyne is a land of gently undulating plains (similar to the Murchison region described below), impressive sandstone ranges such as the Kennedy Range, and moderately high ranges and dissected plateaux separated by sandy lowlands, as evidenced by the countryside near Mt Augustus. This country is sparsely vegetated semi-arid country bordering on arid. It is also sheep grazing country (some cattle grazing in the north and east) fenced into huge paddocks. It was sheep that gave this land its sparse vegetation; overstocking and drought have severely denuded its predominant formation, the mulga shrublands. There is only one township in this immense area (Gascoyne Junction), though far to the east lies the isolated hotel and old mining centre of Kumarina.

Nearer the coast the countryside changes; vast sand plains

dominate the landscape, some of which support sand dunes. Though the countryside is still semi-arid, the vegetation is more dense, acacia and other shrubs being dominant. Adjacent to the major town of the region, Carnarvon, is an activity unusual in the outback: farms drawing water from beneath the sandy bed of the Gascoyne to irrigate tropical fruit plantations.

In the south-west of the region, where the Carnarvon sand plains merge with sand plains more typical of the south-west of Western Australia, is one of the outback's more unusual districts, an area dominated as much by water as by land. **Shark Bay** lies like an afterthought tacked onto the west coast. The land component is comprised of old limestone ridges which form numerous peninsulas and islands upon which are found rocky clifflines, sand dunes and gypsum-covered saltpans. Between the peninsulas are shallow estuaries and bights that support an amazing diversity of aquatic life, in fact nature seems to be more abundant beneath the waters than on the semi-arid land. Partly sheep grazing country, partly national park, the Shark Bay district supports one town (Denham) but a growing number of tourist settlements.

GAWLER RANGES

Rising above a sea of bluebush shrublands dotted with western myalls are rounded hills and ranges, spinifex-clad domes formed by past volcanic activity. Between the ranges are gently undulating plains coursed by dry creek beds. In winter, if the usually reliable rains have fallen, the creeks may briefly run. In summer, after the winter grasses have dried and bleached in the sun, the landscape takes on a sunburnt look; only the bluebush holds its tinges of blue-green. These are the Gawler Ranges, a small region nestled between the cultivated wheatlands of the Eyre Peninsula to the south and the vast desert plains of the Gairdner Plain district of the Far North region to the north. The Gawler Ranges is sheep station country, relatively densely settled by outback standards but virtually unknown to outsiders. There are no towns in the

Gawler Ranges and even its main routes are simply station access roads.

Whilst the Gawler Ranges are mostly rounded hills and intervening plains, there are other landscapes too: areas of sand dunes which support quite dense shrublands dominated by mallee eucalypts; and saltlakes, some of which are vast in size. The southern coast of Lake Gairdner reaches deep into the heart of the Gawler Ranges, snaking between the hills, occupying the valley bottoms. Nearby Lake Everard does likewise. Between these two saltlakes are smaller lakes and claypans. Another lake, Lake Acraman, is believed to be caused by an astronomical event; it occupies a crater formed by a very large meteorite or comet.

The south-east corner of the Gawler Ranges merges into an area dominated by flat-top hills and ridges which rise hundreds of metres above the saltbush plains south-west of Port Augusta. These ranges are related, geologically-speaking, to the Eyre Peninsula formations, but the general appearance of the countryside, and its sheep grazing pursuits, are more in keeping with the outback rangelands of the Gawler Ranges. Though arid-looking, this area houses a significant section of the South Australian industrial heartland: Iron Knob and its related iron ore mining centres of the Middleback Ranges and, on the Spencer Gulf coast, Whyalla, the largest provincial town in South Australia.

GIBSON DESERT

Situated just east of central Western Australia, the Gibson Desert is about as far as it is possible to get from anywhere else in Australia. Though not as large as the deserts which surround it (the Great Victoria, Great Sandy and Western Deserts), it is in fact more 'desert-looking' than these. Vast, slightly undulating gravel plains with low hills and plateaux support tracts of spinifex with clumps or patches of mulga. This is the true Gibson Desert. Elsewhere, still within the region, are sand plains supporting various grasses, again with a mulga overstorey. These plains are less like desert but more similar in appearance to the pastoral country that lies far to the west. The Gibson Desert, like the other 'Great' deserts, is desert in name only. Compared to the arid regions of eastern Australia, the Saltlakes, or Sturts Stony Desert for instance, this country looks to be semi-arid in appearance. Its name 'desert' comes about by it being unsuitable for pastoralism: a spinifex understorey, lack of watercourses, and remote from markets. Nonetheless it has come to the attention of the mining industry in recent years, as well as to the Aborigines who depopulated the area (willingly and otherwise) when the region was incorporated into the Woomera Rocket Range back in the 1950s. This has led, and is still leading, to conflict: the miners wish to exploit a virtually unoccupied region free of encumbrance; Aborigines wish to return to their 'grandparents' country', to be partially free of the ills of non-Aboriginal society.

Tremendously hot in summer, it is surprisingly cool in winter, especially overnight, due to its altitude of around 500m and its remoteness from the sea. Rainfall is low, around 200mm per annum on average, but this figure can vary enormously. The occasional good seasons, which give the vegetation a lush appearance, may be followed by particularly dry seasons that may run for years. Given its natural environment, the Gibson Desert will remain (mining notwithstanding) one of Australia's great wilderness areas.

NOTES

GOLDFIELDS

Stretching over 600km from north to south and over 300km from east to west, the Goldfields region (sometimes referred to as the Eastern Goldfields) takes its name from the numerous gold mines scattered over much of its area. First discovered in the 1890s, the gold of the Goldfields region provided a major impetus in the development of Western Australia. With the discovery came people from the other Australian colonies (later states) as well as from overseas, either as prospectors, miners, or in the service of these people.

They settled a semi-arid environment creating mines, towns and transport networks, concentrated mostly on the greenstone outcrops and ridges wherein the gold-bearing ore occurred. As old mines and townships died, other sites and developments grew to create a unique region characterised today by numerous mine sites, ghost towns and relics of a past era. Towns are aplenty throughout parts of the Goldfields, places like Kalgoorlie, Leonora and Norseman, which have survived not only the downturns of gold mining, but from the development of new mines or the reworking of the old mine dumps made profitable by increasing gold prices. In addition, the discovery of nickel has led to the development of new towns such as Kambalda, Leinster, and the redevelopment of the old gold mining town of Laverton.

The Goldfields is a vast region though, and mining is concentrated, albeit widely, but in specific areas. Elsewhere the outback bush lies silent and virtually empty, occupied by non-Aborigines in some places by sheep stations, in other places as untouched wilderness.

The landscapes of the Goldfields are many and varied. Dominant are the gently undulating plains, two plains really, one slightly higher than the other, each being separated by long but low escarpments locally known as breakaways. These are at most 30m high. The plains themselves are either sand plains, alluvial plains or granite plains; upon the latter rise domes and outcrops of granite rock. Elsewhere are low ridges, in the vicinity of which gold might be found.

These plains support a variety of vegetation, the type and density dependent as much upon rainfall as upon soil type. In the south where the rainfall averages 250mm or more there are eucalypt woodlands housing some very attractive trees: salmon gums and gimlets for instance. On the deep sand plains are tracts of mallee eucalypts and heathlands. Northward (north of about Menzies), the woodlands grade into mulga dominated shrublands. The countryside hereabouts is more typical of the semi-arid rangelands found over much of the outback. Lying within these woodlands and shrublands are some of the region's more pleasant surprises: the saltlakes and claypans which, not only being attractive in their own right, also provide the traveller with some wide views and a feeling of space.

In the north-east this region merges imperceptibly with the interior deserts. Vast sand plains stretch for long distances, interrupted occasionally by saltlakes or low sandstone ranges. These mulga-clad plains support very large cattle stations.

GREAT VICTORIA DESERT

Lying north of the limestone-based Nullarbor Plain, west of the gibber country of Far North South Australia, east of the mulga-clad plains of the Goldfields, and south of the moderately high hills and mountains of the Musgrave and Mann Ranges which make up the Western Desert region, is one of Australia's largest and least populated regions: the Great Victoria Desert. Virtually completely unsettled in the European sense, the Great Victoria Desert is an ocean of sand. Lengthy parallel dunes reach, discontinuously, from east to west across the South Australia-Western Australia border, each dune interspersed with broad flats or swales. The desert supports an amazing array of vegetation ranging from mallee scrubs in the south-east, through to woodlands of belah and western myall, eucalypt woodlands, mulga shrublands and wide tracts of spinifex with sparse overstoreys of mulga, various eucalypts or, in the northern districts, desert oaks.

This desert looks anything but like a desert.

It came to be known as a desert by the explorers; as pastoral country it was inadequate. There were no major watercourses; it had an understorey of spinifex; it is riddled with high sand dunes making access difficult; and it is a long way from anywhere. The environment of the Great Victoria Desert was unsuitable for economic development based on pastoralism, the result being that it remains to this day one of the world's great wilderness areas.

It has not always been a wilderness though. Over thousands of years it has been home to many Aboriginal clans, some of whom have returned to this country to live. Non-Aboriginal occupancy, though, has been tenuous to say the least. While some parts were incorporated in the Woomera Rocket Range and atomic testing grounds at Emu and Maralinga (which led to the development of some desert tracks - the famous Beadell 'Highways'), it is only on the periphery that the land has been settled in the European sense of the word; minor parts of the desert have been incorporated into the back paddocks of vast station properties. Mintabie, on the very fringe of its north-eastern boundary could be considered the region's only township, although there are some Aboriginal settlements on the South Australian side of the border. Hot in summer, mild in winter, the Great Victoria Desert with its 200mm or so average annual precipitation, remains one of Australia's least known areas.

MURCHISON

The Murchison is one of Western Australia's vast regions, which, to the untrained eye, looks little different to the country that surrounds it. Travelling the Murchison, one can appreciate the vast uniformity of the Western Outback. Lying west of the Goldfields, with which it shares numerous common landscapes (there is no distinct boundary), and south of the Gascoyne (ditto), the Murchison is more readily defined by what it is not, that is the wheatlands that occupy what would have been the same country to the south, or the vast scrubby sand plains to the west. For the sake of argument though, these sand plains are included in the Murchison region, for the river that lends its name to the region courses through these plains en route to the sea.

The Murchison is dominated by huge areas of mulga shrublands given over to the grazing of sheep. It is dominated by undulating granite plains above which rise the occasional low rocky range, or sometimes a granite dome. These plains merge eastward into country typical of the Goldfields region; a land of plains, low ranges, breakaways and saltlakes.

Further west the Murchison region is typified by extensive sand plains supporting a multitude of shrubs; this in turn merges into a sandstone plateau (also covered with sand!) deeply dissected by the Murchison River. It is here, near Kalbarri, and on the adjacent coast, that the Murchison region can be described as grand, where the deep Murchison River gorge erupts through a high, cliffed coastline. Though the Murchison region can be fairly described as uniform in its scenery, there are compensations: the massed everlasting wildflower displays in which countless billions of daisies spread their colours from one horizon to the next is truly astounding.

Also of interest is the **Murchison Goldfields** district, an area of old mining townships and ghost towns exhibiting excellent examples of the architecture of the time. While undergoing a resurgence in mining activity in the Meekatharra, Mt Magnet and Cue districts, it is Cue itself that epitomises the Murchison Goldfield towns. Its streetscapes are virtually intact as a living museum of the life and times of the early Twentieth Century.

NORTH-WEST

The North-West is one of those regions that appears distinct from other regions but is difficult to define, especially on its inland margins. There its characteristics merge with its adjacent region, the Gascoyne, itself a difficult region to define except by assuming its boundaries to be the divide separating the Gascoyne River basin from those of its neighbours. This problem is further exacerbated by the political usage of the term North-West as being that area north of the 26 degree latitude.

The readily defined portion of the North-West is characterised by an area of low folded ridges and limestone dunes that form the Exmouth Peninsula. The main terrestrial feature of the peninsula is the Cape Range, with its attendant narrow coastal plains. The Cape Range peters out to the south, though the low ridges and dunes remain, reaching to just south of Quobba. Off-shore lies the North-West's main maritime feature, Ningaloo Reef, a major coral reef on par, as regards with species if not length, with the Great Barrier Reef.

East of Exmouth Gulf lies the Onslow Plain, a long narrow coastal plain of tidal flats and mangroves which merge into a red soil plain dotted with spinifex and anthills. These in turn merge into the northern Carnarvon Dunefield, an area of north-south longitudinal dunes separated by sandy swales. This dunefield extends into similar country included in the Gascoyne region, although it could be said that the northern section of the dunefield is somewhat more arid in appearance and rather more attractive than the scrubby dunes found east of Carnarvon.

The North-West is an arid region and it looks that way due to the nature of its vegetation. Most of the North-West is sheep grazing country, although parts of Cape Range and the Ningaloo Reef have been preserved in parks.

NULLARBOR PLAIN

Stretching for kilometre after endless kilometre, the ever-so-slightly undulating Nullarbor Plain is one of the world's great empty regions. The true Nullarbor, the treeless section, ranges over 600km from east to west. A small portion of this treeless section can be seen from the Eyre Highway near Nullarbor Roadhouse; a significantly larger portion can be seen from the railway.

Surrounding the true Nullarbor is country that can be included in the Nullarbor Plain region as it is underlain by the same limestone rock. This peripheral country is characterised by either its low acacia woodlands, or by its dense mallee scrubs. It is bounded on the east by the uncleared portions of the Eyre Peninsula (the undulating limestone ridges near Yalata); on the north by the Great Victoria Desert dunefield; on the west by the eucalypt woodlands of the Goldfields region; and on the south by the sheer and abrupt cliffs (except for one portion) which plunge into the Southern Ocean. This exception, the Roe Plain, lies west of Eucla. It is characterised by western myalls and saltbush; nearer the coast are mallee scrubs, while on the coast are massive sand patches and dunes.

Though the Nullarbor Plain is seemingly featureless, beneath the surface is another world of immense caves and subterranean lakes, some of which extend for many kilometres their only surface expression being sinkholes, cave entrances or collapsed dolines. Being limestone, there are no watercourses on the Nullarbor Plain, with the exception of very minor creek beds flowing off the Nullarbor Plain escarpment above the Roe Plain.

The arid Nullarbor Plain region is a region of contrasts. Summer temperatures might reach the high forties one day, to be followed by a cool, drizzly day with the temperatures in the low twenties, a result of its proximity to the sea. Another effect of this coastal influence is that daytime temperatures are often moderated by sea breezes, giving the southern Nullarbor a relatively benign climate.

While parts of the Nullarbor Plain remain as unsettled wilderness country (the effects of rabbits notwithstanding), large portions have been extensively grazed by sheep. Like most outback country, though, this type of farming is unable to support large settlements. There are no towns on the Nullarbor, only roadhouses and tiny railway settlements, which support the two transport links that cross it.

PILBARA

Spectacular scenic country is in short supply in the Western Outback, but the vast undulating plains of the Goldfields, Gascoyne and Murchison regions are more than compensated for by the incredible landscapes of the Pilbara. Ranging from coastal plains to high mountain summits, the Pilbara is a region of contrasts. The coastal districts are dominated by sparsely vegetated coastal plains which offer vast views. Tidal flats and mangrove-lined estuaries subtly merge onto granite plains dotted with low hillocks. Further west ranges separate the Pilbara from the North-West; here the coastal country (around Dampier) is one of weird bouldery hills, some of which are marked with Aboriginal petroglyphs, or of rocky mountains dotted with spinifex and snappy gums.

These ranges continue at an angle to the coast, thus forming a southern boundary to the aforementioned coastal districts. For much of its length this is known as the Chichester Range, a long, narrow escarpment constructed of similar rock piles to those seen around Dampier. The Chichester Range forms the northern boundary of a plain that carries the Fortescue River across the breadth of the Pilbara. Across the plain can be seen another escarpment on the horizon, the northern face of the **Hamersley Ranges**. The Hamersley Ranges, a large partially dissected plateau topped with yet higher and higher flat-top summits and ranges, forms the soul of the Pilbara and presents the traveller with some of Western Australia's most spectacular country, comparable to portions of the Kimberley. The escarpment is rent with deep chasms and gorges, or of more open valleys, some of which provide access to the higher country beyond. Given its moderate altitude, the Hamersley district is somewhat semi-arid in appearance, compared to the arid lands of the coastal districts.

South of the Hamersley Ranges, the land falls into the Ashburton River basin, an undulating lowland dotted with low ranges and hills, country somewhat reminiscent of the Gascoyne region which lies adjacent. Eastwards of the

Hamersley Ranges and Fortescue River Valley is an area sometimes known as the **Nullagine Hills,** a lowland of rocky outcrops, low ranges and spinifex-clad plains. This country, around Nullagine and Marble Bar, will be of interest to fossickers.

Although most of the Pilbara has been taken by vast sheep stations, many areas have remained little altered by non-Aboriginal settlement, the country being too rugged or spinifex-dominated to be of any use for grazing. Elsewhere, over the past thirty years, parts of the Pilbara have undergone rapid change as huge iron ore deposits have been exploited. This has led to the development of many mining towns, port towns and related infrastructure, such as railways, roadways, pipelines and powerlines. Given the vastness of the region, this industrialisation seems minuscule.

SALTLAKES

Surrounding the peninsula of high ranges that constitute the Flinders Ranges, restricted by the sand dunes of the Simpson and Strzelecki Deserts, and limited by the sand plains and stony downs of the Far North, the Saltlakes region occupies Australia's sump, a lowland which partially lies below sea level. Part of this lowland once formed the bed of Lake Deiri, Australia's prehistoric and fabled 'inland sea'. Centred upon Lake Eyre, the 'inland sea' drained, as Lake Eyre does today, over one sixth of the continent. Being an internal drainage basin, having no outlet to the sea, salts and sediments were carried and deposited by the inland rivers, forming saltlakes and alluvial plains. Saltlakes characterise this region today for the seasonal rivers: the Diamantina, Cooper, Warburton, Frome, Neales, Macumba, etc, still lead to (and on rare occasions even reach) this lowland sump, only to be evaporated into the atmosphere, thus leaving behind their cargo of salt.

Geologically separate from, but still a part of the Saltlakes region, Lake Torrens occupies a rift valley bounded on the east by the Flinders Ranges and on the west by the

Andamooka Tableland, a stony plain bounded by a steep, east facing escarpment. A dunefield occupies the plains of its eastern shore.

The Saltlakes region is Australia's driest and, in places, its most desolate. Receiving barely 120 to 150mm of rain on average per year, it supports vast areas of saltbush in some places, hardly anything in other places, and no vegetation whatsoever on its lake beds. Nonetheless, parts of this country lie within the dingo fence and support sheep grazing, watered not only from windmills and bores but by run-off from the nearby Flinders Ranges. In other places, particularly in the sand dune country beyond the dingo fence, cattle are extensively grazed on huge properties. Elsewhere, on and near the saltlakes, the land is unoccupied, wild, and little changed since pre-European times.

Water hose, Callana siding, old Ghan railway, west of Marree (Map 6)

SIMPSON DESERT

Occupying a vast tract of land lying to the north of Lake Eyre, and hemmed in by the stony plains and jump-ups of Queensland's Channel Country to the east, and the desert plains and high ranges of Central Australia to the north and west, the Simpson Desert is a large area of virtually unsettled country. Whilst certainly known to Aboriginal groups, the heartland of the Simpson Desert remained unexplored by Europeans until the 1930s; even today parts of this region would not have been visited by Europeans more than once, if ever.

The Simpson Desert's inhospitality to European occupation is due to more than the region's aridity, considered to be mild by Saharan standards (even the Saltlakes and Far North regions look more forbidding); it is due to the nature of its countryside. The Simpson Desert is an area of longitudinal dunes which roughly run north-west to south-east, often for hundreds of kilometres without a break. Separating these dunes, which may reach thirty or more metres in height, are interdunal flats or swales, themselves often sandy, or occasionally gravelly. Fringing the dunes and so stabilising their movement before the wind, are not only various acacias but spinifex, that spiky grass that covers most of Australia's sandy deserts. Spinifex is basically unpalatable to stock. What European occupation there has been, concentrated on the westernmost fringes of the desert, are a few far-flung homesteads, some low-key mining, and the Old Ghan railway with its attendant infrastructure.

WESTERN DESERT

Located west of the Amadeus Lowland and surrounded on three sides by the regions often collectively known as the Western Desert (the Gibson, Great Sandy and Great Victoria), this region includes that country which does not readily fit into the boundaries of either the above listed deserts or of Central Australia. Although it incorporates outliers of the

Amadeus Lowland and Great Sandy Desert dunefields, it is characterised by a number of moderately high and scenic mountain ranges (the Petermann, Rawlinson, Mann, Musgrave and Warburton Ranges as well as a number of smaller and lesser ranges) interspersed with the outlier dunefields mentioned above. The plains country of the Western Desert is characterised by mulga shrublands and desert oak woodlands; the uplands with spinifex and sparse shrublands.

The Western Desert is Aboriginal country. It has never been extensively grazed, nor has it been more that superficially mined. In the time before land rights it was Aboriginal reserves (still is in Western Australia) or a part of the Woomera Rocket Range; in the time before non-Aboriginal contact it was traditional Aboriginal country. Having never been grazed or otherwise occupied, traditional customs and law are still very strong. This land has preserved to a great extent the power of the elders (alcohol and videos notwithstanding) such that the local people still have some control over their lives rather than being dependent on a welfare system, or the largesse of a paternalistic or assimilating government. (Straddling three states, this cannot be said of the Western Australia portion which, until recently, refused to recognise traditional native title.) Many clans within the Western Desert have entered into agreements with mining companies (proving that land rights and the recognition of native title can co-exist with mining companies), which have provided them with a source of revenue; this in turn has been channelled into businesses, such as a small local airline and road haulage companies, which benefit the local communities.

The people of the Western Desert, living on their own land, have created their own opportunities, giving them a sense of pride and honour. That is not to say they have solved all of their problems (what society has?), but it does indicate that non-Aborigines have little to fear from Aboriginal self-determination.

PART TWO

THE ROUTES AND MAPS

How to Use the Maps

Route maps in strip form have been used by travellers, principally motorists, for over 50 years. Traditionally, they have been designed to be read from the bottom up in order to match the direction of travel, while any additional information has been written in normal reading order, from the top down. A disadvantage of this system is that two maps are required for each section of the route: one map for each direction.

In order to save space and repeating the same information, but in a reversed order, the route maps in this book have been designed to be read in both directions.

Virtually all of the maps have been drawn so that they are read from bottom to top when travelling away from the populated south-east and south-west corners of the continent and its capital cities, and from top to bottom when travelling to these populated areas. The accompanying written material for each map has been written to directly cross-reference with the maps so that when you are heading outback from the populated areas, you read this information from bottom to top; when returning, you read from top to bottom.

Each of the maps has been grouped into a series of commonly named routes or assembled into tracts of country. This makes it possible to follow consecutive maps on particular routes. If travelling on a variety of routes (which you will most likely do), or if travelling across country, refer to the appropriate maps (each connecting map number is given within a circle) at either the so-marked intersections or at the top and bottom of each map.

To find a particular route or map, refer to either the Index of Routes and Maps which follows, or to the Key Map on page

The maps themselves use a number of different symbols which are explained below; they also use a number of landform or vegetation terms which are explained in the glossary. Information regarding the written material that accompanies each map is also detailed below. Please note that the maps are not drawn to scale and that direction is variable.

North, as indicated on the maps is approximate, to help position the route maps to any large scale maps you may be using.

List of Symbols Used on Route Maps

Symbol

① ⑬ ㊷ connecting map numbers

 roads, intersections, bridges

 railways, windmills

 towns, townships

 dog fence with gate, or state border

 very small settlements, buildings, roadhouses, railway sidings, ruins

 national park or reserve, prohibited area

 creek or stream, with water-hole; lakes or claypans

 multi-channelled stream

 low hills, ranges, jump-ups, mountains

\+ isolated mountain (some heights given in metres)

All **distances** are in kilometres; measured between towns, townships, intersections, ruins and other features.

Map number and **title** are at top of map.

Left hand margin shows distances in kilometres between fuel supply points marked thus *.

Right hand margin shows a summary of road conditions between these marks *.

Settlements, towns and **townships** providing services are written in capital letters; also included are altitudes (in metres) and population (based on census figures, local knowledge or estimates).

Localities, ruins, stations, etc, not providing services are written in lower case letters.

Also note the following regarding the accompanying written information:

1. **Distances** are approximate; some discrepancies will occur as alignments are shortened, more accurate measurements are taken, etc. They may vary from different sources by a few kilometres. All distances have been rounded up to the nearest kilometre.

2. **Average Vehicles per Day** are based on a variety of sources, some official, some on local knowledge. They represent an average traffic count between settlements during the tourist season, ie in cooler months. Higher counts have

been achieved during school holiday time, lower counts at the beginning and end of the season. During the summer months these figures will drop considerably, by as much as 90% in remote arid areas; this means some routes may not carry any traffic from one day to the next.

3. **Regions traversed** are presented from the bottom of the map upwards.

4. Some **facilities** are included for each settlement to give an idea of their range of services. A more detailed list is provided by the services grid in the appendices.

5. **Landform** and **vegetation** information is presented in the same order as on the map.

6. **Route gradings**, presented under the map title, are detailed below.

Explanation of Route Gradings

Each of the route maps has been graded in order to give the traveller an idea of the road conditions likely to be encountered. These gradings are based on the type of road surface, vehicle suitability and driver experience, and are representative of **dry weather conditions**. The gradings indicate the typical conditions for that section of the route, not necessarily the best or worst.

Grade One:

* Two lane bitumen highway in fair to very good condition. Some roads may be subject to flooding.
* Suitable for all vehicles and caravans.
* Beware of stock grids.
* Exercise caution when passing or overtaking road trains.

Grade Two:

* Single-width bitumen road in fair to good condition.
* Extra care required when passing or overtaking as the wheels on one side will need to run on gravel verges; beware of jagged bitumen edges, windscreen breakages, narrow stock grids.
* Slow down when approaching other vehicles; completely leave the bitumen when passing road trains.
* Some roads may be subject to flooding. Exercise caution in wet weather as road verges may be muddy. Take care on narrow causeways.
* Suitable for all vehicles, and caravans with care.

Grade Three:

* Two-lane unsealed road in fair to good condition, generally well-maintained in normal (dry) periods.
* Surfaces vary from constructed gravel roads to graded natural formations. Heavily used (especially after school holidays, race meetings) or irregularly maintained roads may be pot-holed, uneven or corrugated. Loose gravel and sandy creek crossings will be encountered.
* Exercise care at stock grids.
* Slow down when approaching other vehicles, to reduce dust hazard and windscreen breakages.
* Some routes may be subject to flooding; all routes may be impassable in wet weather.
* Suitable for conventional vehicles with care; or extreme care if towing a caravan, or in adverse conditions.
* **A good clearance is desirable;** small cars may need modifications.
* **Enquire locally before proceeding, especially in summer or during wet weather.**

Grade Four:

* One or two-lane unsealed and irregularly maintained road or track.
* Conditions are generally rough, rocky, pot-holed, corrugated, washed out, sandy, and may have high centre mounds of gravel, large bulldust holes, etc. Creek crossings are often rocky, sandy or washed out.
* Exercise extreme caution at stock grids.
* Routes offer fair travelling after grading, but quickly degenerate with passing traffic. All routes subject to flooding and may be impassable in wet weather, even to 4WDs.
* Slow down when approaching other vehicles to reduce dust hazard and windscreen breakages.
* Suitable only for experienced drivers of conventional vehicles with extreme care.
* A good ground clearance is essential; 4WDs recommended if only for good clearance. Conventional vehicle modifications highly desirable (sump and fuel tank guards, undercarriage protection).
Not recommended for caravans; passable with trailers towed by a 4WD.
* **Always enquire locally before proceeding and inform someone of your travel intentions.**

Grade Five:

* Unsealed and unconstructed tracks receiving no maintenance. Routes negotiate soft and high sand dunes, otherwise conditions are similar to Grade Four routes.
* All routes subject to adverse wet weather conditions; detours and route finding may be required.
* Suitable only for high clearance 4WDs.
* Always enquire locally before proceeding and inform someone of your travel intentions.

MAP 2 THE CENTRAL AND WESTERN OUTBACK

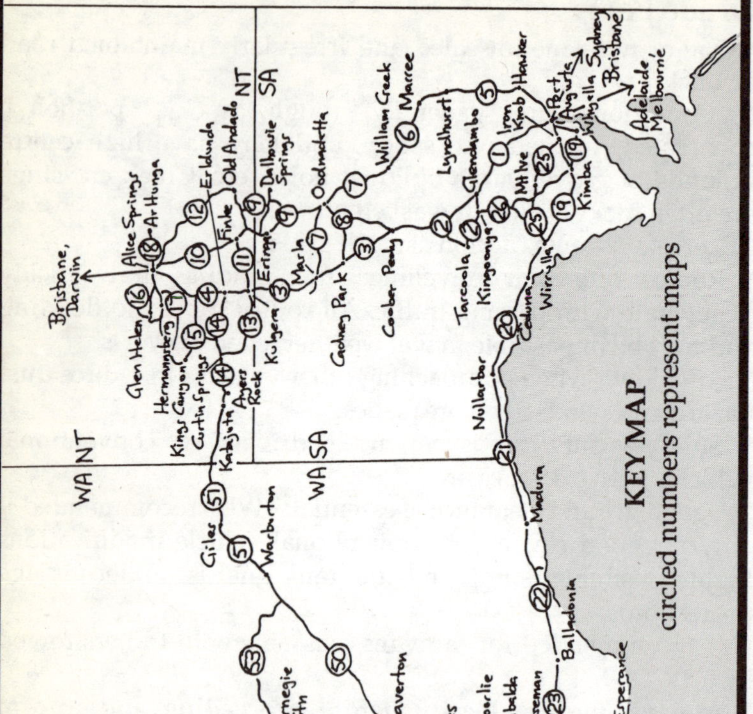

INDEX OF ROUTES AND MAPS

The Legend for the following section is as follows:

1(1) Port Augusta-Glendambo-Port Augusta via Pimba 286km

1 = Map number
(1) = Grade of Road
Port Augusta-Glendambo-Port Augusta via Pimba = Route
286 = Distance

Stuart Highway

Flinders Ranges-Oodnadatta Track

7 (3) William Creek-Marla-William Creek via Oodnadatta 412km

Painted Desert Country

8 (3) Coober Pedy-Cadney Park-Coober Pedy via Oodnadatta 369km

Finke River Country-Simpson Desert

9 (4) Oodnadatta-Old Andado-Oodnadatta via Eringa ruin/Dalhousie Springs 350/357km

10 (5) Eringa-Alice Springs-Eringa via Finke 349km

11 (3) Kulgera-Old Andado-Kulgera via Finke 292km

12 (4) Old Andado-Alice Springs-Old Andado via Santa Teresa 322km

Central Australia

13 (3) Kulgera-Curtin Springs-Kulgera via Mulga Park Stn 265km

14 (1) Erldunda-Katajuta-Erldunda via Ayers Rock Resort 295km

15 (3) Stuart Highway-Kings Canyon/Lasseter Highway-Stuart Highway via Kings Creek 203/166km

16 (1) Alice Springs-Glen Helen (Tylers Pass)-Alice Springs via Namatjira Drive 132km/179km

17 (4) Alice Springs-Kings Canyon/Tylers Pass-Alice Springs via Mereenie Loop road 300/195km

18 (3) Alice Springs-Arltunga (Ruby Gap Gorge)-Alice Springs

Gawler Ranges

Great Northern Highway and northward

Bar-Auski Roadhouse 265/267km

Goldfields Country

31 (1) Southern Cross-Menzies-Southern Cross via Kalgoorlie 356km

32 (1) Menzies-Leinster/Laverton-Menzies via Leonora 245/223km

33 (3) Leinster-Meekatharra-Leinster via Wiluna 349km

34 (3) Paynes Find-Wiluna-Paynes Find via Sandstone 454km

35 (2) Geraldton-Mt Magnet-Geraldton via Yalgoo 343km

36 (3) Mt Magnet-Leinster-Mt Magnet via Sandstone 311km

North-West Coastal highway

37 (1) Geraldton-Overlander Roadhouse-Geraldton via Northampton 280km

38 (1) Overlander Roadhouse-MinilyaRoadhouse-Overlander Roadhouse via Carnarvon 343km

39 (1) Minilya Roadhouse-Fortescue Roadhouse-Minilya Roadhouse via Nanutarra Roadhouse 393km

40 (1) Fortescue Roadhouse-Port Hedland-Fortescue Roadhouse via Roebourne 342km

The Murchison-Gascoyne

41 (3) Mullewa-Dairy Creek Stn-Mullewa via Murchison 421km

West Coast Country

The Pilbara

The Western Deserts

51 (3) Warburton-Ayers Rock Resort-Warburton via Docker River 576km

52 (3) Wiluna-Carnegie Station-Wiluna via Wongawol Station 349km

53 (4) Carnegie Station-Warburton-Carnegie Station via Gunbarrel Highway 493km

Curdimurka siding, old Ghan railway, near Lake Eyre South (Map 6)

THE STUART HIGHWAY

Cutting a swathe across northern South Australia and the Northern Territory, the all-sealed two lane Stuart Highway provides easy access for southerners heading to or from Central Australia and the South Australian opal fields of Coober Pedy and Mintabie. Covering a variety of landscapes, from mulga shrublands to vast never-ending saltbush plains, and culminating in the rocky grandeur of the Centralian mountains, this route is recommended for first-time outback travellers. From the Stuart Highway are unsealed but well maintained roads leading to interesting outback townships: Kingoonya, Tarcoola and Mintabie. Some travellers, even those in conventional vehicles, might wish to spice their travels with a mild adventure along these routes.

Warnings: beware of stock and kangaroos at night; road may be subject to flooding. Make unsealed side trips only in dry weather; enquire locally before proceeding - if unexperienced, stay off the side roads in summer. Department of Defence permit required for entry to Woomera Prohibited Area on the following route: Tarcoola-Stuart Highway via Bulgunnia Station. Permitted required for access to Mintabie.

NOTES

MAP 1 PORT AUGUSTA-GLENDAMBO-PORT AUGUSTA via Pimba

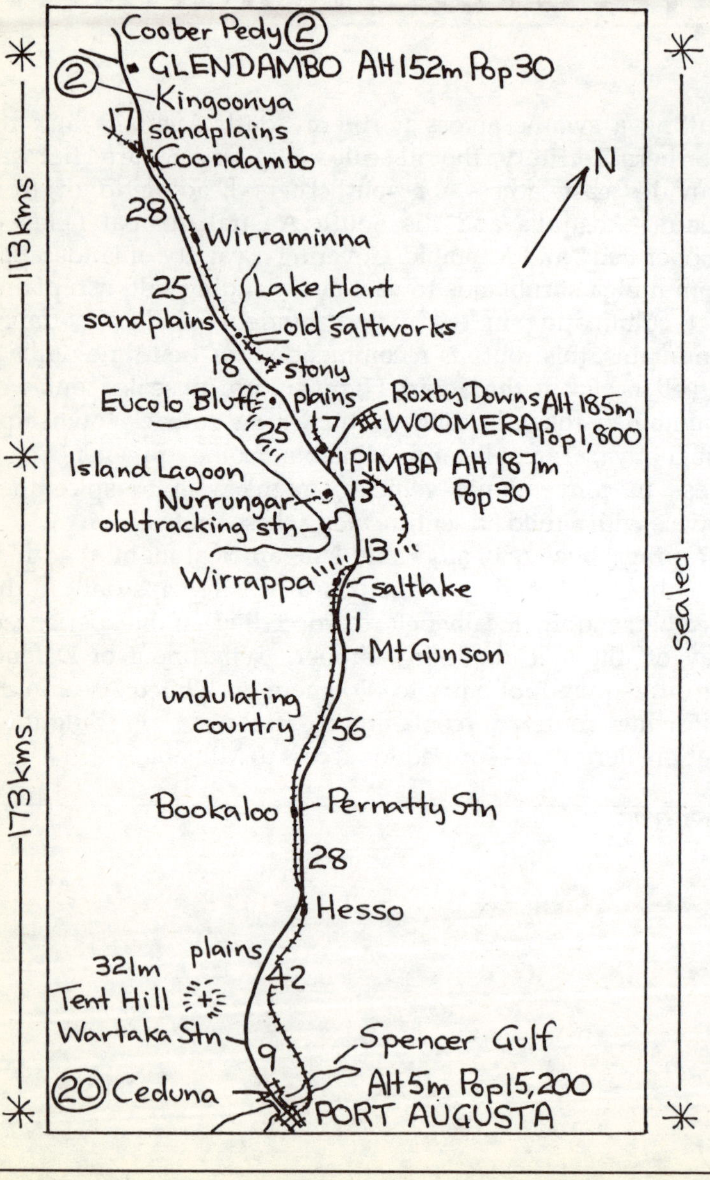

MAP 1 PORT AUGUSTA-GLENDAMBO-PORT AUGUSTA via Pimba

Grade 1

Total Distance: 286km
Average Vehicles per day: 700 west of Port Augusta
Regions Traversed: Far North, (Gairdner Plain)

GLENDAMBO: relatively new settlement servicing the highway. Roadhouse facilities, motel, store.
Sand plains support mulga shrublands with areas of western myall woodlands, each with a ground cover of saltbush.
Coondambo: railway siding.
Wirraminna: railway siding.
Sand plains support tracts of mulga; in some places low sand dunes may be seen. Many saltlakes in this area.

Lake Hart can be clearly seen from the road. A short walk (careful crossing the railway line) leads to the lake's edge and old salt works' remains; very photogenic. On the far side (you need binoculars) is the ELDO rocket launching pad.
Eucolo Bluff: lookout with good views overlooking Island Lagoon saltlake. Bluff separates the sand plain from the gibber-strewn Arcoona Plateau.
Stony plains provide vast views of saltbush.

PIMBA: roadhouse facility and railway settlement with some character. Woomera town visible in the distance. Rail buffs can get some good photographs of railway lines disappearing over the horizon at the nearby station. Motel, store, fuel.

WOOMERA: formerly a closed town but now open to visitors. Houses defence personnel and those connected with the secret Nurrungar Base nearby. Worth exploring the settlement; missile park is interesting. Full town facilities.

Nurrungar: no access. Secret base; though restricted a quick view can be had from the highway where road crosses a shallow valley just west of the old Island Lagoon Tracking Station turn-off. Radomes clearly visible.

Old Island Lagoon Tracking Station: turn-off onto old and potholey bitumen road. Only rubble marks the site of the old station but the view overlooking Island Lagoon and Pointed Island is excellent.

Wirrappa: railway siding in an interesting location: saltlake to one side, steep rocky bluff marking the edge of the Arcoona Plateau on the other.
Undulating country supports stands of mulga shrublands; elsewhere are woodlands of western myall, a low acacia tree which looks like something lifted from the African savanna. Occasional views eastward towards the Flinders Ranges.

Bookaloo: railway siding.
Hesso: railway siding. Numerous western myalls hereabouts; quite photogenic in the right light and especially eerie on cold, foggy mornings.
Plains gradually slope towards the head of Spencers Gulf. Numerous eastward views towards the western ramparts of the Flinders Ranges. Many high residual hills in the area. Plains mostly open with saltbush covering west of Port Augusta.

PORT AUGUSTA: large regional centre sometimes referred to as the crossroads of Australia as it is a major rail and road junction. Good views to the Flinders Ranges and of the northern reach of Spencer Gulf. Some sites worth visiting including Wadlata Outback Centre. Full town facilities. Stock up here if heading north.

MAP 2 GLENDAMBO-COOBER PEDY-GLENDAMBO

via Stuart Highway/Tarcoola

Grade 1 (Glendambo-Tarcoola-Stuart Highway Grade 3)

Total Distance: 252km/378km
Average Vehicles per day: 310 north of Glendambo; 5 or less north of Tarcoola
Regions Traversed: Far North, (Gairdner Plain)

COOBER PEDY: large and interesting opal mining town set upon the barren slopes of the Stuart Range; many underground residences. Worth spending a day or two in this area to visit mines, opal showrooms, underground church, Big Winch lookout, etc. No permit required to fossick on unclaimed mullock heaps; owners' permission required on occupied claims. Beware of hidden shafts - this is a real hazard. Multi-cultural population means a diversity of cafes, clubs and foodstuffs. Full town facilities. Stock up here if heading south.

Stuart Range: really a long escarpment with jump-ups, mesas, etc, locally known as breakaways. Barely visible from the highway although occasional cliffs, rocky outcrops and shallow valleys may be seen to the east.

Undulating country offers far-reaching views across the empty saltbush plains. Occasionally distant jump-ups can be seen on the eastern horizon.

Sand dunes stand isolated from one another on the saltbush plains, their relatively dense shrubby vegetation in stark contrast to the emptiness that surrounds them.

MAP 2 GLENDAMBO-COOBER PEDY-GLENDAMBO
via Stuart Highway/Tarcoola

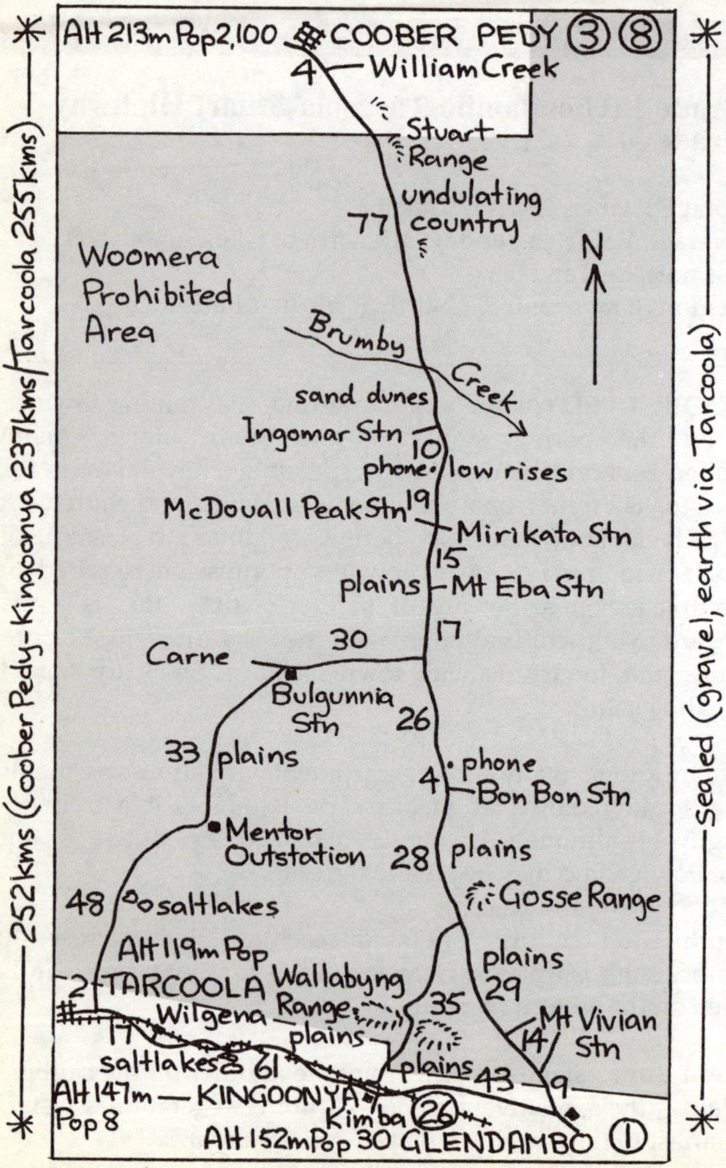

Low rises offer good views to the mulga-clad lowlands to the west and the barren saltbush plains to the east.

Phone (Teal Hole) for emergency use only.

Plains support vast tracts of mulga shrublands occasionally interspersed with patches of open saltbush country. At the McDouall Peak Station-Mirikata Station intersection the old Stuart Highway can be seen.

Phone for emergency use only.

Plains support a covering of mulga shrublands and western myall woodlands. These woodlands are attractive in the late afternoon light.

Gosse Range: low barren rocky range just visible above the tree tops.
Plains with a covering of mulga and/or western myall. Occasional low sand dunes and claypans may be seen.

GLENDAMBO: relatively new settlement servicing the highway. Roadhouse facilities, motel, store.

Stuart Highway-Glendambo via Tarcoola (make local enquiries before proceeding)

Bulgunnia Station: working sheep station. No facilities.

Plains support vast tracts of mulga shrublands with a saltbush understorey.

Mentor Outstation: no facilities available.

Saltlakes edge the road for a short distance providing a break from the surrounding mulga shrublands.

TARCOOLA: former mining settlement, nowadays a major railway settlement of some character. Old mine workings and ruins located a few kilometres north-west of the township. Stop a short while to explore and soak up the atmosphere. Hotel, store, fuel.

Wilgena: railway siding.

Saltlakes visible from the road providing a break from the mulga shrublands.
Plains support a mulga shrubland with a saltbush understorey.

KINGOONYA: interesting old Stuart Highway and former railway settlement, nowadays virtually a ghost town. Abandoned roadhouse photogenic in the right light. All buildings are on private property and some are occupied. Settlement worth a brief stop at least. Limited store and fuel available at caravan park.

Plains support limited areas of mulga and western myall otherwise open tracts of saltbush with a gibber surface.

Stuart Highway-Kingoonya road

Wallabyng Range: low stony range supporting a low saltbush shrubland; rocky outcrops visible. Either side lie plains covered with mulga shrublands and/or western myall woodlands. These woodlands form an attractive backdrop along much of this route; very photogenic in the early morning or late afternoon light.

MAP 3 COOBER PEDY-KULGERA-COOBER PEDY via Marla

Grade 1

Total Distance: 414km
Average Vehicles per day: 310 near Marla
Regions Traversed: Far North, Central Australia

KULGERA: older style roadhouse and small township with some character. Relaxing place; worth stopping for a while. Museum, hotel, motel, store, fuel.

Undulating country offering wide vistas from tops of low rises. Low granite hills; sparse shrublands cover the flats.
Sand plain supports mulga shrublands. Tops of low rises offer fair views. Occasional hills seen in the distance. Creek crossings, especially Marryat Creek, provide shady areas for rest/picnic stops. Emergency phone at Marryat Creek.

Chandler: railway settlement; no facilities.

Indulkana: Aboriginal settlement; no access without a permit. Township visible on the slopes of Mt Chandler from near the Indulkana turn-off.
Low hills of granite are attractive in the late afternoon light. Hills support saltbush and mulga.

Pitjantjatjara Aboriginal Land: freehold land owned by members of the Pitjantjatjara people. No permit required for travel on the highway.

MINTABIE: unusual and rustic opal mining centre with plenty of character. Lack of civic control means plenty of unusual dwellings, no proper roads and a casual attitude; attributes the locals prefer. Well worth visiting. Permit

MAP 3 COOBER PEDY-KULGERA-COOBER PEDY via Marla

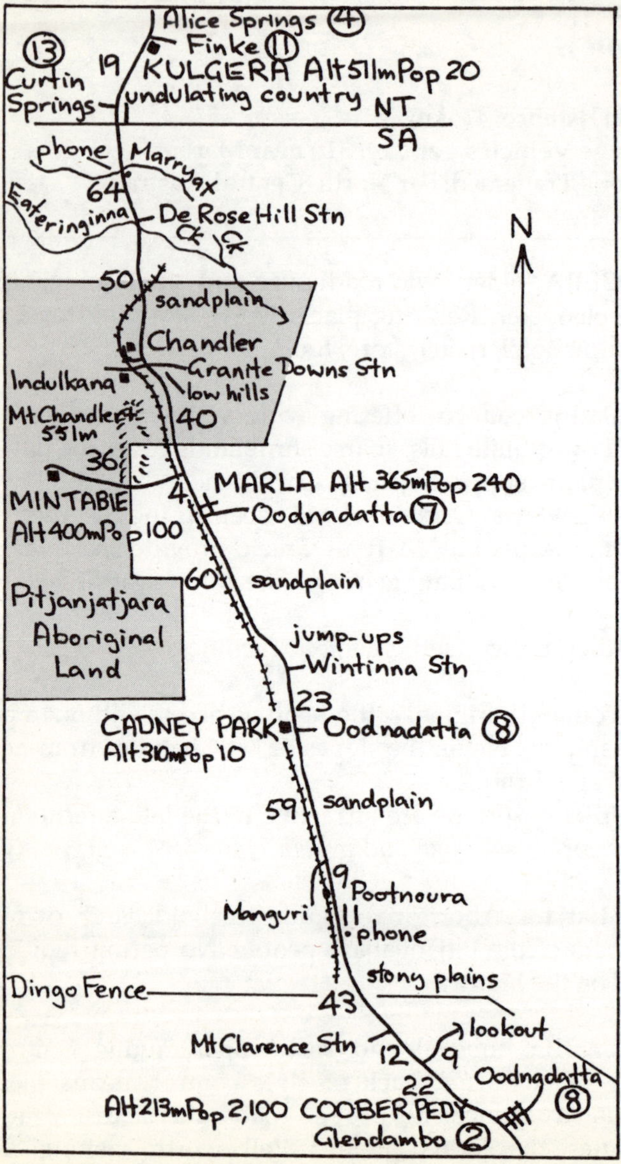

required for entry; easily obtainable from the Marla Police Station. Access road unsealed but in good condition. Stores, fuel.

MARLA: new and modern township servicing northern South Australia. Hotel, motel, store, fuel.
Sand plain forms the eastern edge of the Great Victoria Desert. Mulga shrublands occupy the plains; seasonal swamps supporting canegrass occupy shallow depressions. Occasional views from tops of rises.
Jump-ups can be seen to the east near the Wintinna Station turn-off; of moderate interest in the late afternoon light. Saltbush common.

CADNEY PARK: modern roadhouse facility set in the mulga scrub. A quiet place for an overnight stop. Motel, store, fuel.

Sand plain supports tracts of mulga.

Pootnoura: railway siding; no facilities.
Stony plains offer vast, awe-inspiring vistas. Saltbush country.

Lookout provides excellent views over Breakaway country. Some walks in this area including one to The Castle, a prominent jump-up. Dusk or dawn best for photography. A loop road leads from the lookout joining the Coober Pedy-Oodnadatta road at the Dog Fence. Route okay for conventional vehicles when dry.

COOBER PEDY: large opal mining centre with plenty of character. Many dwellings are underground, but with the advent of air-conditioning newer homes are above ground. Although it looks like a junk yard, this arid and dusty town is worth exploring. There is a lot to see and plenty of characters to meet, though most will say it is not as good as it used to be. Diverse ethnic population means a wide range of foodstuffs

MAP 4 KULGERA-ALICE SPRING-KULGERA via Erldunda

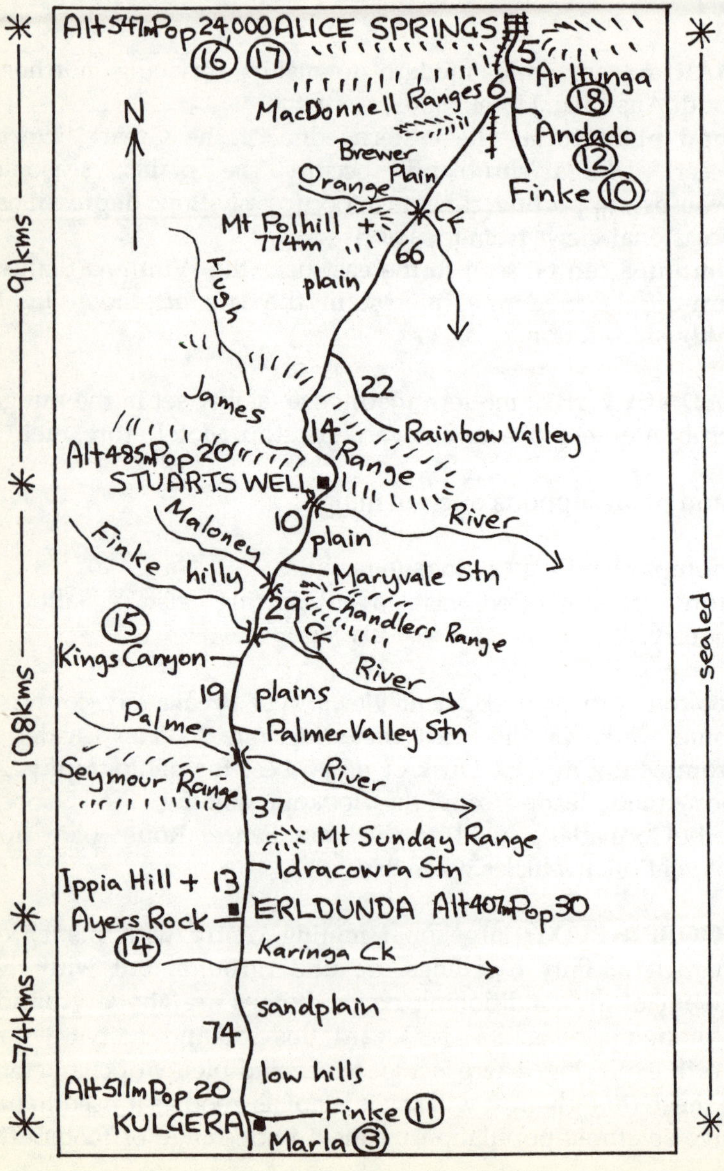

are available. Full town facilities.

MAP 4 KULGERA-ALICE SPRING-KULGERA via Erldunda

Grade 1

Total Distance: 273km
Average Vehicles per day: 270 north of Kulgera
Regions Traversed: Central Australia (Amadeus Lowland/MacDonnell Ranges)

ALICE SPRINGS: major regional centre servicing pastoralists, Aboriginal communities and tourists. Spectacularly situated beneath the red quartzite bluffs of the MacDonnell Ranges. Though the town is mostly modernised and little remains of the 'old Alice', it still retains some character and charm. Numerous tourist facilities available. Stock up here if heading in any direction. Full town facilities.

MacDonnell Ranges: spectacular series of uplifted and tilted ranges which change colour during the day. Very photogenic, especially at dusk and dawn. Road passes through the narrow Heavitree Gap. Lesser ranges rise above the scattered development of South Alice Springs.

Brewer Plain: stony plain supporting a mulga shrubland. Occasional views northward towards the MacDonnell Ranges.

Mt Polhill forms a prominent ridgeline above the plain; mountain is a part of the Waterhouse Range.

Plain south of Mt Polhill supports a mulga shrubland with eucalypt scrubs dominated by blue mallees on the sandy sections.

Rainbow Valley: attractive and multi-coloured clifflines, best seen at dawn and dusk. Camping available adjacent to claypans; access road can be sandy - if unsure seek local information. No facilities.

James Range: moderately rugged rocky ranges supporting spinifex and a variety of sparse, low-growing shrubs. Interesting views from the road; photogenic in the right light.

STUARTS WELL: new roadhouse facility. Adjacent is the Camel Outback Safari which also provides services to travellers. Store, fuel.

Plain south of Hugh River supports open grassy areas. Fair views to the south towards the flat-topped Chandlers Range.

Hilly country near Maloneys Creek is pleasant enough for a brief stop. Rough track on western side of Maloneys Creek passes through a fossil locality. Interesting area to explore on foot for an hour or two. Track leaves highway at Maloneys Creek bridge.

Finke River: broad sandy riverbed lined with superb river red gums. This river is said to be the oldest in the world. Worth stopping for a short while. Occasionally food and snacks are available from a caravan nearby.

Plains and low rises support open grasslands (offering fair views) with patches of mulga.

Seymour Range and **Mt Sunday Range** are just some of the low ranges and hills which loom as purple ridges in the distance. Between these low ranges are some minor sand dunes. Desert oaks and spinifex occupy the sandy country.

ERLDUNDA: busy and modern roadhouse facility with little character. Motel, store, fuel. Area abounds with desert oaks, a graceful, willowy type of she-oak.

Karinga Creek: low lying flood country with saltpans and low dunes.

Sand plain supports a mulga shrubland with a grassy understorey.

Low hills: interesting low granite hills and outcrops; hills rise 50m above the plain. Mulga shrublands on the flats. One access point lies 8km north of Kulgera on eastern side of road (about a kilometre in): worth a quick look.

KULGERA: small township dominated by a roadhouse facility. A relaxing place with plenty of character. Museum, hotel, motel, store, fuel.

NOTES

THE FLINDERS RANGES-OODNADATTA TRACK

Singularly the most spectacular region of the southern outback, the Flinders Ranges is an area of high, upstanding quartzite cliffs, undulating but elevated lowlands and gently sloping piedmont plains. The first part of this route is sealed, taking the traveller past high mountains and rocky bluffs; leading off the route are easily travelled unsealed roads which visit deep valleys and narrow gorges. Further north, prior to the commencement of the Oodnadatta Track at Marree, the route is unsealed.

The unsealed but well-maintained Oodnadatta Track follows probably the world's most ancient trail, an Aboriginal pathway that led from mound spring to mound spring. These natural outlets of the Great Artesian Basin, often set upon a mound of their own making, were utilised by Aboriginal traders transferring goods (pituri, ochre, implements) and knowledge between southern and northern Australia. In their footsteps came European explorers, pastoralists and miners, the Overland Telegraph and the original Ghan railway, each making use of the reliable water supply in this, some of the most arid country in Australia.

Today's Oodnadatta Track provides access to northern South Australia, the Finke River Country, Central Australia and the Simpson Desert. Whilst commonly used by 4WDs, this route is accessible, when dry, to travellers in conventional vehicles, and is recommended to anyone who has an interest in Australia's history or a love of wide open spaces.

Warnings: on the sealed road beware of stock and kangaroos at night; this section is subject to flooding, especially flash flooding. The unsealed road is impassable in wet weather and subject to flooding. Avoid travelling at night. Make local enquiries before proceeding; in summer, inform reliable person of your intentions if travelling between Marree and Marla. If inexperienced, stay out of this area in summer. Desert Parks Pass required to visit Lake Eyre National Park (but not required for Lake Eyre South). Road is generally well maintained but wash-outs can occur after rain, floods. Note: no reliable habitation between William Creek and Oodnadatta (203km).

Dalhousie Springs track, Spring Creek basin (Map 9)

MAP 5 PORT AUGUSTA-LYNDHURST-PORT AUGUSTA via Hawker

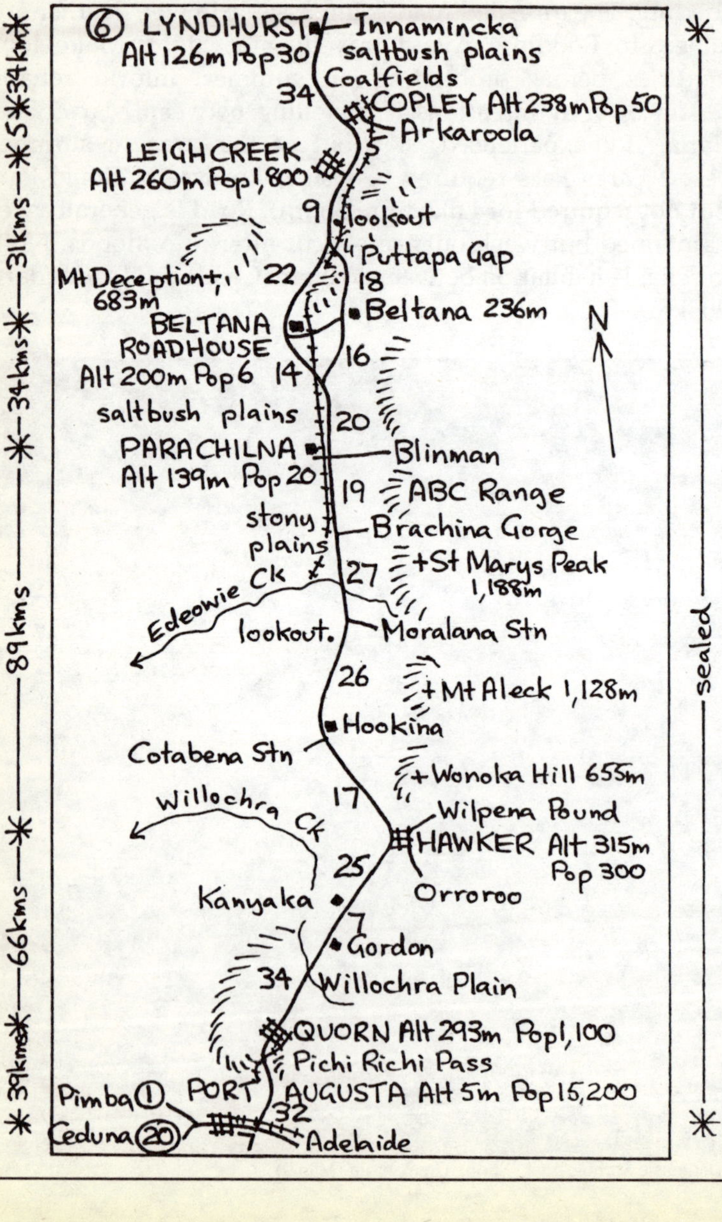

MAP 5 PORT AUGUSTA-LYNDHURST-PORT AUGUSTA via Hawker

Grade 1

Total Distance: 298km
Average Vehicles per day: 180 north of Hawker
Regions Traversed: Flinders Ranges, Saltlakes

LYNDHURST: bush township with plenty of character. Start of the Strzelecki Track. Hotel, store, fuel.

Saltbush plains mark the northern edge of the Flinders Ranges, their purple jagged skylines visible on the horizon.
Coalfields: open cut mining has turned this landscape upside down. Viewing platforms provide scenes of the upheaval; turn-off 12km north of Copley, 3km in.

COPLEY: former railway township, many interesting stone buildings; today virtually a suburb of Leigh Creek. Hotel, stores, fuel.

LEIGH CREEK: modern mining town and district centre with a work camp atmosphere. Limited accommodation facilities. Stock up here if heading north. Stores, fuel.

Lookout south of Leigh Creek definitely worth a look. Excellent view of the flat iron formations of the Mt Bayley Range; also the broad saltbush plains leading to Mt Deception.
Puttapa Gap: attractive rocky gorge with old Ghan railway ruins and relics; wild hops here colourful in spring. Note: road unsealed.

Beltana: historic township well worth visiting; all buildings are privately owned and some are occupied - do not trespass. Information available from roadhouse and old police station.

22km east (not shown on map) is Sliding Rock mine and township ruins; also worth seeing. Note: rough road to Sliding Rock.

BELTANA ROADHOUSE: small roadhouse facility. Information available regarding Beltana ruins. Store, fuel.

Saltbush plains: good views towards the western ramparts of the Flinders Ranges, especially in the late afternoon light; can also be attractive in the showery weather of winter.

PARACHILNA: small grazing and railway settlement. Interesting bush pub. Hotel, fuel. Good camping in Parachilna Gorge on Blinman Road.

Stony plains covered with saltbush. At times, especially on rises, there are excellent views towards the Flinders Ranges, particularly near Edeowie Creek; travelling south the massive buttresses of Wilpena Pound seem to rise above the road.

Lookout south of Moralana Station turn-off: worth stopping at for excellent view of Mt Aleck; particularly interesting with uplifting clouds (common during winter).

Hookina: photogenic stone ruins set on an empty saltbush plain. Distant ranges provide a dramatic backdrop.

Wonoka Hill area: interesting ascent/descent of the ranges; open saltbush-covered hills and rocky ranges.

HAWKER: small grazing and tourist town; interesting stone buildings. Worth stocking up here if heading north. Hotels, motels, stores, fuel. Many farm accommodations in the area.

Kanyaka: old station ruins, worth seeing. Nearby are ruins of Wilson, an old township; a few stone shells of buildings are all that remain.

Gordon: former township of which little remains.

Willochra Plain: saltbush and grass-covered plain which has an air of desolation. Once this area was farmed for wheat, hence the number of township ruins. The aridity of the area could support neither farms nor settlements.

QUORN: attractive town with many fine old buildings; formerly a railway township. From here an historic railway regularly runs through the Pichi Richi Pass following the old Ghan line. A pleasant town in which to spend a few days. Full town facilities.

Pichi Richi Pass: narrow and steep valley negotiating the rugged western rampart of the Flinders Ranges; occasional good views if heading south.

PORT AUGUSTA: large regional centre located at the head of Spencer Gulf; saltbush and salt marshes surround the town. Good views in the afternoon light towards the Flinders Ranges. Worth seeing is the Wadlata Outback Centre. Full town facilities.

NOTES

MAP 6 LYNDHURST-WILLIAM CREEK-LYNDHURST via Marree

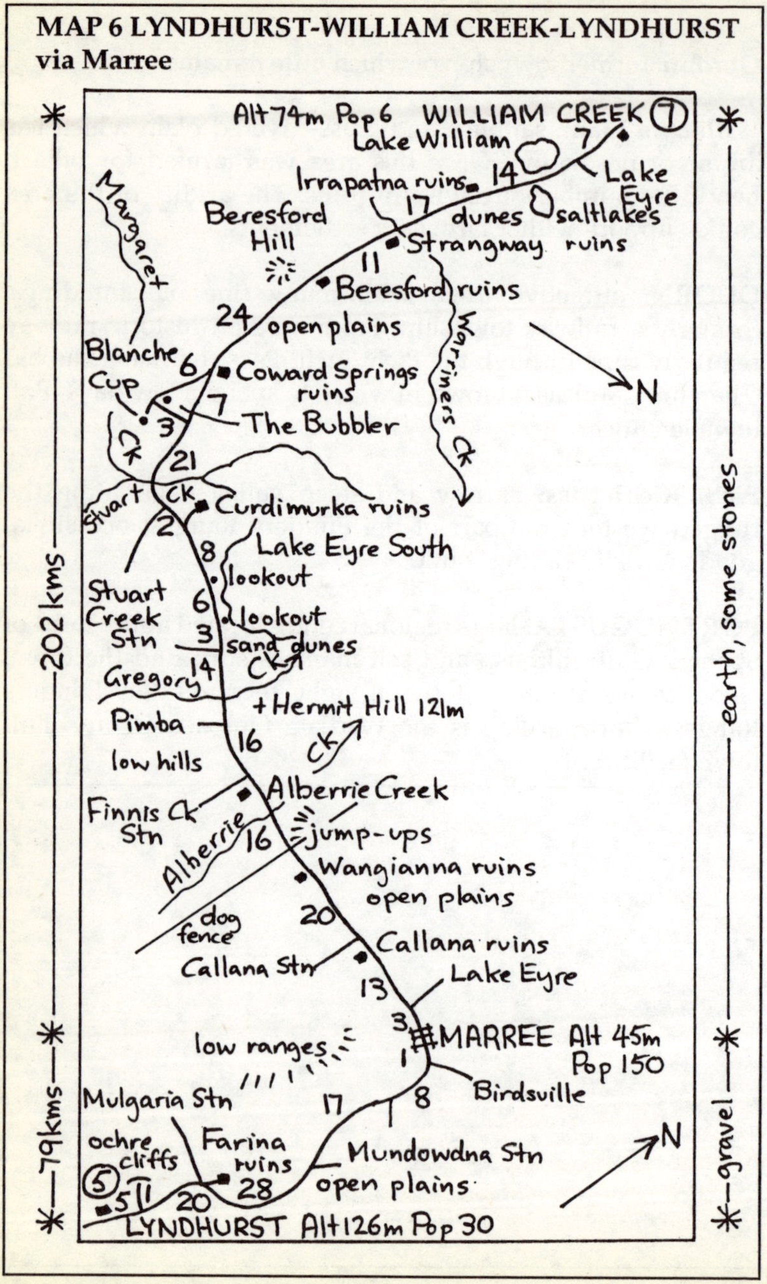

MAP 6 LYNDHURST-WILLIAM CREEK-LYNDHURST via Marree

Grade 3

Total Distance: 281km
Average Vehicles per day: 25 near William Creek
Regions Traversed: Saltlakes

WILLIAM CREEK: bush pub and a few dwellings; former Ghan railway settlement, now South Australia's smallest township. Photogenic buildings, interesting tourist maps. Make enquiries here about 4WD track to ABC Bay on Lake Eyre, one of the most desolate places in Australia (Desert Parks Pass required).

Lake William and adjacent saltlakes: very open plains with interesting lakes; photogenic when full of water. Gypsum cliffs line lakes on northern side of road. Min Min lights have been sighted in this area.

Irrapatna ruins: stone ruin, formerly fettler's hut on old Ghan railway.

Dunes near ruins called the Irrapatna Dunes. Claypans common; vivid red dunes very photogenic. Sand-hill cane-grass and mulga flats with areas of saltbush dominate this area.

Strangway ruins: former overland telegraph repeater station and township, graveyard, flowing bore and mound springs (low reed-topped hill near Warriners Creek). Surrounded by open plains with vast vistas.

Beresford ruins: former fettlers' camp on old Ghan railway: desalination plant, ruined building, flowing bore and dam. Nearby Beresford Hill looms large on the open plains, rising

44m above the plain. Nearby are Warburton Springs.
Open plains extend between Warriners Creek and Curdimurka supporting a cover of saltbush. Low ranges visible to the south are stony plains and jump-up country.

Coward Springs ruins: former railway settlement ruins; old house quite photogenic (beware of deep wells). Flowing bore to the north has formed a wetland; line of Athol pines mark out the old hotel. A seasonal campground operates here during the cooler months: limited facilities, check beforehand.

The Bubbler and **Blanche Cup:** mound springs, both worth visiting. The Bubbler bubbles up sand and water, creating endless patterns. Small creek runs to a wetland, otherwise barren salt flats. Blanche Cup is a high mound spring, reed-lined with blue pool of water. If unsure of track to main road, enter and exit via Coward Springs turn-off.

Stuart/Margaret Creek crossing: salt-encrusted creekline set 12m below sea level.
Curdimurka ruins: preserved ruins and section of train line; a former fettlers' camp on the old Ghan railway - very photogenic. Please do not vandalise. Buildings, desalination plant, flowing bore, absolutely desolate countryside. This area is below sea level.

Lake Eyre South: low dunes provide lookout points over Lake Eyre South saltpan. Very photogenic in dawn/dusk light or when full of water. Rough track to lake edge (walk down); numerous wildflowers after rains. Lake bed is part of Lake Eyre National Park. A walk over the salt surface is very interesting; mounds of salt house small spiders which feed on wind-blown insects. Only idiots attempt to drive on its surface.

Hermit Hill and **low hills** support a low open woodland of eucalypts; structurally this country is a northern outlier of the

Flinders Ranges.
Gregory Creek: interesting old Ghan railway bridge crossing salt-encrusted creek.
Alberrie Creek: old outback style house (very photogenic); do not trespass. Nearby creek of same name set amongst jump-ups; very photogenic from western hillside in afternoon light. Dog fence crosses hereabout; part of the longest fence in the world.

Wangianna ruins: former old Ghan railway siding.
Open plains support vast expanses of saltbush; fair views from tops of rises. Willouran Ranges visible in the south.
Callana ruins: former old Ghan railway siding; water hose and goods platform still visible.

MARREE: former Ghan railway township and pastoral centre; today a grazing and tourist centre. Descendants of the Afghan cameleers live here, as do a number of Arabana people. Interesting buildings, railway ruins, a reconstructed Afghan mosque and the Arabana Centre (a repository and museum of Arabana and other Aboriginal knowledge: well worth visiting) make it worthwhile to spend some time here. Enquire here about road conditions. Hotel, stores, fuel.
Open plains support saltbush; westward lies the Willouran Range.

Farina ruins: old township built as a wheat-growing settlement! Many photogenic ruins, old equipment, railway relics, etc. Worth investigating; please do not disturb anything.

Ochre Cliffs: ancient Aboriginal ochre mine; cliffs display numerous colours - afternoons best for photography. After rain quartz crystals may be seen.

LYNDHURST: small bush township with plenty of character. Hotel, store, fuel.

MAP 7 WILLIAM CREEK-MARLA-WILLIAM CREEK via Oodnadatta

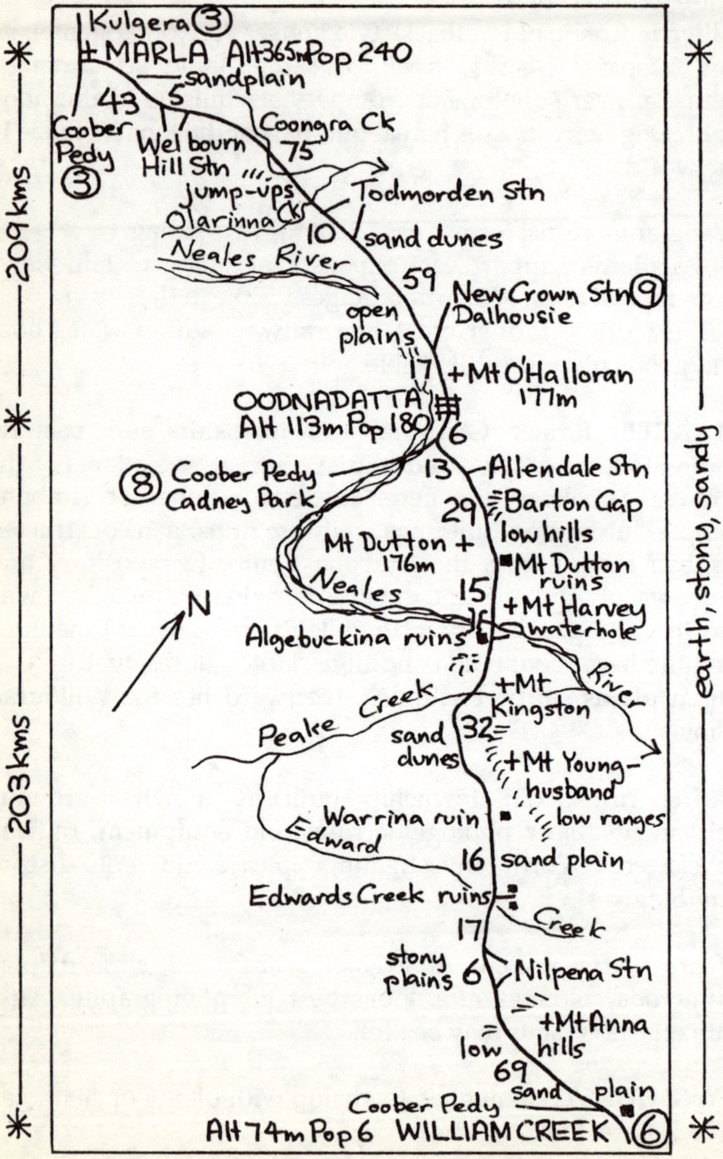

MAP 7 WILLIAM CREEK-MARLA-WILLIAM CREEK via Oodnadatta

Grade 3

Total Distance: 412km
Average Vehicles per day: 25 north of William Creek
Regions Traversed: Far North

MARLA: recently established township providing highway and government services. Modern facilities. Motel, store, fuel. Stock up here if heading south.

Sand plain supports a mulga shrubland. This section of the route follows the old Stuart Highway. Near Welbourn Hill Station turn-off are gibber plains.

Jump-ups line the route and mark the skyline. This saltbush-covered gibber country is attractive in early morning/late afternoon light.

Coongra Creek flood-plain supports a low woodland of coolabahs. Jump-ups visible to the south rise 50m above the plain. Waterholes north of road approximately 3km west of Olarinna Creek.

Sand dunes visible to the north of the road form part of Alberga Dunefield. Dunes support sand-hill canegrass and spinifex; intervening flats covered with mulga.

Open plains provide vast vistas from tops of rises. Saltbush dominates the gibber-strewn countryside. To the south lies the northern branch of the Neales River, marked by a low coolabah woodland.
Mt O'Halloran: rough track (better to walk) leads to a lookout: good views.

OODNADATTA: interesting and photogenic bush township with plenty of character; one of the outback's tidiest towns. Some ruins connected with the old Ghan railway. Sizeable community of Yankunytjatjara people (pronounced 'young goonjarrer'); they refer to Oodnadatta as Tanytjipaka. Worth spending some time here to explore the town and area; also call into the Pink Roadhouse for local information. Hotel, stores, fuel.

Barton Gap: a low pass through a set of hills; good views to the south.

Low hills line the road rising to the heights of Mt Dutton: good views (no track) from the top. Sparse covering of saltbush dominates the landscape. Good views from nearby Cadnaowie lookout.

Mt Dutton ruins: stone fettler's cottage and water tank, part of the old Ghan railway. Located on private property: do not disturb anything. This attractive area supports the tree-lined Ockenden Creek. South of the creek and west of the road, the reed-lined Ockenden Spring can be seen. South of the ruins, purple and red gibbers cover the hills and low rises.

Algebuckina ruins: definitely worth a stop; lots to explore. Stone ruins connected with the old Ghan railway; large red bridge over Neales River (very photogenic) - is one of the longest railway bridges in South Australia. Be very careful if walking on the bridge decking. Old gold mine near northern end of railway bridge (west of the old railway line) and Algebuckina Waterhole (through the gate east of the bridge then a kilometre or so in); good camping, no firewood.

Sand dunes provide a change in countryside; sand-hill canegrass and spinifex grow on the dunes, while mulga and saltbush occupy the intervening flats.

Warrina ruins: former Ghan railway ruin. Nearby a track

leads to the recently restored Peake ruins, a former OT station (not shown on map).
Sand plain supports a sparse covering of mulga and saltbush; some low dunes.

Edwards Creek: former Ghan railway settlement, now abandoned. Many ruins, some quite photogenic; also numerous railway relics. Worth a quick look at least.

Stony plains and low rises support a very sparse growth of saltbush and burrs. Fair views eastward from tops of rises.

Low hills form the southern part of the Denison Ranges, an unspectacular low range of bevelled rocky ridges; numerous dry gullies and rocky outcrops. Fair view to the south about 5km east of Wilyalallina Creek (not shown on map) overlooking a vast expanse of mulga-clad sand dune country - it makes you feel a long way from home!

WILLIAM CREEK: interesting bush township with some character. Hotel, fuel.

NOTES

PAINTED DESERT COUNTRY

These two interconnecting roads, presented as one route, between the Stuart Highway and Oodnadatta Track, pass through some of northern South Australia's remote backblocks country. Crossing broad coolabah-clad drainage channels and sweeping saltbush plains, these roads, though accessible to carefully driven conventional vehicles when dry, are isolated and lonely and recommended for those travellers who seek wide open spaces tinged with an element of adventure. At intervals the plains are interrupted by low jump-up hills, and while each hill is interesting in such an empty space, it is the Arckaringa Hills, on the Cadney Park-Oodnadatta road, which give this area its name, for the Arckaringa Hills present an amazing display of pastel colours on their slopes, a visual delight worth travelling far to see.

Warnings: road impassable in wet weather and subject to flooding. Avoid travelling at night. Always seek local advice before proceeding and inform reliable person of your intentions - stay out of this area in summer unless experienced.

NOTES

MAP 8 COOBER PEDY-CADNEY PARK-COOBER PEDY via Oodnadatta

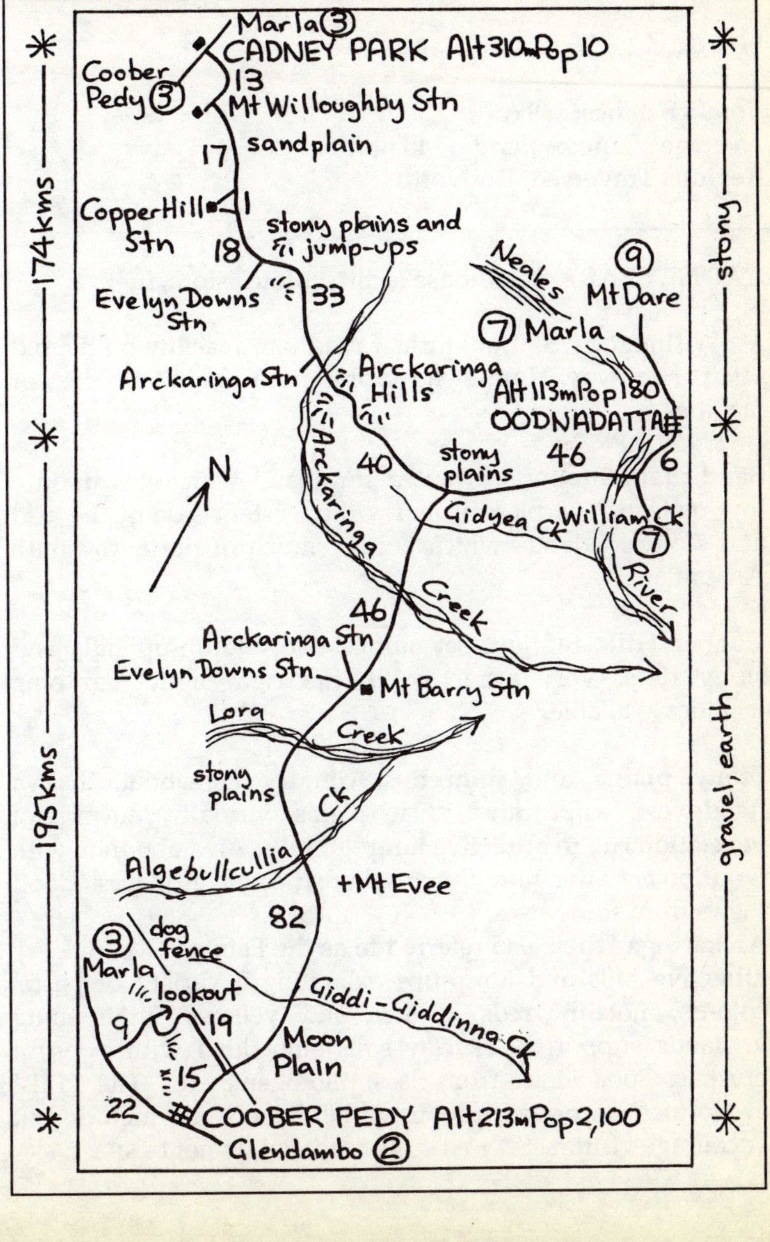

MAP 8 COOBER PEDY-CADNEY PARK-COOBER PEDY via Oodnadatta

Grade 3

Total Distance: 369km
Average Vehicles per day: 40 north of Coober Pedy
Regions Traversed: Far North

CADNEY PARK: roadhouse facility. Motel, store, fuel.

Mt Willoughby Station: former roadhouse facility on the old Stuart Highway. Homestead visible from road. No access or facilities.

Sand plain supports a mulga shrubland which sits upon a low plateau. The plateau marks the western side of the arid and stony lowlands which occupy much of northern South Australia.

Copper Hills Station: set amongst low jump-up hills and stony rises. Very attractive in the right light. Camping facilities available.

Stony plains and jump-ups: country hereabouts has a 'wild-west' appearance. Flat plains virtually devoid of vegetation run to attractive jump-up hills. Area abounds with wildflowers after rain. Some saltbush cover in places. Good views from stony rises.
Arckaringa Hills: also referred to as the Painted Desert. Very attractive hills and jump-ups exhibiting a variety of pastel colours, notably reds, whites and yellows. Intervening lowlands support black clay soils embedded with gypsum crystals. Good views from rises; photogenic area. The 'Hills' are located on private property, the owners of which do not encourage visitors. Stay near the road and do not trespass.

Stony plains exhibit gibbers which run to the horizon. Skyline occasionally broken by distant jump-ups. Arckaringa Hills visible to the west.

Neales River: multi-channelled stream and coolabah-clad flood-plain.

OODNADATTA: interesting township; many historic buildings including old Ghan railway station. Sizeable population of Yankunytjatjara-speaking people who refer to Oodnadatta as Tanytjipaka. Worth half a day here at least, to absorb the atmosphere. Visit roadhouse for stacks of information. Hotel, store, fuel.

Stony plains covered with saltbush line most of the route. Distant views with occasional jump-up hills obtained from tops of rises. Creek crossings support flood-plain clad coolabah woodlands. "Floating mountain" mirages common.

Moon Plain: said to be South Australia's most featureless plain. In some localities there are no visible features between your boots and the horizon in all directions. Gypsum can be seen sparkling in the soft earth.

Dog Fence: part of the longest fence in the world. Junction for loop road to Breakaways Lookout (okay for conventional vehicles when dry). Fossilised shells can be found along this track near a shallow creek bed. Stuart Range, a line of jump-ups, visible to the west.

COOBER PEDY: sizeable opal mining town with many dug-out dwellings, although above-ground buildings are nowadays common. Despite its junkyard appearance there is much to see. Worth spending some time here to absorb the atmosphere. Full town facilities. Stock up here if heading north.

FINKE RIVER COUNTRY-SIMPSON DESERT

Fringing the stony plains of northern South Australia and occupying the westernmost portion of the Simpson Desert where it abuts the landscapes of Central Australia, the Finke River Country is for adventurous travellers. This remote arid land of far flung cattle stations, brooding wilderness country and vivid red sand dunes presents the best aspects of the wild outback: unlimited space, isolation, and a sense of freedom that can move people. It is the sort of country the traveller can revel in; or perish in if unprepared. The landscapes for the most part are dominated by the outlying and peripheral sand dunes of the Simpson Desert, which merge into mulga-clad shrublands on its northern and western margins, and stony saltbush-covered plains in the south. Interrupting this vastness are isolated features: Chambers Pillar, the old Ghan railway and its attendant ruins, isolated homesteads and, most surprising of all, the largest assembly of natural springs in Australia - the Dalhousie Springs.

This part of the outback is not for everyone. Travellers and vehicles need to be well prepared, and additional supplies of food and water should be carried. Very experienced drivers of suitably prepared conventional vehicles can travel here, within limits, but virtually all of this country is unsuitable for the regular family sedan.

Warnings: roads impassable in wet weather and subject to flooding. Avoid travelling at night. Carry an adequate supply of detailed maps and extra food and water. Always make local enquiries before proceeding, and inform reliable person of your intentions. In summer stay out of this area unless very experienced; convoy travel recommended at this time. Roads suitable for very experienced drivers of conventional vehicles with extreme care. The following routes are definitely 4WD only: Hamilton Station-Dalhousie Springs via Pedirka; Finke-Maryvale Station; Chambers Pillar access road. The Kulgera-Finke and Alice Springs-Maryvale Station roads, when dry, are usually okay for all conventional vehicles driven with care. Due to deep sand, conventional vehicles should travel in convoy with a high clearance 4WD between Mt Dare and New Andado. Please note that the Pedirka Track (Map 9) crosses private property and that permission to use it is required from Kidman Holdings.

A Desert Parks Pass is required for travel and camping within Witjira National Park; a Desert Parks Camping Permit is available for one or two nights camping at Dalhousie Springs only. Note: no habitation between Hamilton Station and Mt Dare (141km); Hamilton Station and Mt Dare via Dalhousie Springs (140km); Hamilton Station and New Crown Station (149km); Finke and Maryvale Station (121km); Old Andado and Allambi Station (217km); Kulgera and Finke (150km).

NOTES

MAP 9 OODNADATTA-OLD ANDADO-OODNADATTA via Eringa Ruin/Dalhousie Springs

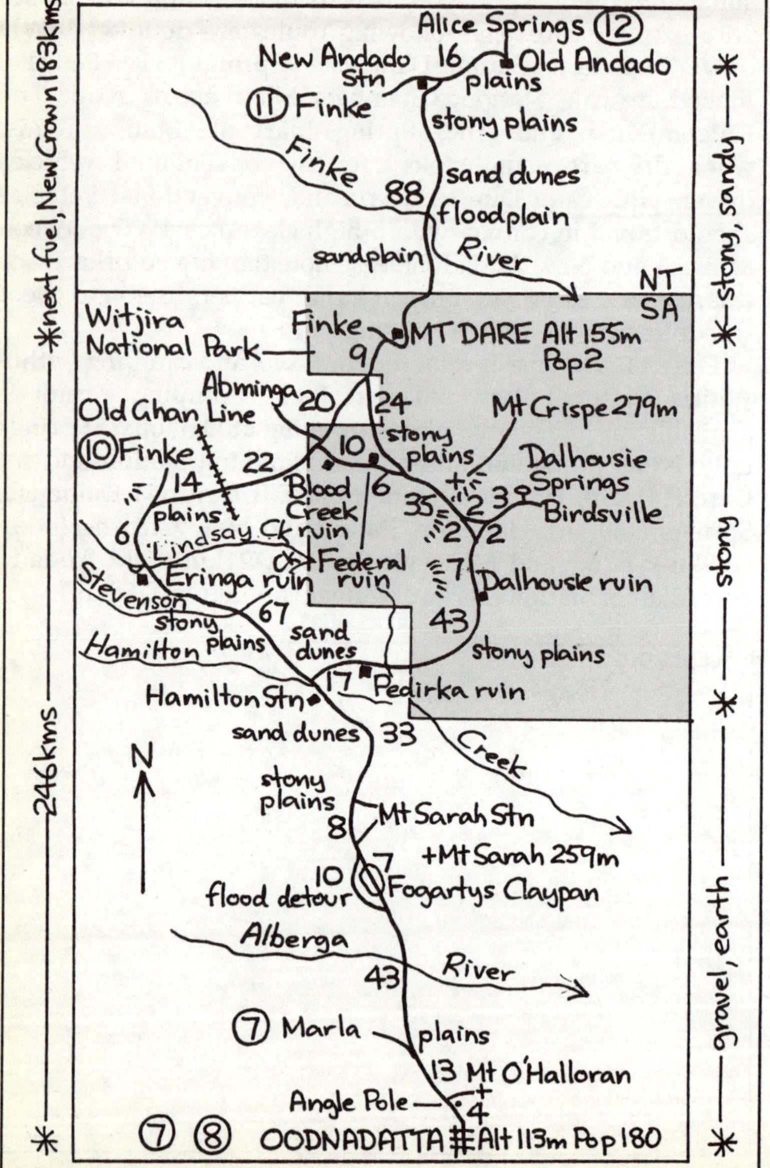

MAP 9 OODNADATTA-OLD ANDADO-OODNADATTA

via Eringa Ruin/Dalhousie Springs

Grade 4 (Hamilton Station-Dalhousie Springs Grade 5)

Total Distance: 350km via Eringa ruin; 357km via Dalhousie ruin
Average Vehicles per day: 5-30 (maximum during winter school holidays)
Regions Traversed: Far North, Simpson Desert

Old Andado: old homestead offering camping facilities and basic accommodation. Awesome location in a remote area. Two high soft sand dunes immediately west of the homestead could prove difficult for low clearance vehicles. No stores or fuel available. Nearest fuel at New Crown Station (111km); next fuel northward at Alice Springs (316km).
Plains support a sparse coolabah woodland subject to flooding; elsewhere are sand plains with low dunes.

New Andado Station: working cattle station; no facilities.

Stony plains support only the barest of vegetation; jump-ups visible on the horizon. Of the occasional shrubs to be seen most are either emu-bushes or dead finish.
Sand dunes form an outlier of the Simpson Desert; low uneven dunes line the road supporting a cover of acacias.
Flood-plain supports a relatively dense growth of coolabahs. In places the flood-plain extends between low-lying dunes. Minor dry channels indicate the Finke River. A number of disused windmills and station relics can be seen at intervals.
Sand plain of deep, soft sand (difficult for low clearance vehicles) abuts the coolabah-clad Finke River flood-plain.

Numerous acacia shrubs.

MT DARE: former station homestead, nowadays offering services for travellers. Call in here for Witjira National Park information, Desert Park Passes, etc. Basic accommodation, store, fuel.

Blood Creek ruin: remains of an old store run by Ted Colson, the first European to complete a Simpson Desert crossing. No buildings, just scattered relics.

Old Ghan Line: sleepers, low embankments and shallow cuttings mark the site of the Old Ghan Railway; worth a quick look at least.
Plains support an attractive array of small gibbers and quartz. Some saltbush ground cover; elsewhere small gidgee trees looking like large Japanese 'bonsais' are very photogenic. Low hills and jump-ups line the route.

Eringa ruin: former station homestead; photogenic ruins and scattered relics. Nearby is an attractive waterhole.

Stony plains along this section of the route occupy two levels: the lower plain supports a thin cover of saltbush and has smallish gibbers; the upper plain is virtually unvegetated and has very attractive large red, purple and black gibbers. Expansive views from the edges of the upper plain. At intervals coolabah-lined creeks cross the lower plains. Shady river red gums line Stevenson and Hamilton Creeks.
Hamilton Station: no facilities. Noteworthy because the road passes through its centre (please slow down); also unusually sited on sand dunes.

Sand dunes support a variety of shrubs; an extension of the much larger Alberga Dunefield. Occasional eastward views to distant jump-ups.
Stony plains: saltbush-covered plains with views to Mt Sarah

and other jump-ups.

Fogartys Claypan: an interesting silk-smooth crossing on a claypan surrounded by low dunes. A wet weather track detours on the western side.

Alberga River: a river red gum-lined watercourse. Shade!

Plains alternate between low sand dunes covered with acacias, saltbush-clad gibbers, gidgee-lined creeks and low jump-ups. North of Oodnadatta is very barren-looking country.

Mt O'Halloran: rough track to top (walking would preserve this track; park at base). Excellent views of the surrounding countryside, including the sweep of the Neales River. A good place to appreciate what Aboriginal dot paintings are attempting to convey.

Angle Pole: a rustic memorial to a pole where the old Overland Telegraph Line changed direction.

OODNADATTA: interesting bush township; numerous historic buildings including those connected with the old Ghan railway. Worth spending some time here to absorb the atmosphere. Hotel, stores, fuel. Stock up here if heading north.

Pedirka Track-Dalhousie Springs Route

Stony plains support a sparse covering of saltbush with a smattering of shrubs, mostly emu-bushes and dead finish. Numerous broad sweeping views.

Federal ruin: former homestead site marked by old yards and scattered relics. Nearby are the remains of a ruined hut.

Mt Crispe: high jump-up located at the southern end of a complex of jump-ups. Stony plains abound (travel here is rough and slow) with expansive views; good photographic opportunities in the right light. Nearby lies Christmas Creek, a bore fed creek with a dense growth of vegetation; quite unusual in this setting. Bore has now been capped.

Dalhousie Springs: thermal and mound springs, natural outlets of the Great Artesian Basin - forms part of Australia's largest spring complex. Swimming in the main pool is a unique and exquisite experience - not to be missed! Please do not use soap or detergent near the pool. Popular camping site but barren, windy, and with no firewood. Surrounding area exhibits salt-encrusted surfaces, barren ground, numerous jump-ups and small melaleuca-lined springs. Nearby is the Spring Creek Basin, a very arid valley with salt-encrusted pans; a wet weather detour is available.

Dalhousie ruins: worth visiting; date palms and stone ruins are very photogenic. Climb the eastern ridge for awesome views.

Stony plains offer expansive views of nothing but rocks; numerous shallow valleys with washed-out creeks. Track often indistinct; offers very slow travelling indeed. Very scary country hereabouts.

Stevenson Creek: shady, dry creek bed lined with river red gums. Located between gibber plains and sand dunes.
Pedirka ruin: old Ghan railway settlement; interesting buildings and graffiti (a fettler's life was lonely!). Old railway bridge nearby; railway relics. Note: this ruin is on private property; do not disturb anything.

Sand dunes: impressive red dunes forming an outlier of the Alberga Dunefield. Acacias dominate the plant life; numerous claypans between the dunes. Beware of on-coming vehicles.

MAP 10 ERINGA-ALICE SPRINGS-ERINGA via Finke

Grade 5 (Eringa-Finke Grade 4) (Maryvale-Alice Springs Grade 3)

Total Distance: 349km
Average Vehicles per day: 5-30 south of Finke (maximum during winter school holidays)
Regions Traversed: Far North, Simpson Desert, Central Australia

---

ALICE SPRINGS: large regional centre spectacularly located amongst the red quartzite ridges of the MacDonnell Ranges. Though mostly a rebuilt town, the place still has character. Wide range of tourist facilities and accommodation. Worth spending a day or two here to learn of Alice's secrets. Stock up here if heading in any direction. Full town facilities.

MacDonnell Ranges: incredible range of bold ridges and deep, narrow gaps. Ranges change colour throughout the day. Road passes through Heavitree Gap. Lesser ranges rise above the South Alice Springs development area.

Brewer Plain: stony plain supporting a mulga shrubland. Occasional low sandstone ridges. On sandy flats grow eucalypt shrubs, typically blue mallee. Northward are occasional views to the MacDonnell Ranges.

Ewaninga: former old Ghan railway siding. A restored fettler's cottage has kiosk, open to service passengers travelling on the restored section of the old railway. Train runs four times a week - highly recommended. Make enquiries at MacDonnell Siding in South Alice Springs. Nearby are the Ewaninga rock carvings set amongst low

MAP 10 ERINGA-ALICE SPRINGS-ERINGA via Finke

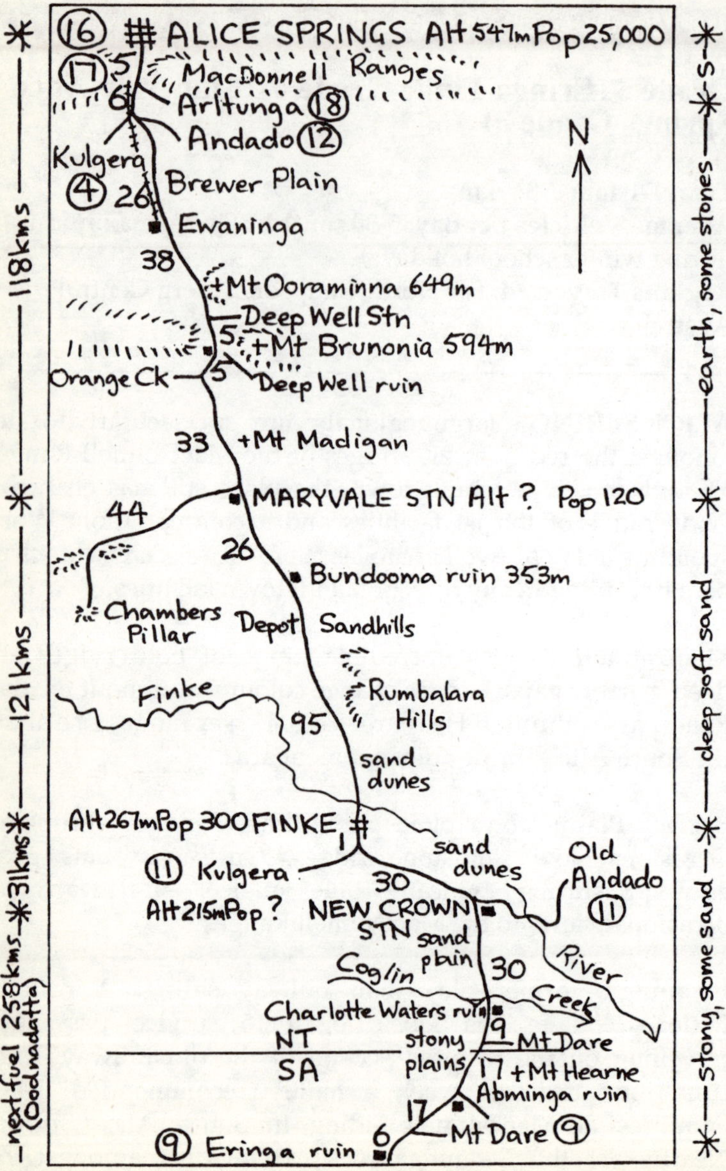

rocky outcrops; adjacent is a photogenic claypan. Definitely worth a look - no camping in conservation park.

Deep Well ruin: little remains of the former Ghan railway siding, but the countryside is worth stopping for. The road and old railway pass beneath Mt Brunonia through a rocky gap; part of the James Range.

MARYVALE STATION: cattle station which provides basic services to travellers. Aboriginal artifacts for sale. Store, fuel.

Chambers Pillar: spectacular rocky outcrop marked with explorers' graffiti. Nearby is the equally impressive Castle, another rocky outcrop. Pillar stands 58m above the plain and acted as a beacon to early travellers. Camping available but little shade. Access road very rough, last 10km definitely 4WD.

Bundooma ruin: old Ghan railway ruin.

Depot Sandhills: forms part of the western edge of the Simpson Desert. Clothed in various acacias and spinifex. Definitely 4WD country.

Rumbalara Hills: low ranges of jump-up hills interspersed with stony plains. Very photogenic in the afternoon light. Various tracks lead through the hills; do not venture here without informing reliable person of your intentions; also seek permission from station owner.

Sand dunes form an outlier of the Simpson Desert. Acacias and spinifex common.

Finke River: deep sandy river crossing set in a bleached, washed-out landscape. Finke River is thought to be the oldest river in the world.

FINKE: former Ghan railway settlement, today an Aboriginal settlement of Pitjantjatjara and Yunkunytjatjara-speaking people. Locally known as Apatula. No photographs to be taken without permission. You may feel as though you are in a foreign country here; please respect cultural differences. Aborigines live for most of the year out of doors. Store, fuel.

Sand dunes are visible to the east; form the western edge of the Simpson Desert.

NEW CROWN STATION: cattle station servicing travellers. Fuel only.
Sand plain supports a mulga shrubland.

Charlotte Waters ruin: former overland telegraph station of which only rubble remains. Nearby Coglin Creek supports a river red gum-lined waterhole. Plenty of shade and mosquitoes.

Stony plains covered with some saltbush; jump-up hills visible in the distance.

Abminga ruins: old Ghan railway settlement well worth exploring. Many ruins and railway relics. Numerous photograph opportunities.

Eringa ruin: old homestead ruin - worth a quick look; beautiful shady waterhole nearby. No facilities available. Next fuel Oodnadatta 179km; nearest fuel Mt Dare 71km.

NOTES

MAP 11 KULGERA-OLD ANDADO-KULGERA via Finke

Grade 4 (Kulgera-Finke Grade 3)

Total Distance: 292km
Average Vehicles per day: 15 east of Kulgera
Regions Traversed: Central Australia, Simpson Desert

Old Andado: old station homestead offering basic accommodation. Outlandish location makes this an interesting place to visit; notify owner beforehand. Two large soft dunes located immediately west of the homestead. No fuel available. Nearest fuel Mt Dare (104km); next fuel Alice Springs (316km).

Plains subject to flooding; support sparse coolabah woodland. Elsewhere these plains are sandy.
New Andado Station: working cattle station; no facilities.

Plains support only the barest of vegetation. Low rises and jump-ups visible in the distance. Claypans common.
Sand dunes: long linear dunes form part of the Simpson Desert. Road winds between dunes. No major crossings but sand may blow onto road. Numerous acacias dominate the interdunal flats; spinifex elsewhere. Very colourful at dawn and dusk. A brief walk onto the dunes recommended - do not lose sight of the vehicle! Broad flats indicate the Finke River crossing.

NEW CROWN STATION: working cattle station offering fuel to travellers; no other facilities. Enquire here about road conditions.
Sand dunes visible to the east; marks the western edge of the Simpson Desert. Jump-up hills lie to the west.

MAP 11 KULGERA-OLD ANDADO-KULGERA via Finke

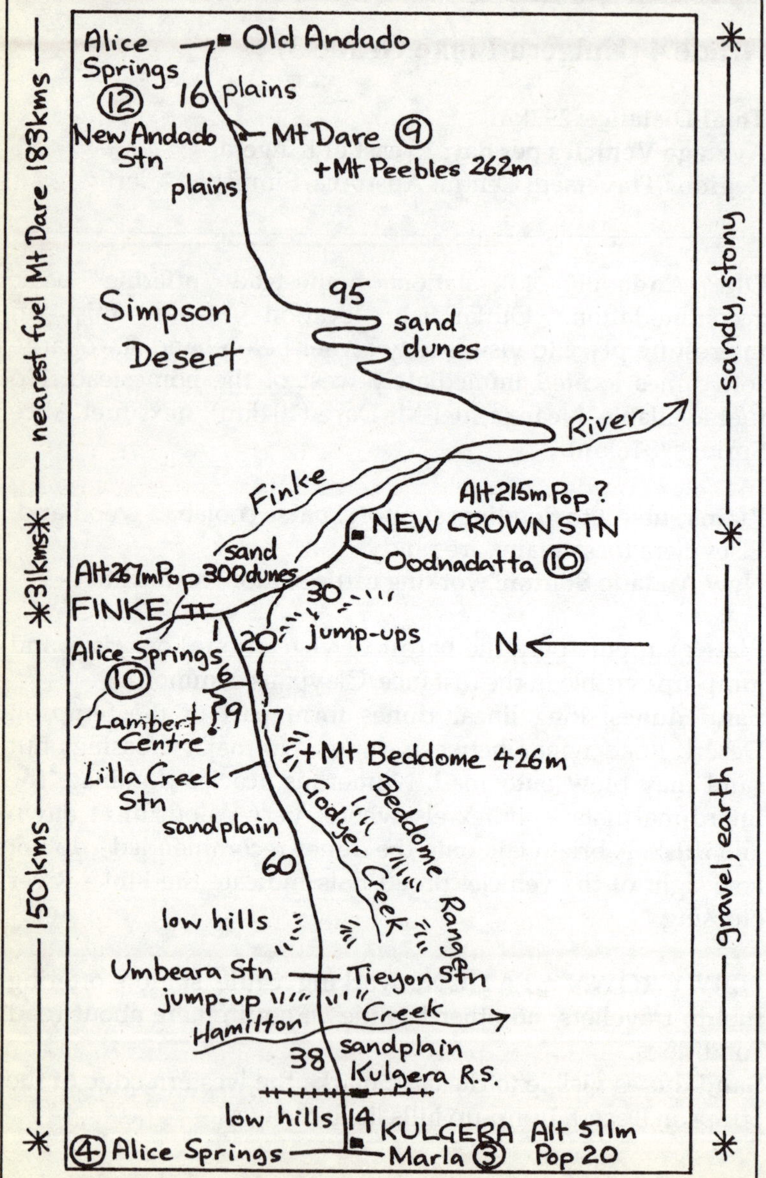

FINKE: former Ghan railway township, nowadays an Aboriginal settlement known locally as Apatula. People mostly Pitjantjatjara and Yunkunytjatjara speakers. Interesting settlement, especially for those who have not visited an Aboriginal community before. Please respect cultural differences; these people live mostly out of doors. Interesting buildings connected with the old railway settlement. Note: no photographs permitted without approval of the Apatula Council. Store, fuel.
Finke River lies just to the north of the township. Broad white sandy river bed is worth a quick look.

Lambert Centre: the latest supposed geographic centre of Australia indicated by a pole. Access track 4WD only: turn left at gate 6.5km in from main road.

Mt Beddome is a high jump-up and typical of the country that reaches far into northern South Australia.
Sand plain with some low dunes; supports a mulga shrubland.
Low hills give the country an arid appearance. These jump-ups support areas of saltbush and patches of mulga.
Jump-up near Tieyon Station turn-off separates quite markedly the more arid eastward-lying lowlands from the less arid westward-lying plateau country. Good views to the east from near top of jump-up.

Sand plain supports a mulga shrubland. Low granite hills may be seen.
Low hills of granite rise dome-like from the plain. Mulga shrublands occupy the granite flats. Some hills have Aboriginal paintings - enquire locally.

KULGERA: older style roadhouse settlement and bush township. Definitely worth a stop. Information available on local and regional tourist features. Old homestead nearby. Hotel, motel, store, fuel.

MAP 12 OLD ANDADO-ALICE SPRINGS-OLD ANDADO via Santa Teresa

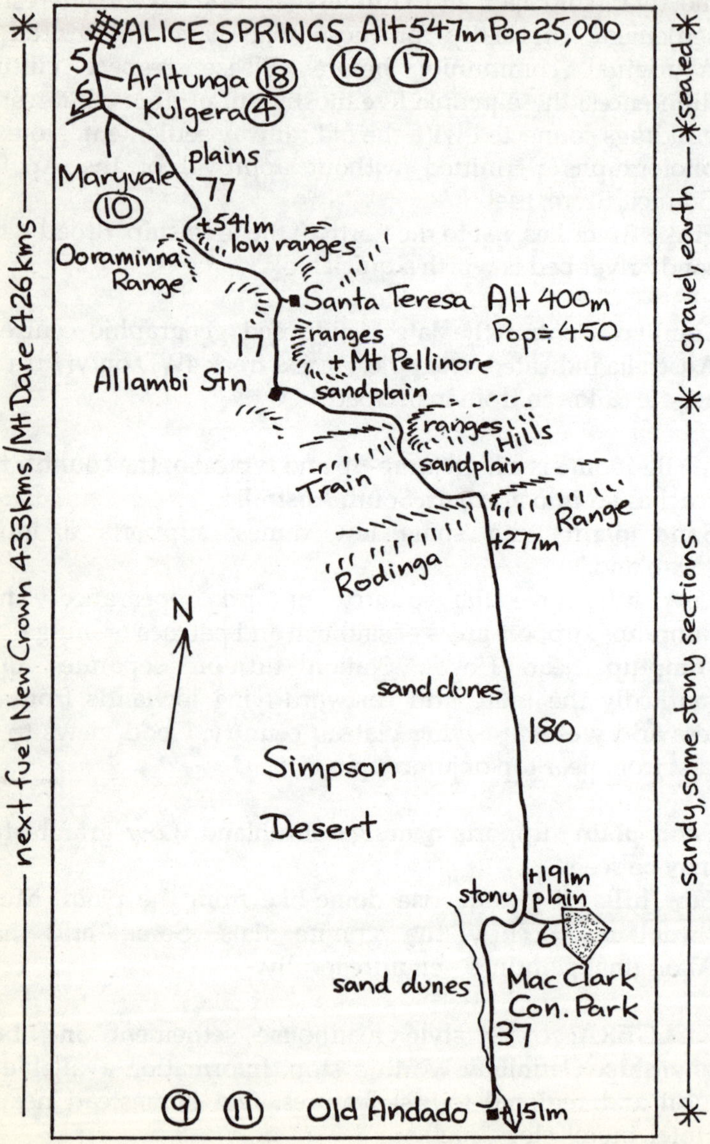

MAP 12 OLD ANDADO-ALICE SPRINGS-OLD ANDADO

via Santa Teresa

Grade 4 (Alice Springs-Allambi Station Grade 3)

Total Distance: 322km
Average Vehicles per day: 5 or less south of Allambi Station
Regions Traversed: Simpson Desert, Central Australia

ALICE SPRINGS: major regional centre servicing the surrounding cattle stations, Aboriginal communities and tourism. Spectacularly situated within the MacDonnell Ranges; the changing colours of the bold quartzite cliffs as the sun moves across the sky is endlessly fascinating. Though modernised, 'The Alice' still has a certain charm. Numerous tourist facilities available. Stock up here if heading south.

Plains provide good views northward toward the MacDonnell Ranges. In the South Alice built-up area (not shown on map) there are low stony ridges. Plains support extensive tracts of mulga shrublands.

Low ranges are sparsely vegetated with shrubs; this open country provides good views, especially from the tops of rises. Extensive wildflower displays after rain.

Ooraminna Range: distant low rocky range visible to the west.

Santa Teresa: sizeable Aboriginal community; permit required for entry. No facilities available for tourists except in an emergency. Township clearly visible from the road.

Ranges line the road providing a moderately interesting backdrop to the countryside. Mulga shrublands dominate the lowlands.

Allambi Station: working cattle station; no facilities.

Sand plain with some low dunes occupies a broad valley lined with rocky ranges. Vegetation dominated by a variety of shrubs; ephemeral herblands occupy the dunes, producing colourful wildflower displays after rain. East of Allambi Station there is a coolabah-clad flood-plain.

Ranges (the Train Hills) form a narrow valley, their upstanding sandstone cliffs producing a scenic backdrop. The ranges themselves are sparsely vegetated with shrubs, mostly emu-bushes. Immediately south of the ranges and to the east are spectacular, if distant, rocky outcrops, pinnacles, spires, etc.

Sand plain with numerous low dunes supports a sparse shrubland and an ephemeral herbland - spectacular wildflower displays after rain. Shrubs include acacias and grevilleas, with stunted whitewood trees occupying the lowest depressions. Good views to distant sandstone ranges.

Rodinga Range: moderately high linear sandstone range abutting a sand plain. Scattered shrubs occupy the lower slopes; the upper slopes are virtually barren but exhibit intricate weathering patterns.

Sand dunes form part of the western Simpson Desert. In the north are views towards the Rodinga Range; elsewhere the view is limited to the relatively densely vegetated dunes that immediately line the route. Numerous wildflowers present after rain; sand-hill canegrass occupies the dune crests, a sparse acacia shrubland occupies the swales. In the south the vegetation is less dense although bare crests are uncommon;

hereabouts occasional claypans are seen. Worth investigating this area on foot (do not lose sight of the vehicle!). For some the closeness of the dunes is claustrophobic.

Stony plain with occasional low rises provides expansive views (anything but claustrophobic). To the west a long linear red-topped dune can be seen. Eastward, in the far distance, are a few scattered waddywoods. Elsewhere this country is very sparsely vegetated; barren areas of gibbers very common.

Mac Clark Conservation Park preserves a scattered stand of tall, spindly waddywood trees, a slow growing acacia thought to have once vegetated today's Simpson Desert. Only three such stands exist in the world. Well worth visiting but access track is washed out. Visitors here are few, the visitors book recording no visits during summer, very few in autumn, and up to 16 days between visits during winter.

Sand dunes form part of the Simpson Desert. Dunes here are less vegetated than further north, with bare red crests of drifting sand - very photogenic. Ephemeral plants and sand-hill canegrass common on the dune's slopes, a sparse shrubland occupies the swales. In some places the swales contain claypans, in other places patches of gibbers. In the south a small flood-plain with stunted coolabahs lines the route.

Old Andado: an old station homestead set amongst two high red-crested dunes. Camping and basic accommodation available (contact owner beforehand). No stores or fuel. Next fuel available at Mt Dare (104km) or New Crown (111km).

NOTES

CENTRAL AUSTRALIA

Made famous in part by the watercolour artist Albert Namatjira, and symbolic of the Australian outback, Central Australia presents the traveller with a bewildering display of natural wonders. Everything you have heard about its landscapes and countryside is true. High rocky bluffs, deep gorges, long linear ridges, prominent peaks, cool waterholes, immense rock domes, vivid red sand dunes, graceful desert oaks and magnificent colour changes on distant cliffs and ranges throughout the day, make Central Australia a magical place to visit. Bear in mind, though, that Central Australia covers a vast area and that many features of interest are separated by kilometres of plains country. Though the plains country may not seem interesting, after a week of exploring rocky gorges and mountain ranges, you may well appreciate its wide open spaces.

Most of the major tourist routes throughout Central Australia are accessible to all travellers, even for conventional vehicles on the unsealed roads, when dry. Nonetheless relatively heavy traffic can make some of these unsealed roads rather corrugated and potholed. Also note that even where the main road is sealed, many of the shorter access roads to specific features may be unsealed and rough. Care will then be required, and caravans may not be accessible.

Warnings: roads subject to flooding (flash flooding in mountainous areas); unsealed roads often impassable when wet. Try to avoid travelling at night, especially on unsealed roads. Note that some unsealed roads may be rough due to relatively heavy usage; travel according to road conditions, not to a timetable. Also, be careful of high speed tourist coaches which do travel to a timetable! Some roads may be unsuitable for the unprepared family sedan. Palm Valley access is definitely 4WD only. Inform reliable person of your intentions during the summer months on the following routes: Kulgera-Curtin Springs via Mulga Park Station and Hermannsberg-Redbank Gorge via Tylers Pass; Mereenie Loop road between either Hermannsberg or Glen Helen-Kings Canyon. Note: no reliable habitation between Hermannsburg and Glen Helen (113km); Victory Downs Station and Mulga Park Station (142km); Hermannsberg-Kings Canyon (174km); Glen Helen-Kings Canyon (237km).

Mt. Conner at Anari Soak (Map 13)

MAP 13 KULGERA-CURTIN SPRINGS-KULGERA via Mulga Park Station

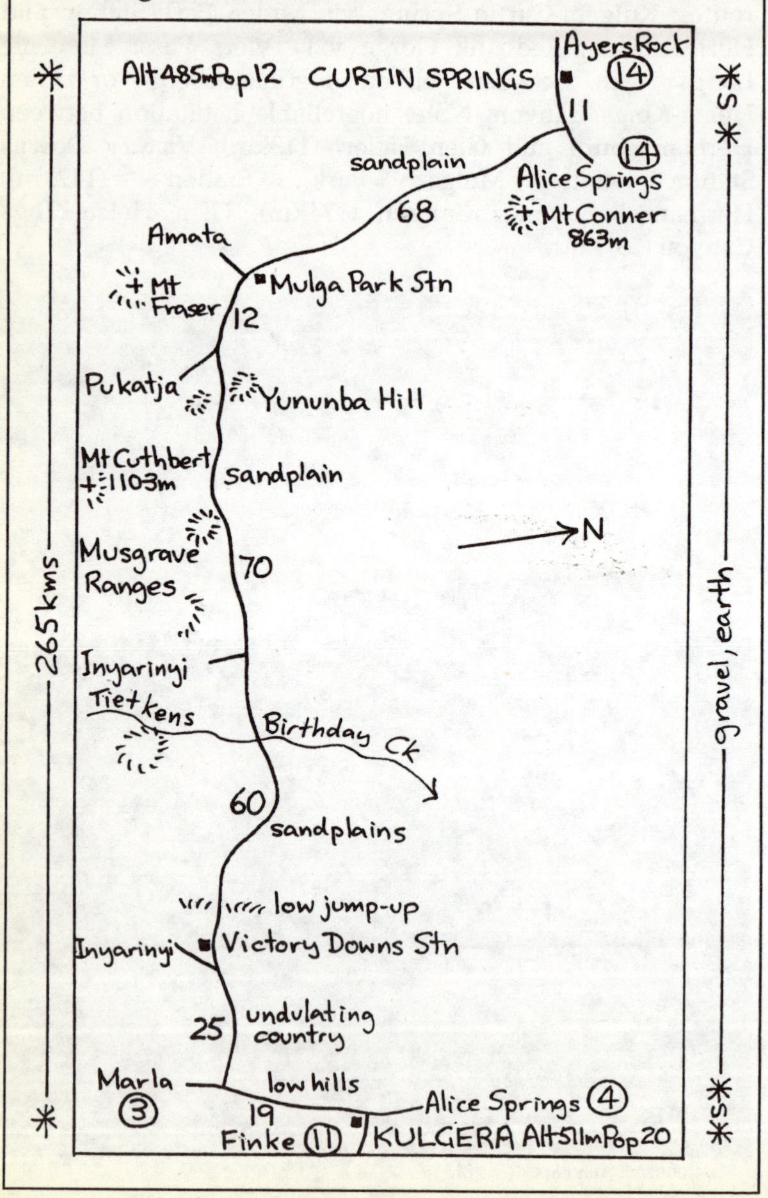

MAP 13 KULGERA-CURTIN SPRINGS-KULGERA via Mulga Park Station

Grade 3

Total Distance: 265km
Average Vehicles per day: 10 south of Curtin Springs
Regions Traversed: Central Australia (Amadeus Lowland)

CURTIN SPRINGS: working cattle station with roadhouse facilities. Plenty of character to this establishment. Good place for an overnight stay to avoid at least one night's accommodation at the expensive Ayers Rock Resort. Motel, store, fuel.

Mt Conner: impressive table-top mountain which rises about 310m above the plain. Best views from rest area 10km east of the Mulga Park turn-off on the Alice Springs road; less impressive from the west and south. Contact Curtin Springs Station for access.

Sand plain and occasional low dunes support mulga shrublands. Occasional views to the south (Musgrave Ranges) from tops of rises. Camels may be seen in this area.

Mulga Park Station: working cattle station; no facilities. A scenic drive can be had by travelling a short distance along the Amata road. Good views of Mt Fraser and distant photogenic views of the Musgrave Ranges. Do not cross state border - permit required. This road was once part of the Gunbarrel Highway.

Yununba Hill: interesting high granite hill adjacent to the road. Photogenic from a distance. Work a quick look on foot - remember you are on private property.

Sand plain supports a mulga shrubland. Numerous views to south of high granite hills and ranges, including the impressive Mt Cuthbert. Occasional low granite hills nearer the road. These hills form outliers of the Musgrave Ranges, South Australia's highest mountain range. Keep a lookout for unusual road signs (often car bonnets) indicating Aboriginal homeland settlements across the state border - some are quite photogenic. This is as close as you will get to Aboriginal homeland communities without a permit.

Sand plains east of Tietkens Birthday Creek support mulga shrublands. Occasional low dunes may be seen.
Low jump-up indicates a change in country; landscape hereabout more open and arid looking. Interesting low cliffline is attractive in the afternoon light.

Victory Downs Station: working cattle station that once offered services to travellers. No facilities.

Undulating country supports open mulga shrublands. Granite hills and low rises visible. Fair views from tops of rises.
Low hills of granite and areas of stunted shrubs give the countryside a broad sweeping outlook.

KULGERA: interesting older style roadhouse and bush township; worth spending some time here to unwind. Information available on the surrounding districts. Hotel, motel, store, fuel.

NOTES

MAP 14 ERLDUNDA-KATA TJUTA-ERLDUNDA
via Ayers Rock Resort

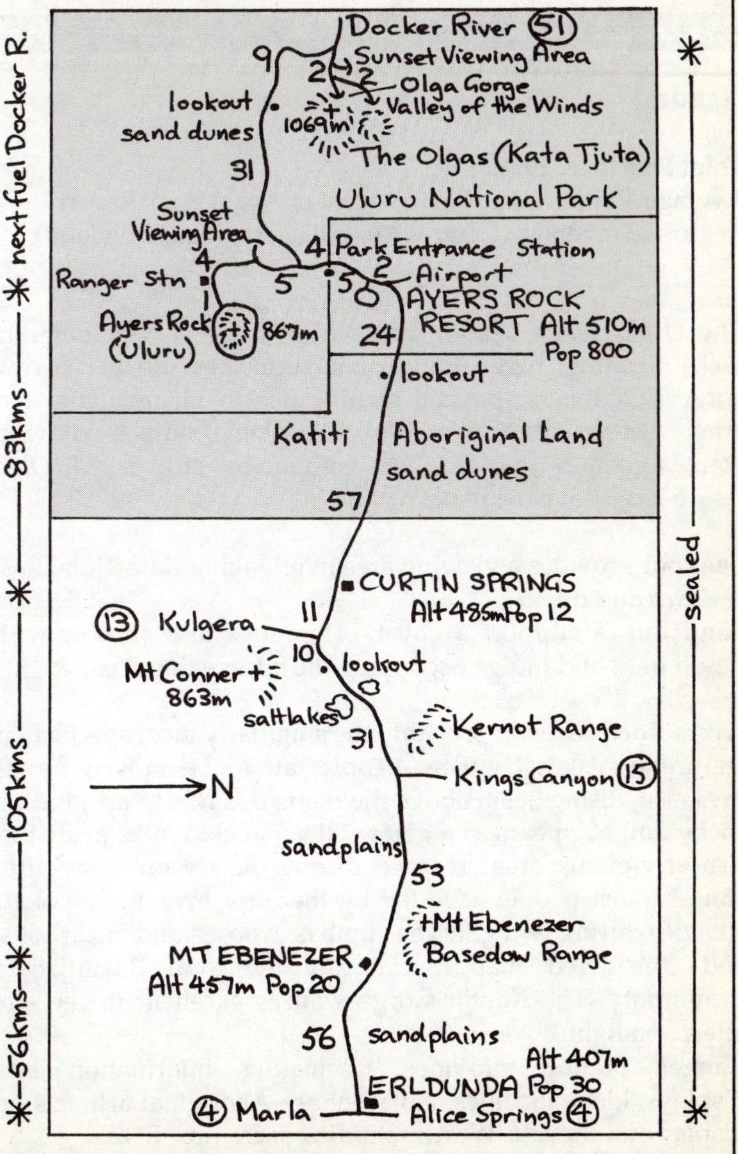

MAP 14 ERLDUNDA-KATA TJUTA-ERLDUNDA

via Ayers Rock Resort

Grade 1

Total Distance: 295km
Average Vehicles per day: 300 east of Ayers Rock Resort
Regions Traversed: Central Australia (Amadeus Lowland)

The Olgas (Kata Tjuta): spectacular range of conglomerate rocks forming high domes intersected by deep, narrow gorges. Of major spiritual significance to Pitjantjatjara and other Aboriginal people. Walks available; **sunset viewing area** as good as that at Uluru without the crowds. Mt Olga rises 546m above the plain.

Lookout provides a viewing area overlooking Kata Tjuta. Best at dawn and dusk.
Sand dunes support a cover of spinifex and shrubs, with desert oaks and mulga occupying the intervening flats.

Ayers Rock (Uluru): probably the singularly most spectacular feature in Australia. Few people fail to be moved by its presence. Rising 348m above the plain, this nearly upstanding rocky range appears as a giant solitary rock. Walks available; **sunset viewing area** crowded during the season - stay after sunset (most people have left by then) for even more colour changes during twilight. The climb is exposed and hazardous, and considered inappropriate by the local Pitjantjatjara community. The Kantju Gorge walk is excellent in the late afternoon light.
Ranger Station provides fascinating information and displays; kiosk facilities. Adjacent are Aboriginal artifacts on display and for sale. Worth spending some time here.

AYERS ROCK RESORT: formerly called Yulara. Overpriced and modern resort with a virtual monopoly on accommodation and services. Excellent for the fly in-fly out tourists; bad news for budget travellers. As no camping is permitted in **Uluru National Park,** all must spend overnight here. Excellent national park displays and information; interesting architecture. **Park fees payable at Park Entrance Station.** Hotels, store, fuel.

Lookout (rest area on left heading west) provides an excellent view of Uluru and Kata Tjuta from atop a sand dune (follow the footprints). At dusk you will find no better nor more moving scene than this first glimpse of Ayers Rock and The Olgas.

Katiti Aboriginal Land: land belonging to Pitjantjatjara and Yankunytjatjara speaking people. No permit required for entry.

Sand dunes line the road forming confused patterns and shapes. Having rarely, if ever, been grazed, the landscape is pristine. Spinifex common on the dunes; desert oaks in-between.

CURTIN SPRINGS: this roadhouse attached to a cattle station has plenty of character and characters. Provides good and cheap bush camping (saves spending at least one night at Ayers Rock Resort). Motel, store (limited), fuel.

Lookout (rest area) gives an excellent and photogenic view of Mt Conner; known as Atila to the Pitjantjatjara people. A short, steep path climbs a dune for further views of Atila and a saltlake; be careful crossing the road.
Saltlakes visible from the road. A short walk here is interesting; park well off the road (not in wet weather).

Sand plains support a covering of mulga shrublands with

open grassy areas. Distant purple ranges seem to float in a grey-green sea.

MT EBENEZER: a recently upgraded older style roadhouse with some character. Owned by the Imanpa Aboriginal Community and an outlet for their artifacts. Pleasant place to relax from driving for a while. Motel, store, fuel.

Sand plains with a few low dunes support a mulga shrubland. Occasional fair views to the south. Desert oaks common amongst the sand dunes.

ERLDUNDA: modern and busy roadhouse complex with very little character. Hotel, motel, store and fuel.

Ochre Pits, Western Macdonnell Ranges (Map 16)

MAP 15 STUART HIGHWAY-KINGS CANYON/ LASSETER HIGHWAY -STUART HIGHWAY via Kings Creek

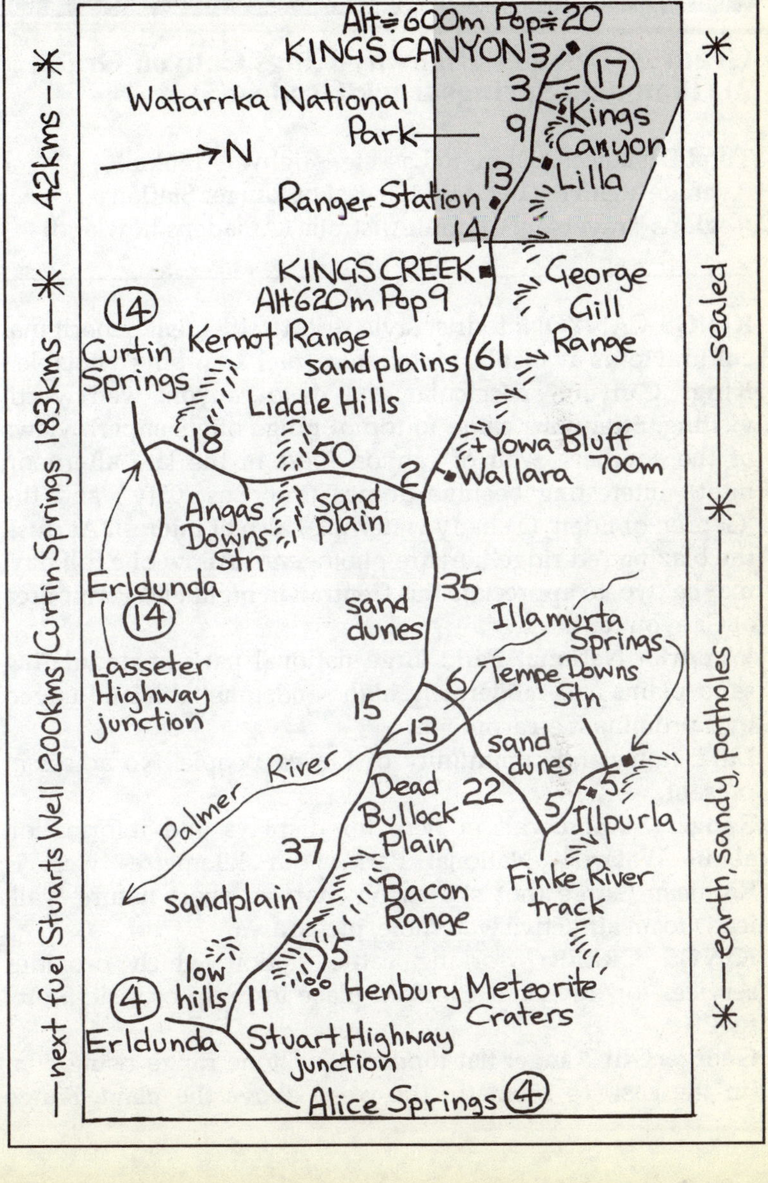

MAP 15 STUART HIGHWAY-KINGS CANYON/LASSETER HIGHWAY-STUART HIGHWAY via Kings Creek

Grade 3 (Lasseter Highway-Kings Canyon Grade 2) (Illamurta Springs track Grade 4/5)

Total Distance: 203km (to Lasseter Highway 166km)
Average Vehicles per day: 100 east of Ranger Station
Regions Traversed: Central Australia (Amadeus Lowland)

KINGS CANYON: tourist style resort settlement. Aboriginal cultural tours available. Motel, store, fuel. Camping available.
Kings Canyon: spectacular and deep canyon; well worth visiting. Strenuous climb to top of range offers superb views of the southern wall of canyon (best in the late afternoon light); interesting beehive domes (the 'Lost City') and the 'Garden of Eden' (a shady waterhole) also of interest. At dusk the blazing red ridgelines are photogenic. Allow one full day, maybe two, to appreciate this Centralian highlight. Picnic area at Canyon car park.
Watarrka National Park: large national park of undulating sand plains and moderately high sandstone tableland edged by a prominent escarpment.
Lilla: homeland community of Luritja people. No access at present.
Ranger Station: call in here for displays and information about Watarrka National Park. Four kilometres west is Kathleen Gorge (not shown on map); a short nature walk leads to an attractive waterhole, picnic area.
KINGS CREEK: working cattle station which provides services for travellers. Pleasant place to camp or visit. Store, fuel.
George Gill Range: flat-topped sandstone range rising 50m (in the east) to 250m (in the west) above the plain. Range

parallels road for some distance. In some places are smooth cliff-faces of Mereenie sandstone, the same rock that forms the walls of Kings Canyon.
Sand plains with low dunes support an attractive desert oak woodland with a spinifex understorey.

Wallara: former roadhouse and accommodation facility which has been pulled down (a pity) set near the base of the striking Yowa Bluff.
Sand dunes support a desert oak woodland with spinifex. This section of the road is often heavily corrugated and potholed.

Palmer River: attractive dry river crossing with plenty of shady river red gums. Interesting spot for a rest break or a short walk. This area is also known as Rodgers Pass.

Dead Bullock Plain: stony plain with low jump-up hills.

Bacon Range: low flat-top range that parallels the road.
Sand plain supports an open shrubland dominated by mulga.

Henbury Meteorite Craters: interesting feature set upon a stony plain and backed by low flat-top ranges. Walking track leads to various craters, including a stream-fed 'wet crater' (beware of mosquitos). Vast views to the north overlooking the Finke River Valley and the distant James Range. Camping available.
Low hills of flat-top ridges dominate this open landscape. Mulga shrublands common.
Stuart Highway junction: locality only; no facilities. Next fuel Stuarts Well (39km).

Angas Downs Road (Desert Oaks Drive)

Lasseter Highway junction: locality only; no facilities. Next fuel Curtin Springs (52km).

Liddle Hills: interesting low range of stony hills. Good views to the south of distant ranges that seem to float on a blue-green sea of mulga.
Sand plain supports an attractive desert oak woodland; spinifex forms the understorey.

Illmurta Springs road

Illmurta Springs: attractive natural springs and birdwatching area; centrepiece of a Conservation Park of the same name. Nearby are stone ruins of a police outpost. A quiet area. Camping available. Northward lies the James Range.
Illpurla: Aboriginal homeland community of southern Luritja people. No access.
Sand dunes support an attractive desert oak woodland. Claypans visible near Palmer River Crossing.

MAP 16 ALICE SPRINGS-GLEN HELEN (TYLERS PASS)-

ALICE SPRINGS via Namatjira Drive

Grade 1 (Redbank Gorge Grade 3) (Tylers Pass Grade 3)

Total Distance: 132km (Tylers Pass 179km)
Average Vehicles per day: 180 east of Glen Helen
Regions Traversed: Central Australia (MacDonnell Ranges)

Tylers Pass: locality only, no facilities. Excellent all round view, especially southward overlooking Gosse Bluff, a comet impact crater. Good views northward toward the high peaks of the Western MacDonnells. Photogenic spinifex-covered hills nearby. Next fuel: Hermannsberg (67km); Kings Canyon (191km).
Amethyst Field: fossicking area of amethysts and smoky

MAP 16 ALICE SPRINGS-GLEN HELEN (TYLERS PASS)-ALICE SPRINGS via Namatjira Drive

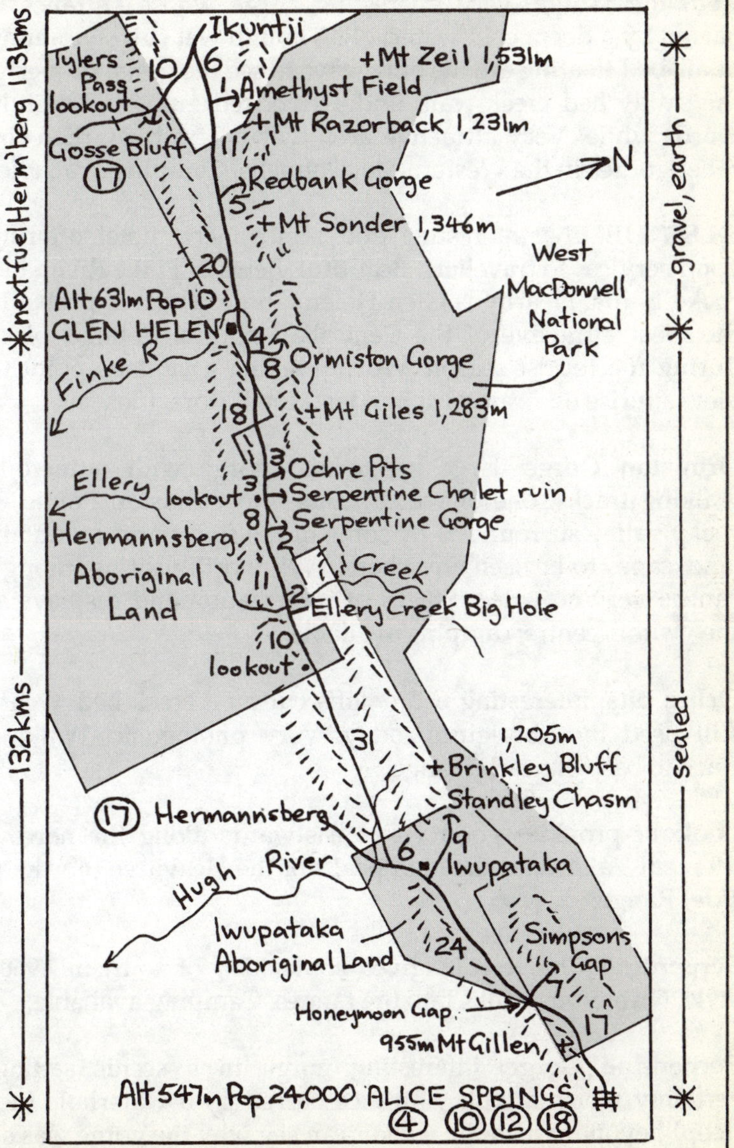

quartz. Interesting outcrop of partially weathered crystals; worth visiting.
Redbank Gorge: very interesting gorge whose entrance is barred by a deep, cold waterhole. Though wet suit swimming or air-bed floating are the only ways to see the gorge properly, the sandy bed creek walk under river-red gums is certainly worth while. Very attractive area that is less busy than the other gorges in the Western MacDonnells. Camping available.

GLEN HELEN: interesting and atmospheric hotel offering good services to travellers. Beautiful views of Finke River and rocky bluffs. Nearby is Glen Helen Gorge which is probably the most attractive of the Centralian gorges. Popular place during the tourist season. Worth seeking a vantage point to view sunrise on nearby Mt Sonder. Hotel, store, fuel.

Ormiston Gorge: large spectacular gorge with numerous walking tracks, one of which leads into Ormiston Pound, a rocky valley surrounded by some of the finest arid mountain landscapes to be seen anywhere. Well worth visiting, though can be very crowded. Stacks of information and displays at the visitors centre; camping available.

Ochre pits: interesting ochre cliffs cut by a creek bed. Ochre still used by Aborigines today. Very photogenic. Walking track to base of nearby range.

Lookout provides good views eastwards along the narrow Mereeni Valley and the high peaks of the Heavitree (northern side) Range.

Serpentine Chalet ruin gives some idea of tourism 1960s style. Numerous walks into the ranges. Camping available.

Serpentine Gorge: interesting gorge in a scenic setting; certainly worth a look. Entrance barred by a waterhole (not deep) beyond which the walker can see why the gorge was so named. A steep climb leads to a spectacular lookout.

Hermannsburg Aboriginal Land: freehold land owned by various Aboriginal groups, notably the Western Arrernte. Permit not required for travel along the main road.

Ellery Creek Big Hole: a smaller gorge, but with a large and attractive waterhole which is always very cold. Interesting rock formations. Note, on leaving, the long, linear ridge adjacent to and south of the main road. This ridge parallels the road well to the west of Glen Helen. Camping available.
Lookout: excellent views to the west. Worth being here at sunrise to see the sunlight strike the high, jagged peaks while the valley below lies in darkness. Spinifex abounds here; very photogenic in the afternoon light. Good eastwards views east of the lookout along the road - near sunset the best time.

West MacDonnell National Park: large national park encompassing some of the finest arid scenery in Australia. The generally sparse vegetation cover allows for the rocky ranges and peaks to be clearly seen along with the daylight colour changes. The vegetation of the park is variable though the following is typical: mulga dominates much of the valley lowlands along with other acacias, grevilleas (beefwood) and hakeas (corkwood). The southern sunny slopes are dominated by spinifex; the northern shady slopes support native figs, eromophilas (native fuchsias), cycads, ghost gums, with cypress pines on the ridgelines.

Iwupataka: formerly known as Jay Creek, this Aboriginal settlement is visible from the road. Various language groups live here, including Western Arrernte and Southern Luritja. No public access.

Iwupataka Aboriginal Land: freehold land occupied by Western Arrernte and Southern Luritja people. No permit required for travel on the main road.

Standley Chasm: narrow gorge of red quartzite which positively glows for ten minutes as the sun passes quickly overhead at midday. Well worth seeing but expect a crowd. This narrow 5 to 9m wide gorge is worth seeing at other times. A walk is required to see the spectacle. Located on Iwupataka Aboriginal Land; no permit required for access; kiosk facilities available. Entry fee payable.

Simpsons Gap: very popular gorge with a cathedral-like atmosphere in a spectacular setting. Interesting rock formations and waterhole. Numerous walks lead into the ranges and to rocky bluffs and lookouts. Ranger station has lots of information and displays.

Honeymoon Gap: small and attractive gap in a narrow, rocky range. Sandy creek bed supports a shady river red gum woodland. A ridgeline of cypress pines is very photogenic in the afternoon light. Road through gap provides an alternative route to Alice Springs.

ALICE SPRINGS: large regional centre with some, albeit hidden, character. Spectacular setting makes up for a loss of charm through overdevelopment. Sunrise and sunset from Anzac Hill, to observe the colour changes on the quartzite bluffs and cliffs of the Heavitree Range, well worth seeing. Numerous tourist facilities, museums, etc, available. Make enquiries here about the Larapinta Trail, a trekking and bushwalking track which, when completed, will run the length of the Western MacDonnells. Trail between the old Alice Springs Telegraph Station and Standley Chasm, and between Serpentine Gorge and the Ochre Pits already completed. Full town facilities. Stock up here if heading west.

NOTES

MAP 17 ALICE SPRINGS-KINGS CANYON/TYLERS PASS-ALICE SPRINGS

via Mereenie Loop Road

Grade 3
(Palm Valley Grade 5)

Total Distance: 300km (Tylers Pass 195kms)
Average Vehicles per day: 140 east of Hermannsburg
Regions Traversed: Central Australia

Watarrka National Park: large national park of undulating sand plains and moderately high sandstone tableland edged by a prominent escarpment.
Kings Canyon: spectacular and deep canyon; well worth visiting. Strenuous climb to top of range offers superb views of the southern wall of canyon (best in the late afternoon light); interesting beehive domes and a shady waterhole (the "Garden of Eden"). Good bushwalks - take water and wear a hat. Area worth at least two days.

KINGS CANYON: tourist style resort settlement. Motel, store, fuel.

Carmichael Crag: prominent rocky mountain rising above a mulga-clad plain; very photogenic in the afternoon light.
Lookout provides good views southward towards Carmichael Crag and northward overlooking sand dune country. Just south is Morris Pass; to the south-east lies Hope Valley. No camping allowed.
Sand plains support sparse woodlands of desert oaks with an understorey of spinifex. Low dunes can be seen. Southward and eastward distant ranges break the horizon.
Aboriginal Land is occupied by Arrernte and Luritja people. Permit required for entry north of Kings Canyon and west of

MAP 17 ALICE SPRINGS-KINGS CANYON/TYLERS PASS-ALICE SPRINGS via Mereenie Loop Road

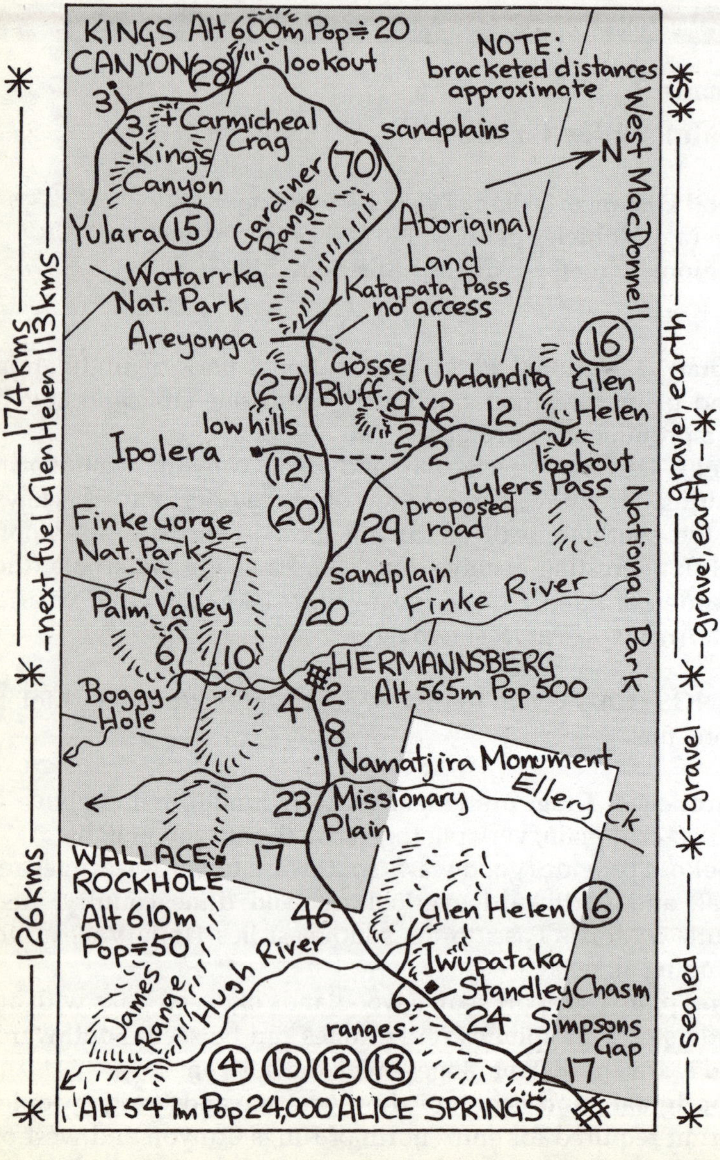

Hermannsberg (Mereenie Loop Road pass).
Katapata Pass: scenic area near the Areyonga turn-off (no access) located in the attractive Gardiner Range. Photogenic area.
Low hills of sandstone can be seen to the south; elsewhere is a sand plain supporting tracts of mulga and occasional desert oak groves.

Ipolera: small Aboriginal community of Arrernte people set near the Krichauff Range. Cultural tours available including the large ground painting of the Spinifex Pigeon Dreaming. Camping available. Store. Fuel may be available; check beforehand.
Sand plain supports a sparse desert oak woodland with an understorey of spinifex; elsewhere are mulga shrublands.
HERMANNSBERG: also called Ntaria by its predominantly Western Arrernte speaking population. Worth visiting for a look at its historic buildings and museum, part of the old Hermannsberg Mission. Buildings quite photogenic. Permit not required for entry to see historic buildings. No access or photographs of the residential areas permitted. Store, fuel available in the settlement and at the Finke River Crossing (Tjuwanpa).
Namatjira Monument: monument to the famous Arrernte artist Albert Namatjira whose watercolour paintings made accessible to the general public the beauty of Central Australia. Good views to the south towards the Finke Gorge.

Missionary Plain: slightly undulating stony plain supporting a cover of mulga. Occasional views northward towards the southern ramparts of the MacDonnell Ranges; southward towards the James Range.

WALLACE ROCKHOLE: Aboriginal homeland community open to the general public. Well worth visiting. This extraordinarily neat and friendly settlement offers services to travellers including camping facilities. Interesting walks (tours available) into the nearby ranges; museum of Arrernte artifacts. Store, fuel.

Hugh River: broad sandy riverbed with attractive river red gums.

Iwupataka: Aboriginal settlement of various language groups; formerly known as Jay Creek. Visible from road; no access.

Ranges line the road, especially to the south. Prominent pink quartzite ridges and clifflines very colourful at dawn and dusk. Good views from tops of rises. After rare winter rains surrounding sand plains support excellent wildflower displays.

ALICE SPRINGS: large regional centre with some character. At busy times the traveller will need to search deeply for the real Alice, but it is there beneath the rebuilt and modernised town. Numerous tourist facilities and activities available. Full town facilities. Stock up here if heading west.

Tylers Pass road

West MacDonnell National Park: spectacular park of high arid ranges, deep gorges and scenic lookouts.

Tylers Pass: locality only; no facilities. Excellent views from nearby lookout (east of road) in all directions. Southward is probably the best obtainable view of Gosse Bluff. Northward, running east to west, are the MacDonnell Ranges, including the high peaks of Mt Sonder, Mt Razorback and Mt Zeil. Attractive spinifex grasslands cover the nearby hills. Permit required south of Tylers Pass. Next fuel: Glen Helen (46km).

Gosse Bluff: ring of mountains formed by a comet impact. Of major significance to Aboriginal people. Hills rise 200m above the plain. Access track may be sandy. Area locally known as Tnorala, and Gosse Bluff is located in the Tnorala Conservation Reserve. Two permits are required for a visit:

one available from Mereenie Loop Road Pass outlets, the other from the Aboriginal Areas Protection Authority, Alice Springs. Note: a proposed road may join Tnorala with the Ipolera turn-off during the currency of this book.

Palm Valley road

Finke Gorge National Park: large wilderness park encompassing part of the James and Krichauff Ranges as well as Palm Valley and the Finke River. Camping available at Palm Valley.

Palm Valley: unusual valley harbouring thousands of palm trees. Shady waterholes and interesting creekbed walks through the palms make this an area well worth visiting. Also of interest is Initiation Rock and the impressive rock-enclosed Ampitheatre with its striking and unusual rocky sandstone structures. Note: access definitely 4WD only.

MAP 18 ALICE SPRINGS-ARLTUNGA (Ruby Gap Gorge)-

ALICE SPRINGS via Ross River

Grade 3 (Ruby Gap Gorge road Grade 5)

Total Distance: 109km (Ruby Gap Gorge 152km)
Average Vehicles per day: 110 near Corroboree Rock; 40 near Arltunga
Regions Traversed: Central Australia (MacDonnell Ranges)

Ruby Gap Gorge: isolated and rarely visited rocky valley exhibiting a fascinating geology of contorted rock strata. Area has a wilderness feel; please take all your rubbish with you and leave no sign of your passing. Access track difficult; inform reliable person of your intentions. Camping allowed.

MAP 18 ALICE SPRINGS-ARLTUNGA (Ruby Gap Gorge)-ALICE SPRINGS via Ross River

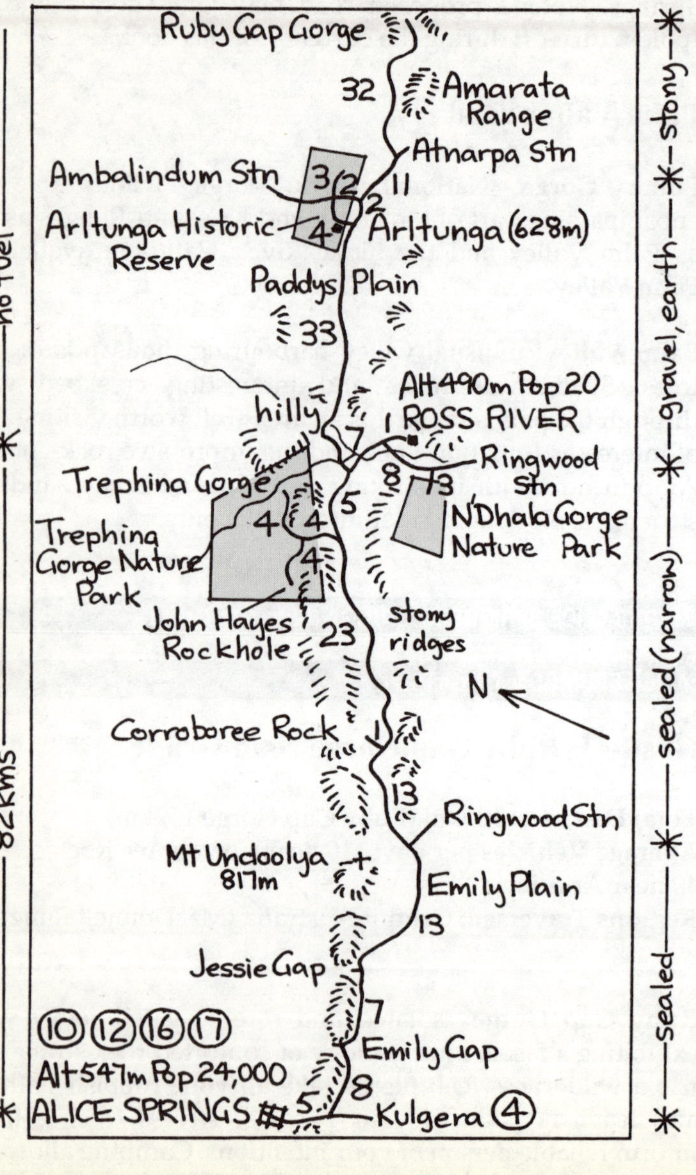

Amarata Range: prominent range rising above undulating stony country that supports shrublands.

Arltunga: ruins of a former gold mining settlement; the first settlement in Central Australia. Although probably over-protected with reconstructed buildings, formalised displays, etc, there is still much to be seen here: old stone building ruins, mining equipment, walk-through mines, old cemeteries, scattered relics (please do not disturb), as well as walking trails, gorges and an impressive Visitors Centre, all contained within the **Arltunga Historic Reserve**. Nearby is a fossicking reserve. No facilities save for a primitive camping area adjacent to the Historic Reserve.

Paddys Plain: an undulating plain covered with grasses and herbs after rain; numerous quartz gibbers may be seen. Excellent views to nearby colourful ranges and stony ridges.
Hilly country provides fascinating views (especially heading west) of the greatly contorted Bitter Springs rock formations - this would be one of the best 'geological views' in Central Australia. A short walk along the Bitter Springs Creek bed is well worthwhile. Countryside hereabout supports ironwood woodlands (those with a drooping crown) as well as mulga shrublands; spinifex common on the rocky slopes.

ROSS RIVER: station homestead primarily nowadays a tourist complex with plenty of character. Interesting historic buildings and ruins set amongst attractive ranges. Hotel, limited stores, fuel. Camping allowed.

N'Dhala Gorge Nature Park: interesting park set amongst dry, rocky ranges; protects countless petroglyphs or rock carvings. This area has a certain mystique. Walking trails; camping allowed. Access track may be difficult; seek local advice.

Trephina Gorge Nature Park: spectacular and wildly scenic park with numerous walking trails, attractive tree-lined watercourses, rockholes, stunning rocky outcrops and bluffs, and contorted geological rock formations. Camping allowed.

Trephina Gorge: very attractive gorge set amongst wild, rocky hills. Well worth seeing.

John Hayes Rockhole: interesting rockhole and creek bed set within a deep rocky gorge; good spot to sit out a hot day. Access road may be rocky.
Stony ridges line the road to the south providing good views; many opportunities to photograph the colourful rock strata. Numerous wildflowers after rain. Northward lies the immense bulk of the Eastern MacDonnell Ranges with its attendant lesser ranges. This is some of the most attractive desert mountain country in Australia.

Corroboree Rock: upstanding ridge of limestone rock, once a storage site of the Eastern Arrernte people. Walking tracks provide excellent views of the colourful nearby ranges.

Emily Plain: a level sandy plain supporting a mulga shrubland; in places low eucalypt woodlands can be seen. Good views northward towards the high quartzite cliffs of the Heavitree Range. The prominent peak (looking eastward) is Mt Undoolya.

Jessie Gap: small interesting gap set within the Heavitree quartzite. Worth a short visit at least. Aboriginal painting on the eastern wall - please respect this artwork.

Emily Gap: interesting small gap with a waterhole; worth a quick look.

ALICE SPRINGS: major regional centre providing a full range of services to travellers. Full town facilities. Stock up here if heading east.

EYRE HIGHWAY and westwards

The Eyre Highway is the major and only readily accessible route between the southern portions of South and Western Australia. While no longer a rugged adventure, today's crossing on the all-sealed road is still a major travelling experience, particularly for those people crossing the Nullarbor for the first time. While the route cannot boast a major hill, and flat to slightly undulating landscapes are the order of the day, there are some dramatic surprises: the Nullarbor cliffs being one. Elsewhere are more subdued but still interesting features: the treeless section of the Nullarbor Plain, limestone caves, giant sand patches, rocky gullies, old ruins, attractive woodlands, areas of uninhabited country, etc. Also of note is the longest length of straight roadway in the world!

Give the Eyre Highway the time it deserves. If driven too fast, this crossing will seem to be boring. It is the little things that make the seemingly boring country interesting. By slowing down you will not miss them.

Warnings: beware of stock, kangaroos, camels and wombats at night. If visiting the cliff side lookouts, stand well back in strong winds. Visit only sign-posted lookouts; other tracks to the cliff tops may be sandy. These lookouts provide good spots for whale watching.

NOTES

MAP 19 PORT AUGUSTA-WIRRULLA-PORT AUGUSTA via Wudinna/Whyalla

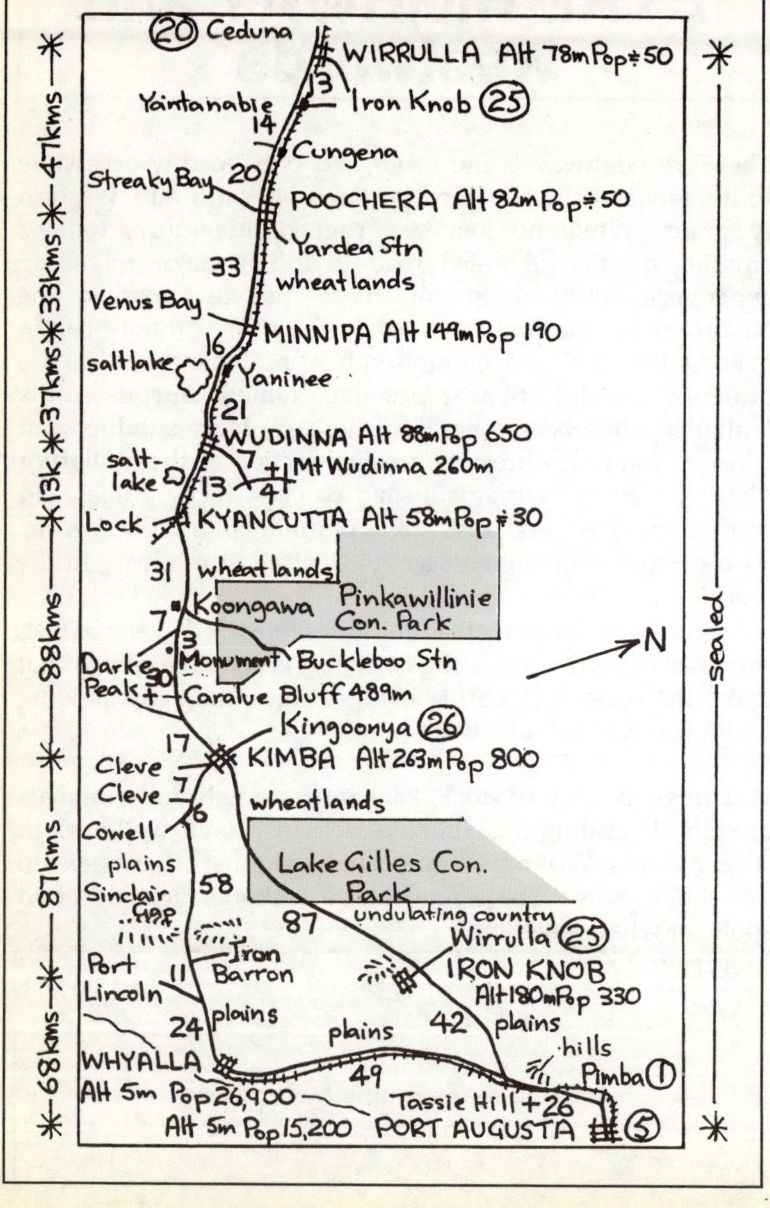

MAP 19 PORT AUGUSTA-WIRRULLA-PORT AUGUSTA

via Wudinna/Whyalla

Grade 1 (Whyalla-Kimba Grade 3)

Total Distance: 373km; 399km via Whyalla
Average Vehicles per day: 660 east of Kimba
Regions Traversed: Gawler Ranges, Eyre Peninsula

WIRRULLA: small wheat-farming township and railway station. Hotel, store, fuel.

Yantanabie: railway siding, no facilities.

Cungena: railway siding, no facilities.

POOCHERA: small wheat-farming township. Hotel, store, fuel.

Wheatlands spread endlessly across the gently undulating plain. Little natural vegetation remains except along the roadside. Mallee eucalypts are dominant.

MINNIPA: small wheat-farming township. Hotel, store, fuel.
Yaninee: railway siding, no facilities. Nearby is a saltlake, Lake Yaninee.

WUDINNA: small wheat-farming town, larger than most in this part of the country. Hotel, motel, stores, fuel.
Mt Wudinna: worth visiting - follow the sign-posted route. Mt Wudinna is a large granite outcrop, a domed and unvegetated inselberg. Excellent views from the sides and top. To the north lies the peaks of the Gawler Ranges; elsewhere

are vast expanses of wheatbelt - very attractive after winter rains. Picnic facilities and shade at base. Nearby is the aptly named Turtle Rock.

KYANCUTTA: small township. Store, fuel.

Wheatlands spread across attractive undulating country. Fair to good views from tops of rises, occasional granite outcrops. Very attractive country after winter rains.
Koongawa: locality only, no facilities.

Pinkawillinie Conservation Park (north of highway). Large area of natural bushland covering a dunefield of longitudinal sand dunes. Dominant vegetation is a mallee eucalypt with a shrubby understorey. Road may be sandy. No facilities.

Monument south of the road commemorates the death of explorer John Drake in 1844. Of interest is the granite rock nearby (Waddikee Rocks); good view from top of rise, interesting crystals in the rock itself. Rock is 2.4 billion years old!

Caralue Bluff: prominent hill rising above the plains. Other ranges to the south include the Darke Peak Range. Picnic area at base of Bluff - beware of sand on the road.

KIMBA: small wheat-farming town. Hotel, motel, stores, fuel.
Wheatlands occupy the undulating plains, land formerly covered with mallee eucalypts.

Lake Gilles Conservation Park: large wilderness park conserving numerous plant and animal species. Mallee eucalypts dominate the countryside covering an area of longitudinal sand dunes. Limited 4WD access to Lake Gilles saltpan. No facilities.
Undulating country supports mallee eucalypts. Long distance views along the road from tops of rises; views include

Middleback Ranges, visible to the east.

IRON KNOB: small iron ore mining town of some character situated at the foot of the Middleback Ranges. Good views northward, in the late afternoon light, towards the Gawler Ranges. Hotel, motel, stores, fuel.

Plains covered with low saltbush shrubs offer vast vistas. Distant ranges on the skyline. At intervals groves of western myalls may be seen.
Hills line the road at Lincoln Gap. Good views northward towards the head of Spencer Gulf and the western ramparts of the Flinders Ranges. For an interesting alternative route, follow the old highway via El Alamein Army Camp (not shown on map).

PORT AUGUSTA: called the crossroads of Australia due to major rail and road junctions. Some features of interest include the Wadlata Outback Centre and the Australian Arid Lands Botanic Gardens. Lookout in Port August West offers views over the head of Spencer Gulf and the Flinders Ranges (late afternoon best). Stock up here if heading west. Full town facilities.

Port Augusta-Kimba Road via Whyalla

KIMBA: small wheat-farming township. Hotel, motel, stores, fuel.
Plains support wheatbelt country in the west, and mallee eucalypt shrublands in the east. At the sign-posted Secret Rocks (not shown on map) there is a granite outcrop offering views - a good spot for a rest or picnic.

Sinclair Gap divides the Middleback Range into two parts: North and South Middleback. North of the gap lies the peak Iron Warrior.

Plains support covering of saltbush; the views are occasionally restricted by acacia shrubs. Westward the outline of the Middleback Ranges can be seen.

WHYALLA: large industrial centre with some character. Some tourist features include lookouts (Hummock Hill has the best view) and a museum. Enquire locally for directions to historic Lowly Point lighthouse on Spencer Gulf. Full town facilities.

Plains support a saltbush cover with western myall woodlands. Whyalla steelworks dominates the skyline to the south.

Point Sinclair, south of Penong (Map 20)

MAP 20 WIRRULLA-NULLARBOR-WIRRULLA via Ceduna

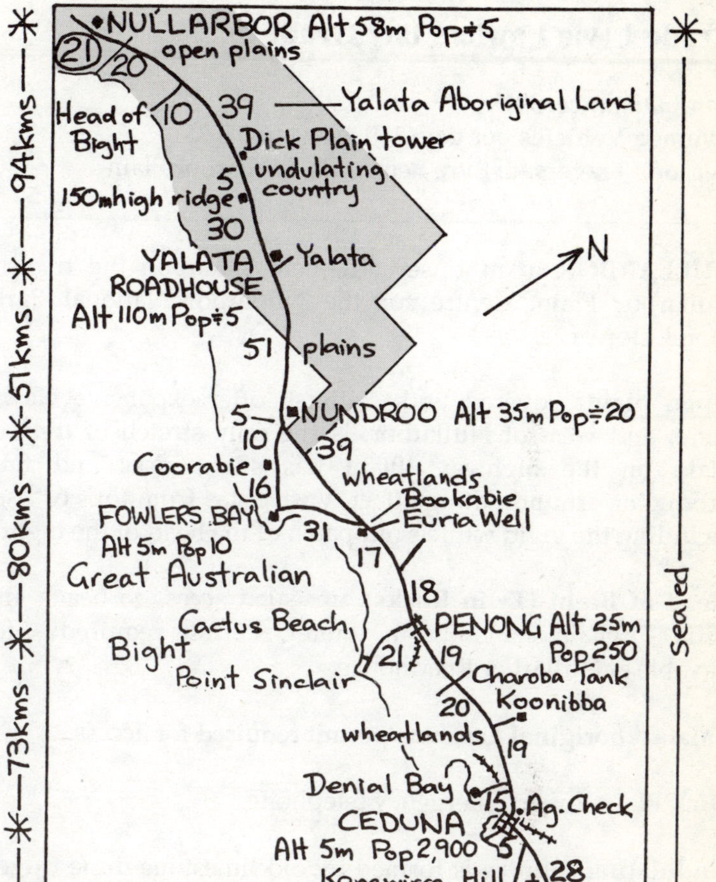

MAP 20 WIRRULLA-NULLARBOR-WIRRULLA via Ceduna

Grade 1 (via Fowlers Bay Grade 3)

Total Distance: 391km
Average Vehicles per day: 250 near Nundroo
Regions Traversed: Eyre Peninsula, Nullarbor Plain

NULLARBOR: roadhouse settlement set upon the treeless Nullarbor Plain. Centre for the Nullarbor National Park. Motel, store, fuel.

Open plains covered with saltbush offer expansive views. Here, and west of Nullarbor, is the only stretch of treeless plain on the highway. Plain has slight rises and falls producing an undulating effect. Vast vistas from tops of rises including the vivid white sand patch of the head of the bight.

Head of Bight (Twin Rocks): unsealed access to beach and cliffs - whale watching in winter. Permit required - fee payable at Nullarbor Roadhouse.

Yalata Aboriginal Land: no permit required for access.

Dick Plain tower: emergency telephone.

Undulating country is formed by old limestone dune ridges. Countryside dominated by a eucalypt shrubland of mallees with a shrubby understorey, notably saltbush.

High ridge presents a long vista westward down the road. From its base, looking eastward, the ridges appears as a hill.

YALATA ROADHOUSE: Aboriginal-owned roadhouse set amongst the old limestone dune ridges. Plenty of shady camping spots. Artifacts for sale. Nearby is the Yalata Community - no access at present. Store, fuel.

Plains and low rises covered with mallee eucalypts. Long road vistas from tops of rises. Eastward the country is cleared.

NUNDROO: roadhouse facility set upon a cleared plain. A few stone ruins are located west of the roadhouse. Motel, store, fuel.

Wheatlands occupy the vast undulating plains; vast views from tops of rises. Northward are occasional glimpses of uncleared country, the southernmost dunefields of the Great Victoria Desert.

Bookabie: locality only, no facilities. A few stone ruins dot the plain.

PENONG: small attractive wheat-farming town. Many interesting stone buildings. Numerous transportable windmills surround the town, extracting water from the limestone beneath. Hotel, store fuel.

Cactus Beach: famous surfing beach in a spectacular setting. Worth visiting. Basic camping available. Unsealed access.

Point Sinclair: attractive bay and jetty (fishing); a good spot for lunch. On the way is the pretty Pink Lake. Gypsum crystals found in this area. Unsealed access.

Wheatlands cover the undulating plains. Little natural vegetation remains except for the mallee eucalypts growing along the road reserves. Northward lies the Yumbarra Conservation Park preserving a vast tract of the Great Victoria Desert dunefields and vegetation. Limited access, no facilities.

Koonibba: Aboriginal settlement, no facilities.

Denial Bay: attractive bay-side settlement with a jetty. Popular with fisherfolk.

Ag. Check: agricultural check point. No fruit, vegetables or plants to be carried eastwards.

CEDUNA: major town of Eyre Peninsula's west coast. Attractive place with white stone buildings set beside Murat Bay. Nearby is the port and older style settlement of Thevenard (the local fishing spot); worth a quick visit for views back towards Ceduna. Full town facilities. Stock up here if heading west.

Kongwirra Hill: notable if only for its Telecom tower. Vast views westward towards Ceduna.

Wheatlands occupy the gently undulating downs. Area virtually devoid of natural vegetation except along road reserves.

WIRRULLA: small wheat-farming township. Hotel, store, fuel.

Fowlers Bay road

Coorabie: farming locality only, no facilities. Interesting stone buildings. Southward road crosses numerous saltpans. High sand dunes visible in the distance.

FOWLERS BAY: interesting bay-side historic settlement partially engulfed by dunes. Worth visiting: photogenic ruins, old jetty, ghost town atmosphere (some people live here, do not trespass). Reasonable fishing. Beware of sandy patches on the road leading to the highway. Camping available, limited supplies, fuel.

MAP 21 NULLARBOR-MADURA-NULLARBOR via Eucla

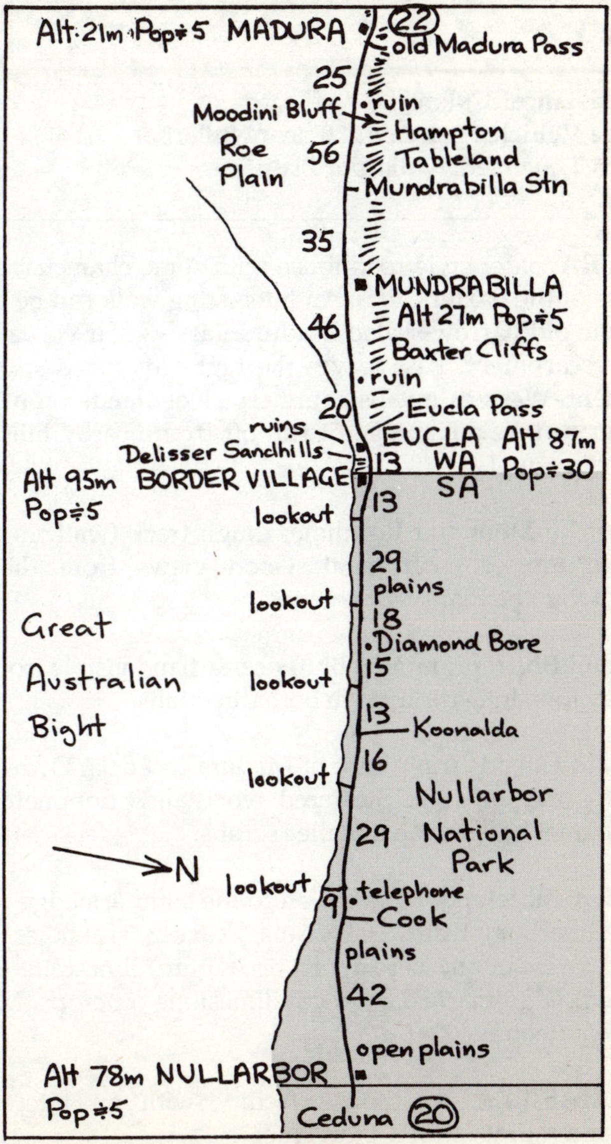

MAP 21 NULLARBOR-MADURA-NULLARBOR via Eucla

Grade 1

Total Distance: 379km
Average Vehicles per day: 250 near Nullarbor
Regions Traversed: Nullarbor Plain

MADURA: older style roadhouse with some character, set at the base of the Baxter Cliffs. An interesting walk can be taken along the old narrow-sealed Madura Pass - good views from top of escarpment. Pass leaves the highway just east of the settlement. Western myalls common - woodlands on base of escarpment take advantage of run-off from nearby hillslope. Motel, store, fuel.

Ruin set by Moondini Rockhole; rough track (walkers only) leads to top of escarpment. Good views from the top overlooking Roe Plain.

Moondini Bluff: prominent bluff or headland visible from the highway for a long distance in both directions.

Roe Plain extends from west of Madura to Eucla. Occasional claypans may be seen. Scattered woodlands dominated by western myalls; occasional mallee scrubs.

Hampton Tableland: name given to the southern edge of the true Nullarbor Plain. Claypans, caves, sinkholes and rockholes common, set upon or within limestone rock. Tableland edge marked by rocky limestone outcrops. Mallee scrubs common.

MUNDRABILLA: roadhouse facility with an interesting aviary and murals. Motel, store, fuel.

Baxter Cliffs: name given to the southern edge of the Nullarbor Plain (Hampton Tableland); forms part of the presumed longest unbroken cliffline in the world (375km). Numerous limestone outcrops and bluffs; minor rocky creeklines.

Ruin: remains of old stone building. Good views over Roe Plain from near ruin. Beware of deep, uncovered well. Fair views eastward along highway toward the white Eucla dunes (Delisser Sandhills).

Eucla Pass: interesting rocky valley through which the highway ascends/descends the Baxter Cliffs. Illuminated white cross nearby, dedicated to all Christians.

EUCLA: large roadhouse settlement, virtually a township. Good views from the settlement overlooking the Roe Plain and Delisser Sandhills. Nearby (6km, take the narrow bitumen-sealed old Eucla Pass road behind the motel) are the Eucla **ruins,** a former telegraph station now mostly covered by sand. Old stone buildings - very photogenic. About a kilometre away on the coast (walk slightly west of south) are the remains of the old Eucla jetty. A stroll through the dunes is interesting, especially in the early morning (before footprints mar the landscape) - interesting ripple patterns in the sand. Looking inland from atop a high dune towards the Baxter Cliffs and Roe Plain provides awesome views. This area around the ruins is part of the Eucla National Park.

BORDER VILLAGE: roadhouse facility set right on the state border. Motel, store, fuel.

Lookout: good views overlooking the Great Australian Bight and large dunes called the Merdayerrah Sandpatch.
Plains form the southern part of the Nullarbor Plain. Vegetation here quite dense due to proximity to the ocean, dominated by mallee eucalypts. Shrubs stunted near cliff top.

Wildflowers often seen in this area.
Lookout: expansive views from atop a high cliff; the southern margin of the Nullarbor Plain. Sheer drop to ocean, about 85m; stand well back in winds.

Diamond Bore: locality only. Telephone available.

Lookout: excellent views of cliffline and ocean. Sheer drop; very dangerous.

Lookout: good views overlooking the Great Australian Bight. Beware of strong winds.

Nullarbor National Park: large national park of former grazing leases, conserving an expansive portion of the Nullarbor Plain. Make enquiries at Nullarbor Roadhouse.

Lookout: good views of cliffline and ocean. Be careful in winds. Emergency **phone** nearby.
Plains support a shrubland of mallee eucalypts.

Open plains support a low shrubland of saltbush; part of the true treeless Nullarbor Plain.

NULLARBOR: roadhouse facility. Motel, store, fuel.

NOTES

MAP 22 MADURA-BALLADONIA-MADURA
via Cocklebiddy

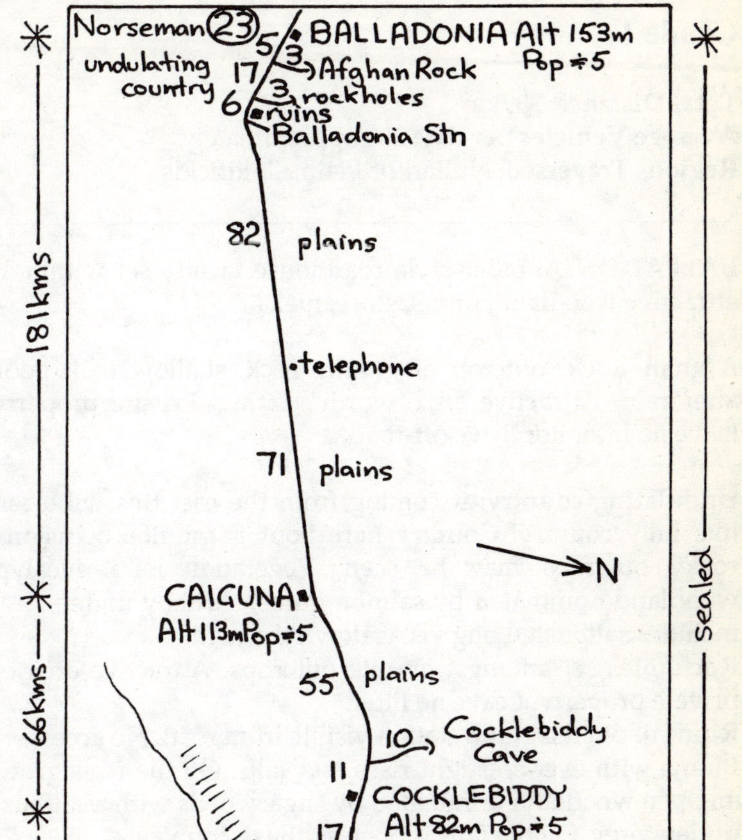

MAP 22 MADURA-BALLADONIA-MADURA via Cocklebiddy

Grade 1

Total Distance: 339km
Average Vehicles per day: 250 approximately
Regions Traversed: Nullarbor Plain, Goldfields

BALLADONIA: older style roadhouse facility set within an attractive woodland. Motel, store, fuel.

Afghan Rock: outcrop of granite rock; shallow rock pools after rain. Attractive area, worth visiting. Private property: leave no litter nor drive off-road.

Undulating country: if coming from the east this will seem like hilly country! Country hereabout is granite; occasional rocky outcrops may be seen. Vegetation is a eucalypt woodland dominated by salmon gums; shrubby understorey includes saltbush. Long vistas down the road.
Rockholes set amongst granite outcrops. Attractive area on private property. Leave no litter.
Ruins of old telegraph station visible from road. No access.
Plains with ever-so-slight rises and falls. On the rises grows an open woodland dominated by sugarwoods with a saltbush understorey. On the falls is open saltbush country.
Telephone situated virtually in the middle of what is probably the longest straight stretch of roadway in the world: approximately 145km. Uninhabited country hereabout.
Plains support sugarwood woodlands with some mallee eucalypt shrublands near Caiguna.

CAIGUNA: roadhouse facility with friendly birdlife! Motel, store, fuel.
Plains with ever-so-slight rises and falls. Expansive areas of

grassland and saltbush. Broad vistas from tops of rises. Some areas of mallee eucalypts.

Cocklebiddy Cave: undeveloped cave with no facilities. Turn-off adjacent to truck parking area (eastern end). Rough track suitable for conventional vehicles with extreme care - drive slowly. Cave appears as a collapsed doline (big hole in ground). A small creek and rough foot-track lead into the doline. Do not enter cave proper without climbing equipment. Warning: sheer unprotected cliff on virtually all sides. Interesting pristine area; disturb nothing and take all rubbish with you.

COCKLEBIDDY: older style roadhouse facility. Old mission ruins out the back. Motel, store, fuel.

Eyre: former telegraph station settlement, now the centre of a bird sanctuary. Visitors welcome but booking required. Access definitely 4WD. Rough track to top of escarpment accessible to conventional vehicles with extreme care. Excellent views from **lookout**, overlooking Roe Plain, the sand dunes at Eyre, and the Great Australian Bight. Beneath the cliffs are the ruins of the old Burnabbie Station - lonely country indeed; part of the Nuytsland Wilderness.
Claypans occupy the lower portions of the plain; surfaces covered with saltbush. Elsewhere are extensive tracts of eucalypt mallee shrublands.
Hampton Tableland: name given to that portion of the Nullarbor Plain which abuts the escarpment, or southern edge of the plain. Escarpment referred to as the Baxter Cliffs.
Lookout at top of Madura Pass provides good views overlooking the Roe Plain. Note the density of vegetation at the foot of the escarpment, making use of the run-off from the cliffline.

MADURA: roadhouse facility in an interesting location. Motel, store, fuel.

MAP 23 BALLADONIA-COOLGARDIE/KALGOORLIE-

BALLADONIA via Norseman

Grade 1

Total Distance: 359km (Kalgoorlie 380km)
Average Vehicles per day: 600 north of Norseman
Regions Traversed: Goldfields

COOLGARDIE: interesting historic mining town. Numerous old buildings; very photogenic. Worth spending some time here exploring the streets. Visit the cemetery, Prior's museum (unbelievable!), bottle museum, photogenic Catholic Church, climb Toorak Hill for reasonable views (ask locally for directions) or The Bluff, a 15m high breakaway on the Ora Banda road (ask locally) - good views over the town and old mining areas. Hotels, motels, stores, fuel.
Undulating country supports a cover of quite tall salmon gums; very attractive in the afternoon light. Also note the beautiful bark on the gimlet trees (shorter than the common salmon gums with flat crowns) - very photogenic, especially up close.

Emu Rocks: outcrops of granite by a rest area. Pretty spot.
Larkinville: old mining area. Access via track. Enquire locally.
Lookout set upon Mt Edwards, a rocky outcrop. Good views of the surrounding countryside. Access road okay.

WIDGIEMOOLTHA: old mining township, now virtually a ghost town. Worth a quick look. Ask about access to Ted's Show (5km south), a low-key gold mine. Hotel, store, fuel.
Yilgarn Wilderness: vast uninhabited area of sand plains, saltlakes, low ranges.
Higginsville: locality only, no facilities. Old mining area and

MAP 23 BALLADONIA-COOLGARDIE/KALGOORLIE-BALLADONIA via Norseman

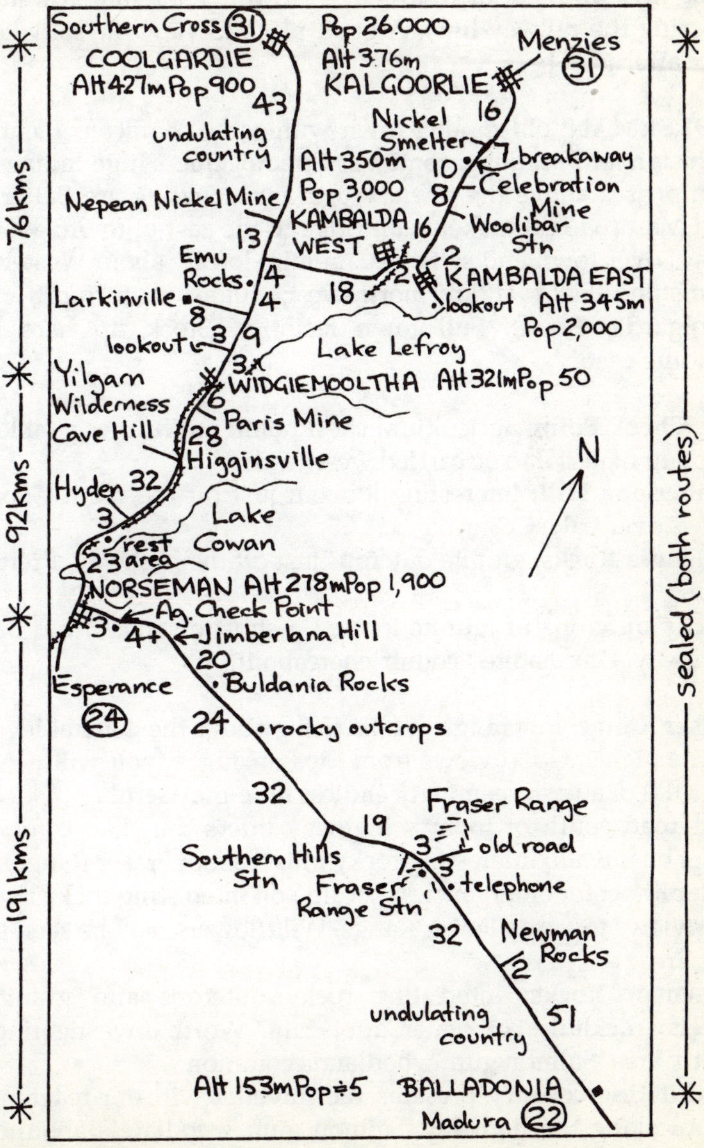

railway station. A pleasant spot for exploratory rambles.

Rest area located next to Lake Cowan shoreline (careful crossing the railway line). A good place to view the saltlake. Late afternoon best.

NORSEMAN: old mining town with some character. Plenty of historical buildings; some very photogenic. Huge tailings' dump rises above the town. Worth investigating are Battery and Mararoa Hill lookouts on ridge to the east of town; good views over town and saltlakes. Enquire locally about Western Gemstone Field (17km north-west; 10km to turn-off on Coolgardie Road). Full town facilities. Stock up here if heading east.

Ag. Check Point: agricultural checkpoint; no fruit, vegetables or plant material to be carried westwards.
Jimberlana Hill: interesting lookout just off the road. Good views over Lake Cowan.
Buldania Rocks: granite outcrops just off the highway. Pretty area.
Rocky outcrops of granite located a short distance from the highway. Uninhabited country hereabout.

Fraser Range: low range of hills rising above the general level of the plains. Good views from tops of ridges (you will need to walk) of a vast, seemingly endless blue-grey scrub.
Old road south of today's highway offers the chance for a quiet bushwalk. Interesting rocky hills (part of Fraser Range).
Telephone: for emergencies. Located on interesting rocky rise. Fair views towards Fraser Range. Wildflowers may be seen in this area.
Newman Rocks: interesting rocky outcrops and granite sheets; rockholes of water after rain. Worth investigating; pretty area. Salmon gum woodlands common.
Undulating country presents the traveller with far-reaching views along the highway. Salmon gum woodlands abound;

attractive in the afternoon light. Adjacent to the road are numerous claypans. Worth exploring on foot (park well off the road!) - very photogenic. Beyond the road lies uninhabited wilderness country.

BALLADONIA: roadhouse facility in an attractive setting. Motel, store, fuel.

Kalgoorlie Road

KALGOORLIE: large regional and mining centre. Many historic buildings; very photogenic. Worth spending a couple of days to explore the town and vicinity. Mine tours, museums, historic displays, viewpoints. Visit the Golden Mile, see the Hay Street brothels, call into the Boulder Block (old buildings). Good view overlooking Kalgoorlie-Boulder about a kilometre south of Boulder on the Kambalda road. Full town facilities.

Breakaway: attractive break in slope some 20m high and about 1km long; numerous colours, notably pinks, yellows and browns. Mornings best for photography. Access by foot, approximately 150m from road. Park well off the road.

Celebration Mine: old mine ruins; very photogenic, especially the headframe. Rusty tanks and dumps in area; worth exploring. Look for track in; mine roughly 600m from road.

KAMBALDA EAST: relatively modern nickel mining town set amongst the salmon gums. Nearby is the large saltlake, **Lake Lefroy.** Good view over lake from lookout. Stores, fuel.

KAMBALDA WEST: modern mining town, developed to house the overflow from Kambalda East. Unlike the hilly Kambalda East, this settlement is built upon a plain. Worth a quick look. Full town facilities.

MAP 24 NORSEMAN-ESPERANCE/LAKE KING-NORSEMAN

via Salmon Gums

Grade 1 (Norseman-Lake King Grade 3)

Total Distance: 202km (Lake King 257km)
Average Vehicles per day: 360 south of Norseman/35 Lake King road
Regions Traversed: Goldfields, Wheatbelt

ESPERANCE: large country town and port servicing the surrounding hinterland; also a major coastal resort town. Spectacular coastal scenery nearby. Good fishing grounds - enquire locally. Worth spending some time here. Full town facilities.
Lookout provides good views over Esperance, its surrounding saltlakes, and the granite islands and headlands of the coast.

GIBSON: small wheat-farming township. Fair broad views south of Gibson towards the coast. Hotel, store, fuel.
Wheatlands occupy the broad plains. Attractive after winter rains; bleached and glary after the summer drought. Little natural vegetation remains, except along roadside reserves.

Scadden: locality set amongst the broad-acre wheat farms.

GRASS PATCH: small wheat-farming township. Store, fuel.

Wheatlands spread across the slightly undulating plains. Little natural vegetation remains.

SALMON GUMS: slightly larger wheat-farming township set amongst salmon gums. Hotel, store, fuel.

MAP 24 NORSEMAN-ESPERANCE/LAKE KING-NORSEMAN via Salmon Gums

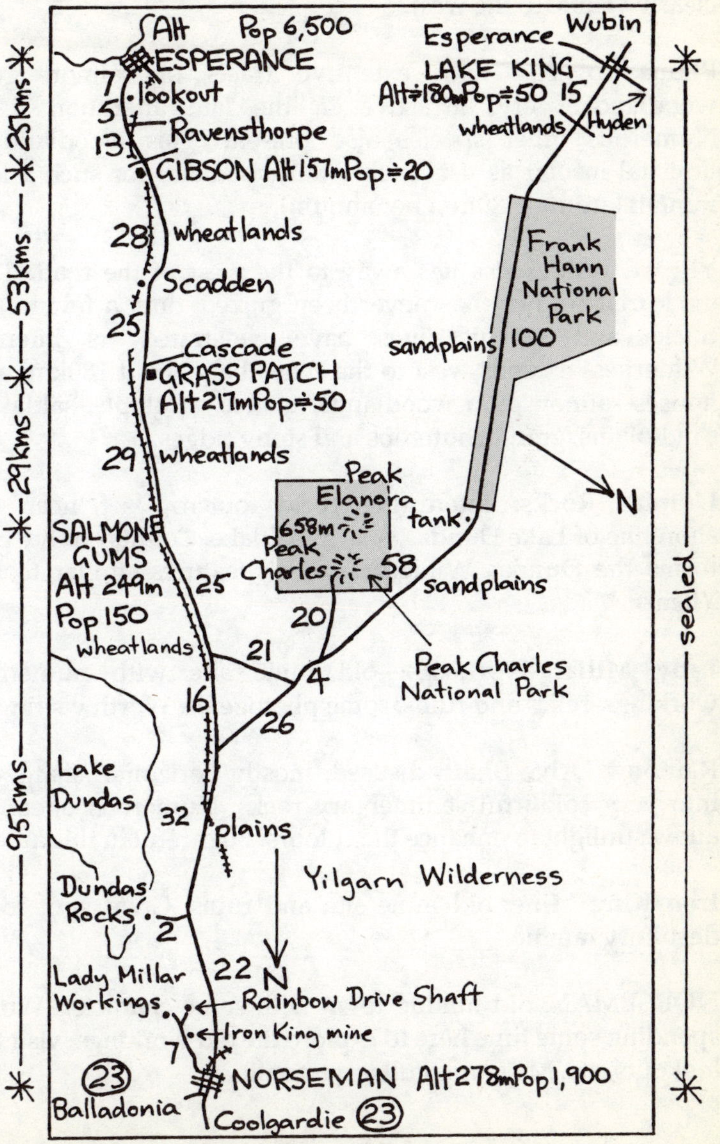

Wheatlands occupy the plains. Uncleared remnants of natural vegetation, notably salmon gum woodlands. Peak Charles clearly visible to the west.

Plains covered with extensive tracts of salmon gum woodlands; very attractive in the late afternoon light. Numerous other species also present. This woodland is unusual insofar as it is such a tall woodland for such a low rainfall (around 280mm per annum).

Yilgarn Wilderness lies away to the west of the road. This uncleared country has never been grazed; only a few minor tracks and seismic lines have penetrated its interior. Wilderness extends west to the Wheatbelt (about 180km) and houses salmon gum woodlands, mallee eucalypts, saltlakes, sand plains, granite outcrops and stony ridges.

Dundas Rocks: interesting rocky outcrop set near the shoreline of Lake Dundas, a large saltlake. Country to the east forms the Dundas Wilderness, with features similar to the Yilgarn.

Lady Millar Workings: old mine site with numerous workings, relics and ruins; some photogenic. Worth visiting.

Rainbow Drive Shaft: disused, mostly horizontal shafts cut into very colourful sedimentary rocks. Numerous openings allow sunlight to enhance the colours. Be careful in this area.

Iron King Mine: old mine site and ruins. Good spot for a desultory ramble.

NORSEMAN: old mining town with some character. Worth spending some time here to explore the old workings, visit the lookouts, etc. Museum. Full town facilities.

Lake King road

LAKE KING: small wheat-farming township. Hotel, store, fuel.

Wheatlands form the eastern edge of the vast and not often inspiring Western Australian wheatbelt. The contrast between the wheatbelt and the country to the east is apparent. Interesting to note that since the wholesale land clearance, rainfall is less in the Wheatbelt than in the adjacent wilderness.

Frank Hann National Park: mostly a broad road reserve preserving sand plain vegetation. Numerous types of heaths and mallee shrublands common.

Sand plains might look dreary from a fast vehicle, but they support a staggering array of plant species, almost as much as a rainforest! Numerous heaths, mallee shrublands and salmon gum woodlands. Sand plain forms southern part of the Yilgarn Wilderness.

Tank provides an emergency water supply. Of note as one of the few man-made constructions (besides the road) in this countryside.

Sand plains of heaths, scrubs and woodlands. In spring this area provides a welter of wildflowers; not necessarily massed displays of single species, but a huge range of different species. Worth exploring on foot. Park well off the road and do not lose sight of the vehicle!

Peak Charles National Park: park preserving sand plain country; also houses a rocky range dominated by Peaks Charles and Elanora. Camping available.

Peak Charles: high rocky peak set upon a vast sand plain. Lower slopes of Peak (reaching the vast rock sheets) easy to climb; higher portions of the Peak require care. Vast excellent views overlooking the Yilgarn Wilderness to the north. Also apparent are the in-roads made by the wholesale land clearances for wheat farming to the south and east. Plans were once afoot to clear the Yilgarn and Dundas Wilderness for cropping.

Madura Pass, Nullarbor Plain (Maps 21 and 22)

GAWLER RANGES

Lying to the north of the Eyre Peninsula, the Gawler Ranges are a little-known region of moderately high hills and ranges, interspersed with attractive undulating bluebush plains. One of the few areas of the outback to receive fairly reliable winter rains, it presents a green face to the traveller who ventures into this area during late winter or spring. Dotted across the plains are western myalls, a low acacia reminiscent of the trees of the African savanna with flattened crowns and attractive foliage.

The Gawler Ranges will be of interest to those travellers seeking to spice their east-west (Nullarbor) crossing with a mild adventure by avoiding the long straights of the Eyre Peninsula wheatlands, or those Western Australian travellers heading to or from Central Australia; the Wirrulla-Kingoonya road is an unsealed short-cut that passes through attractive range and desert country. Be warned, though, this is backblocks country with virtually no services, and the roads, while serviceable, do not encourage high speeds.

Warnings: roads unsuitable for travel in wet weather and may be subject to flooding. Avoid travelling at night. Make local enquiries before proceeding. Stay out of this area in summer unless experienced. Numerous grids and stock races will be encountered. No fuel available between Wirrulla and Kingoonya (251km).

NOTES

MAP 25 IRON KNOB-WIRRULLA/SKULL TANKS-IRON KNOB via Mt Ive

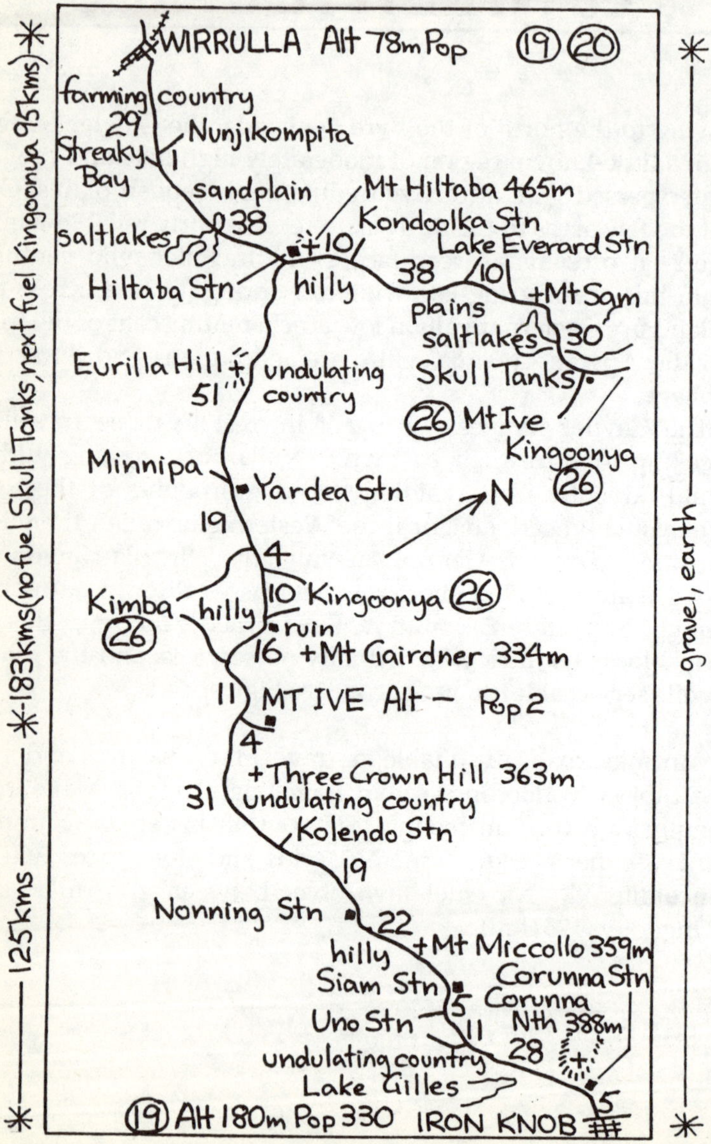

MAP 25 IRON KNOB-WIRRULLA/SKULL TANKS-IRON KNOB via Mt Ive

Grade 3

Total Distance: 308km (Skull Tanks 328km)
Average Vehicles per day: 20 near Mt Ive
Regions Traversed: Gawler Ranges, Eyre Peninsula

WIRRULLA: small wheat-farming township and railway station. Hotel, store, fuel.

Farming country supports extensively cleared tracts of land utilised for cropping and sheep grazing.

Sand plain with low dunes supports a dense eucalypt mallee scrub dominated by red mallee with a spinifex understorey; various acacia shrubs are also seen.
Saltlakes and claypans line the road, providing a break from the dense mallee scrub that surrounds them.

Hiltaba Station: working sheep station; no facilities.

Undulating country dominated by a sparse woodland of western myall with a bluebush understorey. At intervals, rounded rocky hills rise above the lowlands, forming an attractive backdrop. Good sweeping view obtained from tops of rises.

Yardea Station: working sheep station; no facilities.

Hilly country rises above the western myall-bluebush lowlands; the rounded summits appear very striking under a partly cloudy winter sky. Nearby lies an arm of Lake Gairdner (not shown on map). Very attractive area hereabouts.

Ruin of an old stone building; very photogenic set as it is upon a bluebush plain.

MT IVE: working sheep station that caters for tourists; attractively set amongst rounded ranges and rolling hills. Ideal location to explore the Gawler Ranges; enquire locally. Basic accommodation, limited store, fuel.

Undulating country provides many good views across the western myall woodlands; bluebush common in the understorey. Occasional high rounded hills seen to the north; plains and distant ranges visible to the south. At intervals patches of belah (tall tree with straggly foliage) may be seen.

Nonning Station: large working sheep station clearly visible from the road. Interesting buildings; no access or facilities.

Hilly country, especially north of the road near Mt Miccollo. Good views eastward as road ascends/descends from one level to another. A few scattered mallee eucalypts may be seen, otherwise area dominated by western myall and bluebush. Upon the nearby rocky hill summits are tracts of spinifex.

Siam Station: working sheep station; no facilities.

Undulating country supports empty treeless plains of saltbush; expansive views from tops of rises. Westwards low rounded hill summits can be seen; southwards the low-lying Lake Gilles is visible; eastwards the prominent ridgeline of the Baxter Hills and Corunna North is clearly visible; south-eastwards the Iron Knob open cut mine can be seen.

Corunna Station: working sheep station spectacularly situated at the base of Corunna South. Interesting buildings and excellent sweeping views; no access or facilities.

IRON KNOB: interesting mining town set at the foot of the Middleback Ranges. Worth a quick look at least. Hotel, motel, store, fuel.

Hiltaba Station-Skull Tanks road

Skull Tanks: intersection only; no facilities. Nearby is a large shed tank (a large corrugated iron roof catchment feeds into tanks underneath) that is worth investigating - interesting, barely decipherable graffiti from the depression days. Over a rise, a few hundred metres away, is a very attractive saltlake. Next fuel: Kingoonya (95km).

Saltlakes near the road are arms of Lake Everard. Western myalls may be seen in this area.

Plains support a variety of plant life: western myall and bluebush in the north; areas of sand-hill and dune wattles; patches of mallee scrub, etc.

Hilly country supports a western myall woodland with a bluebush understorey. Attractive rounded rocky hills nearby; good sweeping views.

NOTES

MAP 26 KIMBA-KINGOONYA-KIMBA via Mt Ive

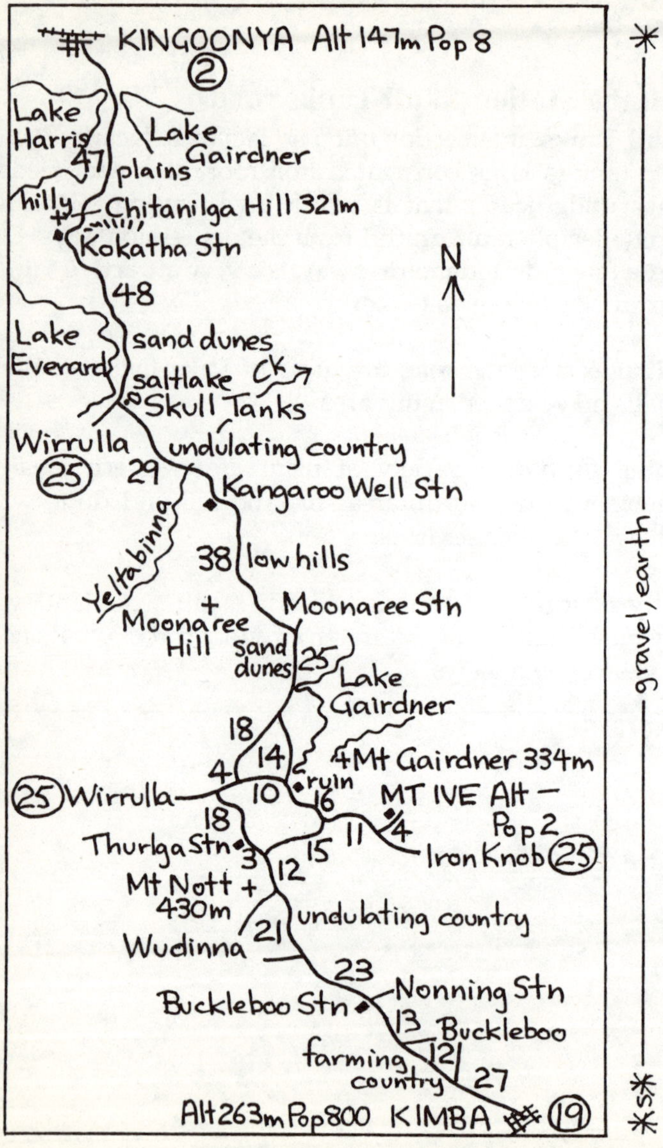

MAP 26 KIMBA-KINGOONYA-KIMBA via Mt Ive

Grade 3

Total Distance: 338km (370km via Mt Ive)
Average Vehicles per day: 20 north of Skull Tanks
Regions Traversed: Eyre Peninsula, Gawler Ranges, Far North

KINGOONYA: former old Stuart Highway and railway settlement; today virtually a ghost town. Interesting township with one of the widest main streets in Australia. Many old buildings, some of which are occupied - do not trespass. Limited stores and fuel available at the caravan park.

Lake Harris and Lake Gairdner just visible across the plains, as evidenced by their glistening salt surfaces.
Plains support vast tracts of salt bush; expansive views. Occasional western myalls may be seen. Further south, western myall woodlands with understoreys of bluebush are more common.
Hilly country covered with saltbush provides excellent vistas. Occasional rocky outcrops may be seen.

Kokatha Station: working sheep station; no facilities.
Sand dunes are quite densely vegetated with various acacias, mostly sand-hill and dune wattles. Cypress pines may also be seen.

Lake Everard inlets edge the road in a number of places, providing good open views of the surrounding desert country. Many sand dunes in this area including some with bare crests.
Skull Tanks: intersection only; no facilities. Nearby is a shed tank (a roofed catchment feeding water to tanks underneath)

that is worth investigating. Nearby, over a rise, is a small saltlake; well worth the walk - very photogenic.

Undulating country surrounded by low hills; occasional good views from tops of rises. Western myall woodlands with bluebush understorey dominates the landscape. Some relics of the sheep grazing industry can be seen along this and more southerly sections of this road.

Kangaroo Well Station: working sheep station; no facilities.
Low hills with rounded summits rise above the undulating lowlands. Western myall and bluebush common. Occasional good views.
Sand dunes support dense thickets of eucalypt mallee scrubs with a spinifex understorey.
Lake Gairdner inlet lies close to the road; worth investigating on foot. Fairly long distance view to the lake.
Ruin is set amongst attractive rounded hills which rise above bluebush-clad lowlands. Ruin very photogenic. Nearby is another arm of Lake Gairdner.

MT IVE: working sheep station set amongst attractive rounded hills and ranges. Tourist facilities available including private access to the Gawler Ranges - enquire locally. Basic accommodation, limited stores, fuel.

Thurlga Station: working sheep station; no facilities.
Undulating country supports a western myall woodland with a bluebush understorey; in some places groves of belah (a tall shaggy-looking tree) may be seen. Occasional rounded hills are visible, especially to the north and west.
Buckleboo Station: farm property on the edge of the station country; no facilities.
Farming country mostly cleared for cropping and sheep grazing occupies these slightly undulating lowlands.

KIMBA: wheat farming town. Hotel, motel, stores, fuel.

GREAT NORTHERN HIGHWAY and northwards

Running north-south across the bulk of the western rump of Western Australia, the all-sealed Great Northern Highway passes through what some people see as one of the most dreary landscapes in Australia. This is not true, although some sections (Meekatharra-Kumarina for instance) come close. North of the Tropic of Capricorn the countryside is a delight, with fantastic mountain ranges, rocky gorges, vast desert plains and river red gum-lined creeks. South of Meekatharra, while not scenically grand, the road traverses one of the most interesting areas in the outback, the Murchison Goldfields. Dotted at intervals are the remains of old mining towns, interspersed with the still surviving towns dependent on not only mining but grazing. Time spend in these places, chatting with the local characters, will enhance anyone's travels.

Added to this is one of Australia's greatest features: the incredible massed wildflower displays which literally run to the horizon. Occurring most years at the end of the winter rains (late August-September) these displays, everlastings mostly, present a bewildering range of colours varying from white, to yellow, to pink. Elsewhere are more subtle displays as the individual plants of the sand plain country present a range of colours and forms; these, to be appreciated, need to be examined close-up.

Warnings: beware of stock and kangaroos at night. Road may be subject to flooding. On the unsealed deviations (not the major highway) make local enquiries before proceeding;

inform a reliable person of your intentions, particularly in summer. The Woodstock-Marble Bar road is not recommended at this time unless you are experienced. Unsealed roads may be rain-affected and are subject to flooding.

NOTES

MAP 27 DALWALLINU-CUE-DALWALLINU via Mt Magnet

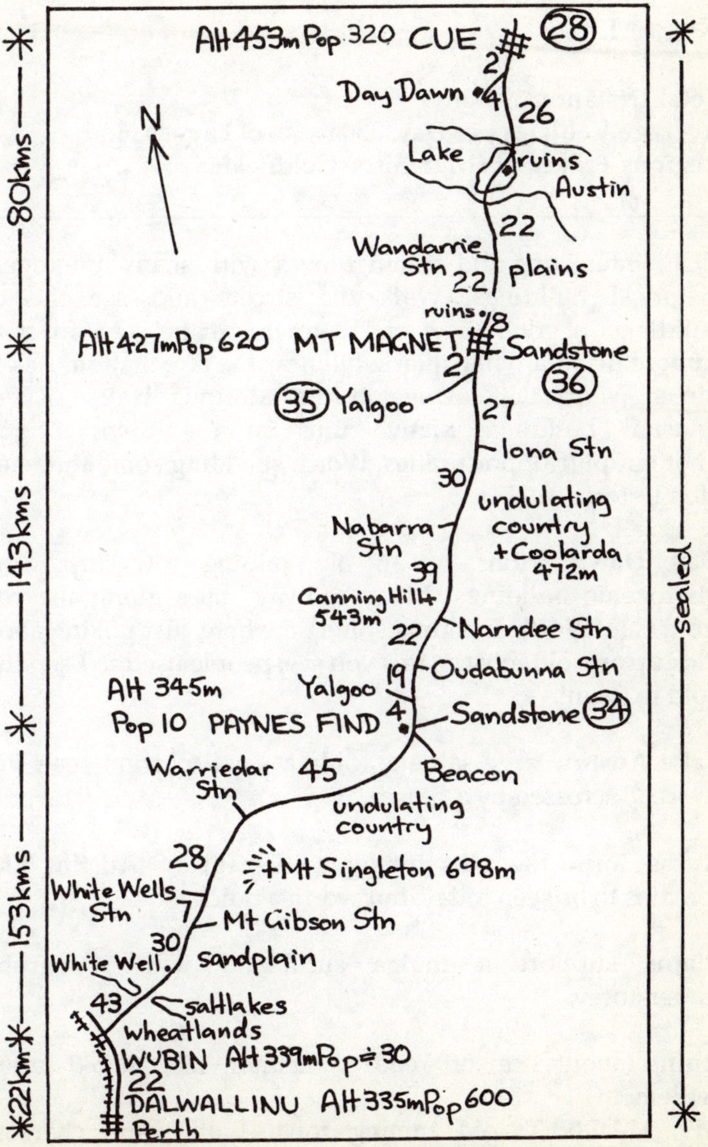

MAP 27 DALWALLINU-CUE-DALWALLINU via Mt Magnet

Grade 1

Total Distance: 398km
Average Vehicles per Day: 230 north of Paynes Find
Regions Traversed: Murchison Goldfields

CUE: interesting old mining town with many photogenic historical buildings. Walk the streets and see the old buildings; a good view of the town can be seen from the Kintore Blow, a white quartz hill near the Fire Station. Ask for directions to the corrugated-iron Masonic Hall - a very unusual building. Many ruins in the town - good photographic opportunities. Worth spending some time here. Hotel, stores, fuel.

Day Dawn: ruins of an old mining township. Some photogenic buildings. Many railway relics along the road from Cue. Worth spending some time here, just poking about. Pick up any old tobacco tins you see; people used to keep their gold in them!

Lake Austin: large saltlake (only a small portion seen from the road) crossed by a causeway.

Ruins form the old mining settlement of Austin. Little remains to be seen today, but worth a quick look.

Plains support a mulga shrubland with a shrubby understorey.

Ruins (about 1km off road) of Lennonville, an old mining settlement.
MT MAGNET: old mining town with some character.

Interesting main street with impressive buildings. The old open-air picture theatre is of interest. Town is undergoing a change with new mining ventures in the area. Good area for gemstone prospecting - enquire locally. Hotels, stores, fuel.

Undulating country offers vast vistas from tops of rises. Occasional low ridges break the skyline. Excellent wildflower displays literally cover the plains as far as the eye can see. A staggering experience for first-timers. The flowers (mainly everlastings) come in a variety of colours. Wildflowers usually present after winter rains (late August-September). Mulga shrublands common.

PAYNES FIND: a small old mining settlement with some character. Interesting bush pub. Hotel, fuel.

Undulating country offers fair views from tops of rises. Occasional low ridges dot the skyline. At times the high bulk of Mt Singleton can be seen. Fair to very good wildflower displays after winter rains (late August-September). Mulga shrublands common with an overstorey of eucalypts. Some patches of mallee eucalypts.

Sand plain country is more typical of the uncleared Wheatbelt landscapes. Dense thickets of various acacias common with a variety of shrubs and heaths in the understorey. Good wildflowers at end of winter (not so much the massed displays of further north, but an incredible variety of different flowers).

White Well: an old stone circular well located by the road, probably made by the monks of New Norcia. About 500m off the highway a track leads through wattle thickets to a large exposed expanse of rock - good spot for a picnic.

Saltlakes edge the road. Fair views across the cleared countryside.

Wheatlands occupy the gently undulating plains. Fair views from tops of rises.

WUBIN: small wheat-farming township. Hotel, store, fuel.

DALWALLINU: larger wheat-farming town serving the surrounding district. Hotel, motel, store, fuel.

NOTES

MAP 28 CUE-KUMARINA-CUE via Meekatharra

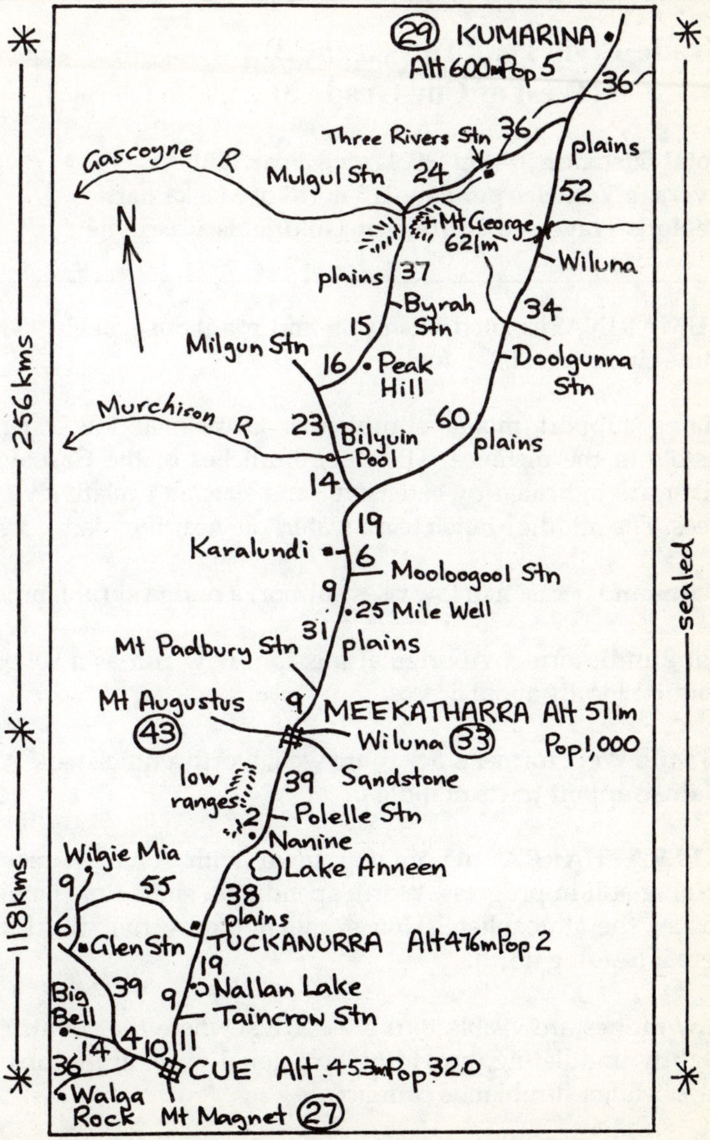

MAP 28 CUE-KUMARINA-CUE via Meekatharra

Grade 1 (via Peak Hill Grade 3)
(West of Cue Grade 3)

Total Distance: 374km (393km via Peak Hill)
Average Vehicles per day: 215 north of Meekatharra
Regions Traversed: Murchison Goldfields, Gascoyne

KUMARINA: isolated bush pub and roadhouse facility with some character. Hotel, fuel.

Plains support mulga shrublands. Occasional low ranges visible in the distance. The three branches of the Gascoyne River are indicated by extensive sand flats and relatively tall trees. The middle branch has a waterhole near the road.

Plains and occasional low rises support a mulga shrubland.

Karalundi: former Aboriginal mission, now run as a school. Enquire locally about access.

25 Mile Well: former stock route well; worth a quick look.
Plains support tracts of mulga.

MEEKATHARRA: old mining town with some character. Mining still in progress. Worth spending a short time here to absorb the atmosphere. Hotels, motel, stores, fuel. Stock up here if heading north.

Low ranges are visible to the west. Elsewhere the country is slightly undulating, providing occasional views from tops of rises. Mulga shrublands common.

Nanine: old mining settlement; a few ruins remain. Worth exploring on foot. Country hereabout degraded by mining but interesting nonetheless. Good views to the south overlooking **Lake Anneen.**

Plains support mulga shrublands. Attractive countryside in this area. Small lakes and flood-plains support areas of grassland and saltbush. Old railway line on the eastern side is of interest.

TUCKANURRA: old mining settlement and railway ruins. Interesting old store still operates as a 'corner store'. Worth stopping just to soak up the atmosphere. Camping available. Enquire here about back-track access to Wilgie Mia ochre mines (Grade 4 route) - you will need a mud-map. Store only, no fuel.

Nallan Lake: attractive area even when lake is dry. When the lake is full this place is a delight. Good wildflowers after winter rains (late August-September); not massed displays but pretty nonetheless. Leave no litter.

CUE: interesting historic mining town. Many old buildings - very photogenic. Worth spending some time here to walk the streets. Hotel, stores, fuel.

Three Rivers Road via Peak Hill

Plains support extensive tracts of mulga. Low ranges and hills dot the landscape.

Peak Hill: old mining settlement of some interest. Current mining activities may limit access. Worth investigating.

Bilyuin Pool: large waterhole on the Murchison River; rarely ever dry. Attractive area with shady river red gums. On northern side of the road are the ruins of the old Bilyuin Hotel.

West of Cue

Wilgie Mia: old Aboriginal ochre mine definitely worth visiting (enquire locally in Cue about road conditions - road usually suitable for conventional vehicles with care). Located in the Weld Range. On the eastern side at the car park (good views to south) there is a tunnel that leads to the Aboriginal mine. You will need old clothes (very dusty) and a torch. This walk is worth it but take care. The Aboriginal part of the mine is a very impressive hole with fascinating ochre colours running through its sides. These colours seem to glow in the half-light. Access to the Aboriginal mine is possible from the western side of the range (rough track - drive very carefully) but it is not possible to enter the mine from this side. Nonetheless the cavity dug by these early miners is impressive.

Afghan Rock (not shown on map) is passed en route to Glen Station and Wilgie Mia, approximately 45km from Cue on the northern side of the road. Rock lies about 500m from road (access via a track). This high granite dome provides good views.

Big Bell: old mining town with many ruins. Worth exploring. Recent mining activity may restrict access to some parts of the old settlement.

Walga Rock: gallery of Aboriginal rock paintings depicting snakes, emus, kangaroos, etc, as well as a Dutch ship that visited the Western Australian coast in the 17th century! Climb the rock for excellent views. This is a clean area; please take all rubbish with you.

MAP 29 KUMARINA-AUSKI ROADHOUSE/ ROY HILL STATION-KUMARINA via Newman

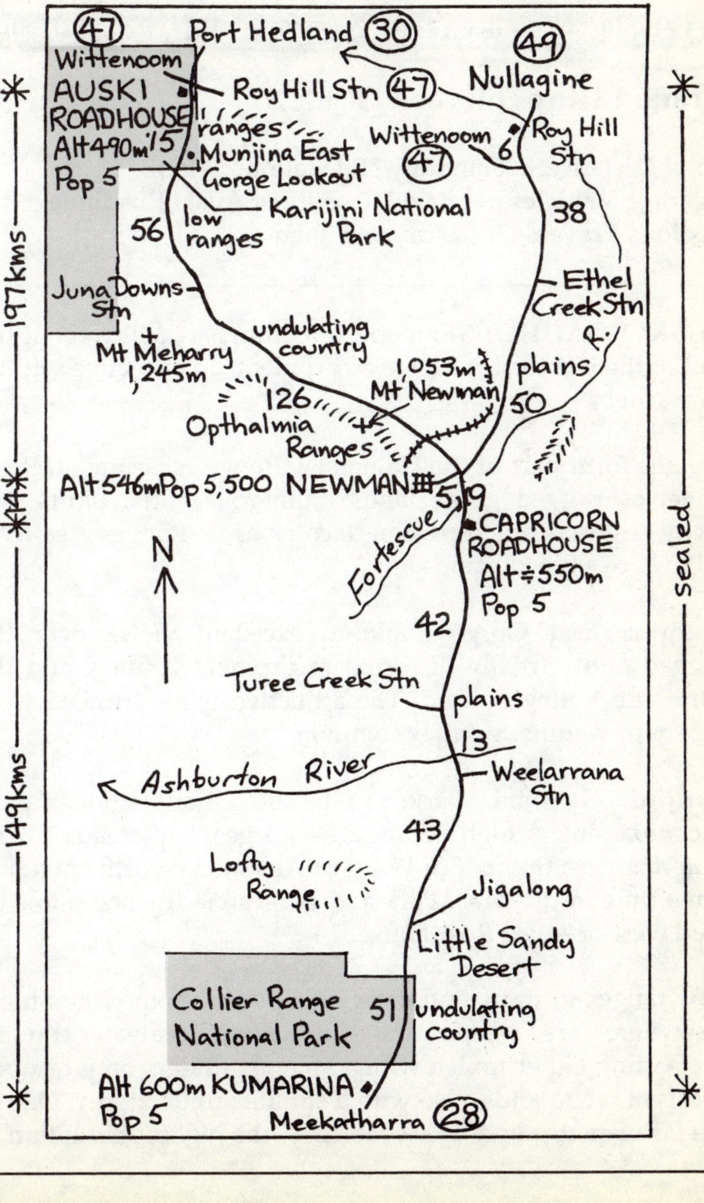

MAP 29 KUMARINA-AUSKI ROADHOUSE/ROY HILL STATION-KUMARINA

MAP 29 KUMARINA-AUSKI ROADHOUSE/ROY HILL STATION-KUMARINA

Grade 1 (Roy Hill road Grade 3)

Total Distance: 360km (Roy Hill Station 257km)
Average Vehicles per day: 110 south of Auski Roadhouse
Regions Traversed: Gascoyne, Pilbara

AUSKI ROADHOUSE: modern roadhouse facility set at the foot of the Hamersley Range escarpment; an attractive setting. Store, fuel.

Ranges form part of the Hamersley Range escarpment. Road traverses rugged gorge lands; numerous cliffs, bluffs and rocky residual outcrops. Spectacular area. Ranges rise over 200m above the lowlands.

Munjina East Gorge Lookout: excellent views over the rugged and partially dissected escarpment country and the Fortescue Valley beyond. The attractive white-trunked trees are snappy gums. Spinifex common.

Karijini National Park: vast and mountainous park encompassing high ranges, gorges, plateaux and watercourses; the roof of Western Australia. Worth spending some time in this area. Park and gorges readily accessible by road west of Auski Roadhouse.

Low ranges form upland areas on a plateau some 700m high. Elsewhere are plains and undulating plateau country supporting either mulga with a spinifex understorey or open eucalypt woodlands, also with a spinifex understorey. One of the far distant ranges is Mt Meharry, the highest mountain in

Western Australia.

Undulating country provides excellent views of the Opthalmia Range, a high, upstanding range rising some 500m above the lowlands. Vegetation varies between mulga shrublands and open eucalypt woodlands.

NEWMAN: attractive mining town constructed during the late 1960s. Huge iron ore open cut mines nearby. Mine tours available; good views of town and district from Radio Hill lookout. Enquire locally about scenic drives in the area. A good place to stock up on supplies. Museum. Full town facilities.

Fortescue River crossing: attractive area with plenty of shady river red gums.

CAPRICORN ROADHOUSE: a fairly modern roadhouse with some character. Often used by Newman people having a day out. Store, fuel.

Plains support extensive tracts of mulga. Elsewhere are open areas of spinifex which provide vast views to distant low ranges - very attractive in the late afternoon light. Floodout country is also passed; these attractive areas support tall gums with a grassy understorey.

Little Sandy Desert: outlier of the Great Sandy Desert. Attractive red sand dunes, quite densely vegetated, line the road. Photogenic in the late afternoon light.

Collier Range National Park: undeveloped wilderness park conserving areas of high ground (the Collier Range). Areas of spinifex on the higher country, mulga on the lower country. Some hills visible, rising above the general level. A bush camping area is available just north of Kumarina.

KUMARINA: isolated bush pub and roadhouse. Hotel, fuel.

Roy Hill road

Roy Hill Station: working cattle station; no facilities. Next fuel at Nullagine, 92km north. Just north of the station turn-off is the Fortescue River crossing, a nice area with shady gums.

Plains seem to extend forever. Vegetation ranges from open eucalypt woodlands with a spinifex understorey, dominated by attractive white-trunked gums, to areas of saltbush and, north of Newman, mulga shrublands. The open country provides vast views to far-off ranges; north of Newman the Opthalmia Range is visible to the south.

NOTES

MAP 30 AUSKI ROADHOUSE-PORT HEDLAND/ MARBLE BAR-AUSKI ROADHOUSE

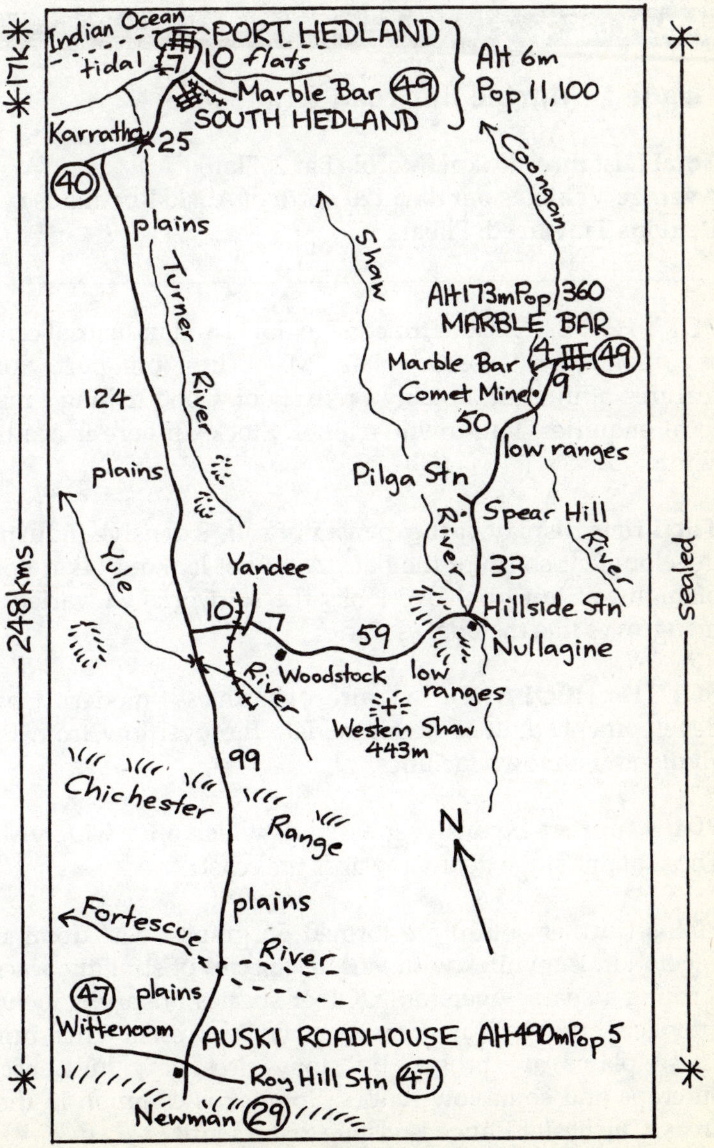

MAP 30 AUSKI ROADHOUSE-PORT HEDLAND/MARBLE BAR-AUSKI

ROADHOUSE

Grade 1 (Marble Bar road Grade 3)

Total Distance: 265km (Marble Bar 267km)
Average Vehicles per day: 120 north of Auski Roadhouse
Regions Traversed: Pilbara

PORT HEDLAND: unattractive regional and industrial centre set upon a vast coastal plain. Major iron ore port. Some features of interest, notably Pretty Pool. Good fishing - make local enquiries. Full town facilities. Stock up here if heading south.

Tidal flats display vast expanses of salt. Extensive industrial development south of the flats. A tourist lookout (4km north of highway junction) overlooks the saltworks. A variety of mangroves line the tidal estuaries.

SOUTH HEDLAND: a fairly charmless modern town development, built to accommodate the overflow from Port Hedland. Full town facilities.

Plains support expansive grasslands which offer wide vistas. These plains slope gently towards the coast.

Plains (further south) are formed on granite. The dominant vegetation is spinifex with various species of straggly acacias forming a sparse overstorey. Other species of shrubs include grevilleas and hakeas. Grasses may be present after rains. These plains are broken by stony rises, low hills, rocky outcrops and some low ranges. Spinifex is common in these areas. Chichester Range is visible to the south.

Chichester Range: long escarpment rising above the plains. Range rises to 400m above sea level (170m above the plains). Rocky outcrops common with spinifex the dominant vegetation.

Plains form a gently sloping plateau which slopes towards the Fortescue River valley. Broad vistas to the south taking in the rugged escarpment of the Hamersley Ranges. Vegetation dominated by spinifex with various acacias. Mulga common near the Fortescue River.

Fortescue River forms a shallow and broad valley with no distinct watercourse. Grassland areas.

Plains formed by outwash from nearby Hamersley Ranges. Good views of ranges to the south. Spinifex common with various acacias and some eucalypts.

AUSKI ROADHOUSE: modern roadhouse facility. Store, fuel.

Marble Bar road

MARBLE BAR: interesting old mining township with plenty of character. Visit the Ironclad Hotel, photograph the attractive stone-built (mornings best) Government building, ask locally for directions to One Mile Gorge. Spend some time here to absorb the atmosphere. Hotel, motel, stores, fuel. Stock up here if heading south.

Marble Bar: a colourful bar of jasper (mistaken for marble) crossing the Coongan River. Wetting the jasper brings up the colours. Worth seeing. A kilometre back towards town, and just north of the road, is Chinamans Pool - very pleasant spot.

Comet Mine: an old mine with a 75m high chimney. Many

old buildings - very photogenic - some of which are still in use. Gemstone displays. A kilometre west of the road (3km north of the mine) is Flying Fox Lookout - very good views.

Low ranges form a harsh but attractive landscape, especially in the late afternoon light. Snappy gums common with spinifex in the understorey. Uninhabited country lies to the north-west.

Spear Hill is an interesting dome-like hill of pink granite over 2km long. Hill is covered with large boulders and tall minnirichi trees (once used for making spear tips). The local Njamal people once used the summit of the hill for initiation ceremonies. Numerous engravings on low hills in the district. No public access without permission of the Department of Aboriginal Sites (WA Museum), local Aboriginal groups and the local landholder.

Hillside Station: working cattle station; no facilities.

Low ranges rise abruptly from the plain. Snappy gums and spinifex common.

Woodstock: a former grazing homestead, now a ranger's residence for the Abydos-Woodstock Aboriginal Cultural Preserve. Numerous rocky outcrops, appearing as conical heaps of rounded boulders, support literally thousands of engravings, many of which are human figures engaged in fighting, hunting or copulation. This area exudes a profound spirit. Public access to the engravings is restricted; permission required of the Department of Aboriginal Sites (WA Museum).

NOTES

GOLDFIELDS COUNTRY

While the Goldfields Country can make no claims of scenic grandeur, it is still perhaps one of the most fascinating regions of outback Australia. Dotted throughout its vast, slightly undulating plains, occasionally interrupted by solitary hills and ridges, are a multitude of old mining settlements, ghost towns and modern mining enterprises, most of which are devoted to the extraction of gold, and more recently, nickel. The Goldfields' settlements exude character and interest. They are fine 'outdoor museums', the history of which is still remember by people living today.

Joining these towns and settlements are good to excellent sealed and unsealed roads readily travelled by the family sedan. The routes pass through country which supports attractive salmon gum woodlands in the south, and vast tracts of mulga (with massed displays of everlastings after the winter rains) in the north. The countryside is fairly uniform though occasional surprises do occur: a glimmer of a saltlake or claypan through the trees, a rocky hill that beckons to be climbed, or the discovery of an old stone ruin set by a disused railway line. Then there are the old mining settlements and their ruins which just beg to be explored for a few hours or days. Pottering over the rubble and ruins with the promise of unearthing a small nugget of gold (check the old tobacco tins!) makes for an interesting travel experience.

Warnings: beware of deep mine shafts in mining areas. On the sealed roads beware of stock and kangaroos at night. Unsealed roads are usually okay after showers, but seek local advice - creeks may be flooding. In summer, always seek local advice and inform a reliable person of your intentions on these roads; avoid travelling at night.

MAP 31 SOUTHERN CROSS-MENZIES-SOUTHERN CROSS via Kalgoorlie

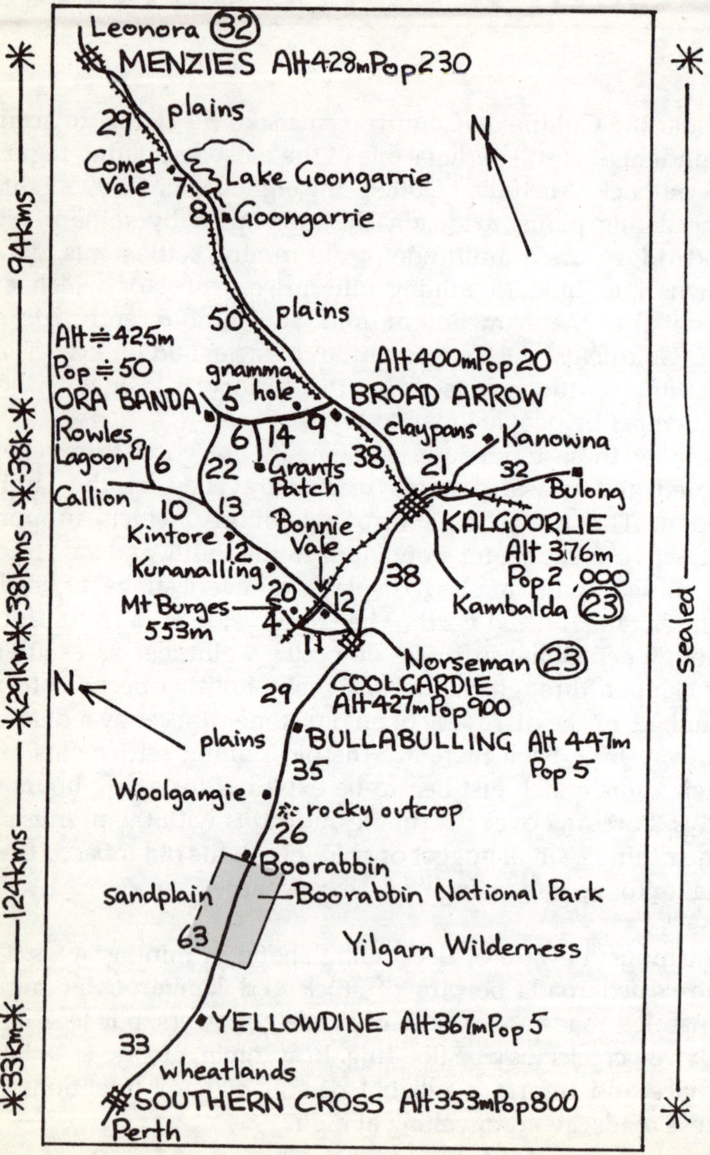

MAP 31 SOUTHERN CROSS-MENZIES-SOUTHERN CROSS via Kalgoorlie

Grade 1 (Ora Banda road Grade 3)
(East of Kalgoorlie Grade 3)

Total Distance: 356km
Average Vehicles per day: 950 west of Coolgardie
Regions Traversed: Wheatbelt, Goldfields

MENZIES: old mining township with plenty of character. Photogenic buildings and ruins. Worth seeing: old railway station, town hall, state battery. Reasonable views from Tank Hill east of town. Hotel, store, fuel.
Plains support open eucalypt woodlands with some she-oaks.

Comet Vale: old mining settlement, a stone ruin being the sole remains. Worth a quick look.

Lake Goongarrie: 300m access track leads to edge of lake (dry weather only!) - track leaves the main road in a shallow dip between two rises. Worth stopping here: good views across the saltlake including mirages, interesting rocky outcrops, good walking country.

Goongarrie: old mining and railway settlement; a few buildings remain. To the north (2.5km) is a level, open area with old workings; good fossicking area.
Plains support tracts of eucalypt woodlands dominated by salmon gums, gimlets, etc. Other trees include York and coral gums, Goldfields blackbutt and mallee eucalypts. Beneath are various shrubs, including jam trees and poverty bush. This is an unusual woodland given its proud stature in such a low rainfall area (approximately 240mm per annum). Numerous drainage lines, evidenced as sandy flats, cross the road.

BROAD ARROW: old mining settlement of which little remains. Many corrugated iron structures, some of which are inhabited. Do not trespass. Hotel, fuel.

Claypans common on the plains; area supports saltbush and she-oak woodlands. Salmon gum woodlands are more common further south.

KALGOORLIE: major mining town and regional centre with plenty of character. Grand buildings line a particularly impressive main street; side streets too have a share of interesting and photographic buildings. Mine workings and remains common. Also of interest is Kalgoorlie's sister settlement - Boulder with its many interesting buildings. Tourist features include mine tours, Goldfields and School of Mines museums, Two-Up School (6km north of the Broad Arrow road), Hay Street brothels, The Golden Mine Loop Line (a restored railway), etc. Full town facilities. Stock up here if heading north.

COOLGARDIE: historic mining town with many photogenic buildings. Worth spending some time here to absorb the atmosphere. A pleasant place to walk the streets. Fair views overlooking town and surrounding district from Toorak Hill or The Bluff (on the Ora Banda road near the end of town). Nearby (on the Kalgoorlie road) is Fly Flat, an old prospecting area - access may be restricted by mining activities. Hotels, motel, stores, fuel.

BULLABULLING: interesting bush pub and former railway station on the narrow gauge railway. Hotel, fuel.

Plains support an attractive salmon gum woodland with a shrubby understorey.

Woolgangie: locality only, no facilities. Located just north of the highway. Old narrow gauge railway siding. Many rocky

outcrops in this area.
Boorabbin: locality only, no facilities. Ruin set near the highway.

Boorabbin National Park: small park conserving sand plain vegetation. No facilities. To the south and north (away from the road) extends the vast and virtually untouched **Yilgarn Wilderness**, a region of saltlakes, claypans, sand plains and low, rocky rises.

Sand plains support a wide variety of vegetation including casuarinas, grevilleas, hakeas, etc. Good wildflowers on the shrubs after winter rains (late August-September). Undulating country hereabout provides fair distant views from tops of rises.

YELLOWDINE: old railway settlement. Current settlement has plenty of character. Worth stopping just to look. Hotel, motel, fuel.
Wheatlands are apparent by the cleared countryside. Some patches of native vegetation remain, particularly along the road reserve.

SOUTHERN CROSS: interesting old mining town with some character. Today the town serves as a wheat-farming settlement. Hotel, motel, store, fuel.

Ora Banda road

Gnamma hole: rock hole set into a granite outcrop. Interesting feature. Located about 20m north of the road.

Grants Patch: old mining area. A few scattered shacks still remain. Enquire locally about access to a fossicking area nearby.

ORA BANDA: old mining settlement with plenty of

character. Numerous ruins and mining relics; scattered shacks throughout the bush (some may be occupied); old restored hotel. A pleasant place to spend a few days. Hotel, store, fuel.

Rowles Lagoon: reserve and picnic area set by a freshwater lake. Open area but surrounded by shady scrub and trees.

Kintore: old mining settlement evidenced by stone ruins. A kilometre south are mine dumps and attractive gullies set into colourful sandstone; located west of the road.

Kunanalling: old mining settlement with impressive stone ruins about 150m off the road (western side). Climb the low hill about 400m to the north for good views.

Bonnie Vale: old mining area as evidenced by many dumps.

Mt Burgess: highest point in the district rising 120m above the plain. A good hill to climb for interesting views; the area has a remote feel to it. Pass through gate north of railway line for about 2km. Rough, washed-out track leads up the hill (unsuitable for vehicles). Inform someone of your intentions.

East of Kalgoorlie

Kanowna: old mining town which once had a population of 12,000. A few ruins remain today; rubble more common. A pleasant place for walking and just poking about. Good views from hill on eastern side when entering the settlement.

Bulong: old mining settlement of which little remains. A pleasant place to while away an afternoon.

NOTES

MAP 32 MENZIES-LEINSTER/LAVERTON-MENZIES via Leonora

Grade 1 (Laverton road Grade 1) (Kookynie road Grade 3) (Lawlers road Grade 3/4) (Mt Morgans road Grade 3)

Total Distance: 245km (Laverton 223km)
Average Vehicles per day: 280 east of Leonora
Regions Traversed: Goldfields

LEINSTER: modern mining town housing workers from the nearby Agnew Nickel Project. Enquire locally about attractive breakaway country near the town. Motel, stores, fuel.

Ford Run Plateau supports an extensive tract of mulga shrublands.
Teutonic: mining settlement.

Plains support extensive tracts of mulga shrublands. Massed wildflower displays of everlastings may occur after winter rains (late August-September).
Mt Davis: rocky hill set near the road. Good views.

LEONORA: old mining town with plenty of character. Interesting old buildings, some very photogenic. State battery worth visiting; fair views from Tank Hill east of the town. Stock up here if heading north.

Gwalia: definitely worth visiting. An old but relatively intact mining settlement. Photogenic old pub and many interesting houses, some of which are still occupied. Worth spending a few hours here to walk the streets, take photographs, etc. The various styles of corrugated iron buildings are unbelievable. Nearby is the Sons of Gwalia mine. Some services may now be available.

MAP 32 MENZIES-LEINSTER/LAVERTON-MENZIES via Leonora

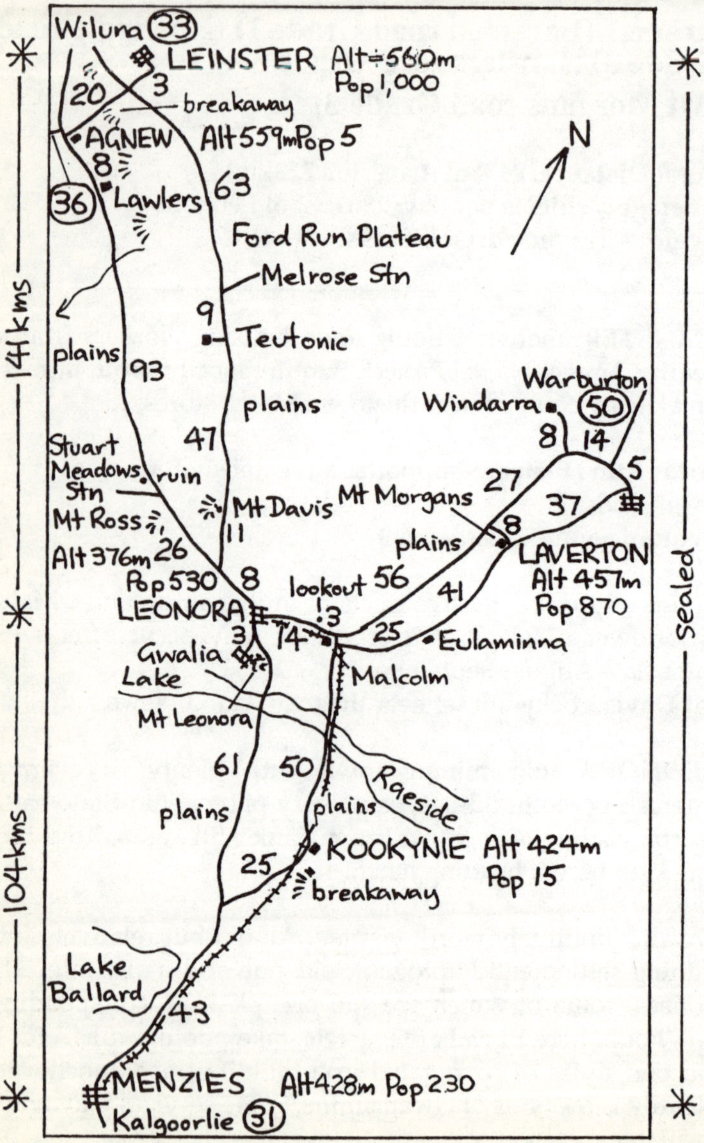

Mt Leonora: high hill rising 100m above the plain. Climb is relatively easy (best access on eastern side from the Menzies road). Excellent views from top.

Lake Raeside: saltlake occupying what is probably a former river channel. Supports a cover of saltbush and samphires. Of minor interest mainly because it is roughly 270km long, Australia's longest lake.
Plains support extensive tracts of mulga. Wildflowers may be present after winter rains (late August-September).

Lake Ballard: large saltlake lying west of the main road.

MENZIES: interesting old mining settlement; worth stopping for a quick look at least. Old photogenic buildings. Hotel, store, fuel.

Lawlers road

Breakaway offers fair views over the plains to the west.

AGNEW: old mining township with character. Interesting old row of shops and bush pub. Photogenic mine site about a kilometre west of the township. Photogenic headframe. Hotel, store, fuel.

Lawlers: old mining settlement now just a pile of rubble. One ruin remains. Still worth investigating if only to potter around. 1km east is the old mine: ruins, dumps, etc.
Plains support tracts of mulga; numerous dry creek crossings lined with river red gums. Breakaway country lines the eastern horizon for some distance.
Ruin near Stuart Meadows Station turn-off is an old government stock well. Interesting stonework and pulley.

Mt Ross (near above turn-off) offers good views of surrounding countryside.

Laverton Road

LAVERTON: a partly modernised older style mining town. What character it once had has now all but gone. Some interesting buildings still remain nonetheless. Town currently houses workers from the nearby Windarra Nickel Mine. Hotel, motel, stores, fuel. Stock up here if heading east.

Windarra: large nickel mine of the 'Poseidon Share' fame. Mine not open for inspection but view can be had from top of Mt Windarra, a hill rising 60m above the plain.
Plains support extensive tracts of mulga. Wildflowers (everlastings) may be present after winter rains (late August-September).

Malcolm: locality only; no facilities.
Lookout (sign-posted) provides good views. Nearby is a 50m easily-climbed hill that offers very good views.

Mt Morgans road

Mt Morgans: interesting old mining settlement set upon a low ridge. Ridge offers good views. Stone ruins nearby - very photogenic. Worth spending some time here to explore the area. A good area for walks.

Eulaminna: a kilometre off the road to the south is a large slag heap, the remains of a copper smelter.

Kookynie road

Lake Raeside: saltbush and samphire-covered saltlake, the longest lake in Australia.

Plains support tracts of mulga; wildflowers after rains.

KOOKYNIE: old mining town with interesting buildings and ruins - many quite photogenic. Some buildings are still occupied. Fair views from 10m high tailing dump at northern end of the township. Many mine relics. A pleasant place to spend some time. Just south is a chimney, the sole remains of Niagara mining township. Ask locally about directions to Niagara Dam, an attractive scenic area with **breakaways.** Hotel, fuel.

Old house, Gwalia (Map 32)

MAP 33 LEINSTER-MEEKATHARRA-LEINSTER via Wiluna

Grade 3

Total Distance: 349km
Average Vehicles per day: 60 east of Meekatharra
Regions Traversed: Goldfields, Murchison Goldfields

MEEKATHARRA: interesting old mining town and pastoral settlement with some character. Hotels, motel, stores, fuel. Stock up here if heading south.

Plains support open shrublands of mulga. Fair views across the plains from tops of rises.
Low rises form slight undulations in the countryside. Mulga shrublands common.
Plains support mulga shrublands, the road cutting a straight line through the scrub.
Low rises support mulga shrublands. Occasional fair views from tops of rises. Isolated low hills break the skyline.

WILUNA: old mining town currently undergoing a small mining boom. Unfortunately many of the old photogenic buildings have been bulldozed. Sizeable Aboriginal population, mostly of people who occupied the desert lands until recently. Aboriginal culture still very strong here: clans include Budidjara, Gadudjara, Mandildjara, Ngadadjara and Wanman groups. Hotel, store, fuel.

Wiluna Mine: definitely worth seeing. Many photogenic ruins and relics; a fascinating place.

Lake Way: large saltlake, a small portion of which lies near the road by a major creek crossing. Large river red gums line the creek.

MAP 33 LEINSTER-MEEKATHARRA-LEINSTER viaWiluna

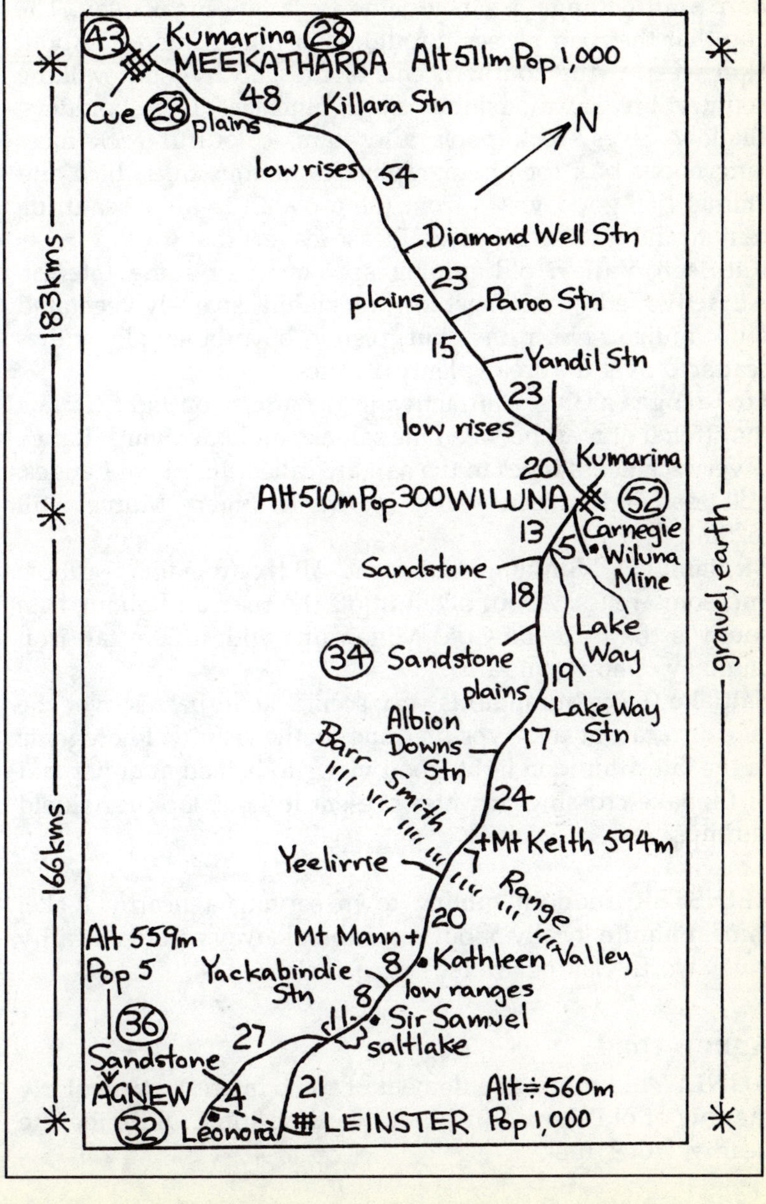

Plains support vast tracts of mulga; in some places there are open eucalypt woodlands with a spinifex understorey.
Barr Smith Range: a fancy name for a low breakaway. The gap that the road passes through is of minor interest. About 1km west of the southern end of the gap is good walking country; breakaway exhibits crags, pinnacles, large boulders, shallow caves, rock pools after rain, colourful rock faces (afternoons best for photography), numerous trees, bird and animal life, good views from the top - all in all a beautiful, remote and untouched place. Please leave it that way.
Kathleen Valley: old mining settlement of some interest. Attractive setting amongst low, rocky hills sparsely vegetated with mulga. No ruins, but plenty of rubble; old mines scattered over the area - plenty of relics.
Low ranges are very attractive in the afternoon light (in fact the stretch of road between the saltlake and Barr Smith Range is very scenic). Ranges to the east are called the Violet Ranges. Hill east of Kathleen Valley known as Bigery Mumal Hill (625m).
Sir Samuel: old mining settlement. All that remains is rubble and some relics. About 300m in off the road and about 1km south is the Bellevue Gold Mine ruins with a 50m tall iron chimney - photogenic area.
Saltlake (Lake Miranda) is very scenic. Road passes over the lake on a causeway. Gypsum dunes in the vicinity. Photogenic in the late afternoon light; good views to be had at either end of the lake crossing. If water present in lake, look for shield shrimps.

LEINSTER: modern mining town serving a nearby nickel mine. Enquire locally about scenic breakaway country nearby - well worth visiting. Motel, stores, fuel.

Agnew road

AGNEW: old mining settlement of some interest, particularly the row of old shops. Bush pub worth visiting. Old mine site nearby. Hotel, fuel.

MAP 34 PAYNES FIND-WILUNA-PAYNES FIND via Sandstone

Grade 3

Total Distance: 454km
Average Vehicles per day: 40 north of Paynes Find
Regions Traversed: Murchison Goldfields, Goldfields

WILUNA: old mining town currently undergoing a small mining boom. Many of the old photogenic buildings have been torn down. Large Aboriginal population of former desert dwellers. Aboriginal culture is still very strong here; some people lived traditional lives up until 25-30 years ago. Hotel, store, fuel.

Wiluna Mine: definitely worth seeing. Incredible photogenic ruins; numerous mine relics.

Lake Way: large saltlake east of the road. Near a river red gum-lined creek, a portion of the lake lies just to the east.

Barr Smith Range: fancy name for a breakaway which, on this road, is not that spectacular. Sparse covering of eucalypts and acacias with spinifex in this area.

Yeelirrie: station homestead and site of a future uranium mine. No facilities.

Breakaways rise above the general level of the plains. Minor creeks and drainage lines in this area; quite attractive in the afternoon light.
Plains support vast tracts of mulga shrublands; some open patches of eucalypts and acacias with spinifex.

Booylgoo Range: prominent range in this generally flat

MAP 34 PAYNES FIND-WILUNA-PAYNES FIND via Sandstone

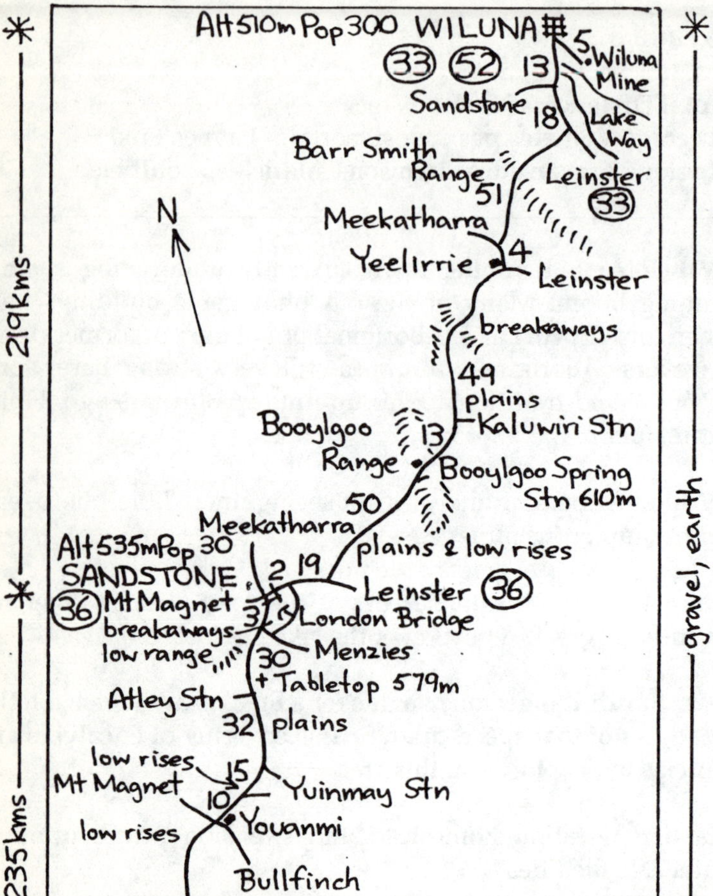

country rising a hundred or more metres above the plains. Mulga common.

Booylgoo Spring Station: working station; no facilities. Of interest because of cold temperatures recorded here: -6C, one of the coldest temperatures recorded in Western Australia.
Plains and low rises support tracts of mulga. Fair views from tops of low rises; breakaways may be seen.

SANDSTONE: interesting old mining township with many photogenic buildings and ruins. Golf course also of interest - red earth clearings running through the mulga. Worth spending some time here to explore the area. If nothing else, visit **London Bridge,** a natural arch set into a breakaway. Other features of interest include old mine sites, wells, state battery, underground brewery, etc. Hotel, store, fuel.

Breakaways offer fair views to the south.
Low range (the Black Range) lies to the west. Isolated hills rise above the general level of the mulga-clad plains.
Plains support extensive tracts of mulga. Everlastings in massed displays may be present after winter rains (late August-September).
Low rises offer fair views across the countryside.

Youanmi: remains of an old mining town - no ruins, just old fence lines, rusted metal and rubble. Nearby is a huge dump and a modern mining camp. No facilities.

Low rises offer fair views along the road. Mulga common.
Sand plain supports a variety of shrubs and heaths, country reminiscent of the uncleared portions of the wheatlands further south. Some low rises offer distant views along the road and over the sand plain wilderness. Worth stopping for a brief look at some of the plant life; the variety is amazing. Good wildflower display (not a massed display like the everlastings) after winter rains (late August-September).

Low hills provide a brief but vastly different landscape. Low craggy outcrops, breakaways, gullies, etc. Fair views of not much in particular from hill tops.

Plains support eucalypt woodlands with shrubby understoreys, patches of mulga and acacia thickets.

PAYNES FIND: old mining area, a bush pub and a few shacks. Of interest if heading outback; 'seen it before' if returning to the coast. Hotel, fuel.

Our Lady of Mount Carmel Church, Mullewa (Maps 35 and 36)

MAP 35 GERALDTON-MT MAGNET-GERALDTON via Mullewa

Grade 2

Total Distance: 343km
Average Vehicles per day: 250 east of Yalgoo
Regions Traversed: Wheatbelt, Murchison Goldfields

MT MAGNET: interesting old mining town with photogenic buildings. Enquire locally as to ruins in the area; also the gemstone fossicking areas. Hotels, motel, stores, fuel.

Plains support vast tracts of mulga shrublands. Massed displays of everlastings after the winter rains (late August-September) - well worth seeing. Occasional low hills dot the horizon.
Low hill north of the road provides a change in the scenery.

YALGOO: interesting old mining township with plenty of character. Enquire locally about the Fields Find, Gullewa and Yuin Reef ghost mining settlements nearby. Old court house museum worth visiting, as is the restored chapel overlooking the township. Hotel, store, fuel.
Low hill (Mullyakko Hill) overlooks Yalgoo, providing a scenic backdrop.

Wuraga: old mining township marked by rubble and ruins. Worth a quick look at least.
Plains support mulga shrublands; further west are quite dense acacia thickets.

Pindar: agricultural locality; no facilities.

Farmlands spread across the mostly cleared plains; cropping common.

MULLEWA: interesting agricultural town with some character. Worth stopping here to see Our Lady of Mount Carmel Church, a most fascinating building of the Romanesque style - very photogenic. Built of local stone. Take time to appreciate this architecture. A museum is attached. Worth a quick look is the local zoo. Hotel, motel, stores, fuel.

Tenindewa: agricultural locality; no facilities. Nearby is the historic Tenindewa Pioneer Well, a good example of stonework. Just off the Yuna road lies an ancient glacial bed.

Farmlands occupy the undulating plains and downs. Expansive views may be seen from the tops of rises. Some remnant patches of natural vegetation remain.

Greenough River (barely more than a creek except after winter rains) occupies a deep valley. Good views in this area.

Hilly country is very attractive, especially after the winter rains. Good views to the west from the lookout at the top of the hills.

Farmlands occupy a lowland plain; some low hills break the horizon. Landscape brown and dry after summer; green and lush after winter.

Moonyoonooka: locality on the outskirts of Geraldton.

GERALDTON: large seaside regional centre; attractive downtown and foreshore area, especially the Gregory Street historic buildings precinct. Various lookouts and museums. Grand cathedral (designed by Father John Hawes, the same person who designed the church in Mullewa) is worth visiting. Many other tourist features; enquire locally. Full town facilities. Stock up here if heading east.

MAP 35 GERALDTON-MT MAGNET-GERALDTON
via Mullewa

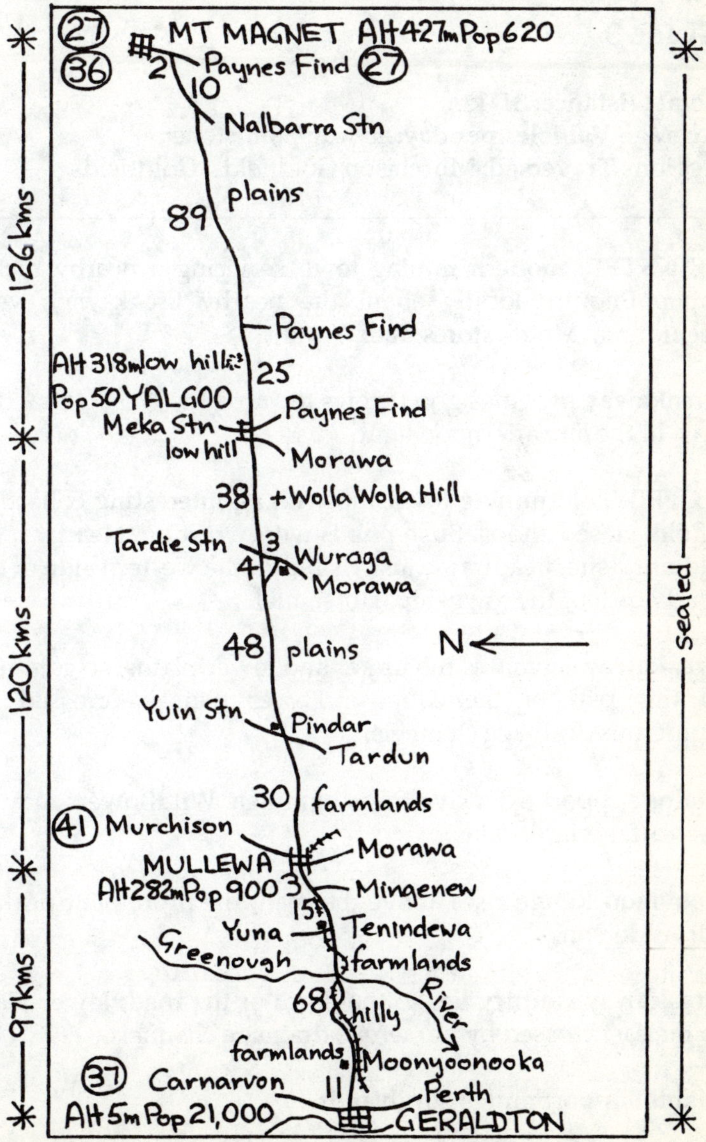

MAP 36 MT MAGNET-LEINSTER-MT MAGNET via Sandstone

Grade 3

Total Distance: 311km
Average Vehicles per day: 45 near Sandstone
Regions Traversed: Murchison Goldfields, Goldfields

LEINSTER: modern mining town servicing a nearby nickel mine. Enquire locally about the nearby breakaway; very scenic area. Motel, stores, fuel.

Breakaway provides good views towards the west. Attractive area in the late afternoon light.

AGNEW: old mining township with an interesting collection of old, closed shops. Bush pub is worth visiting. Nearby is an old mine site; headframe just visible on the western side of the road north of the township. Hotel, fuel.

Breakaway separates the upper and lower plains, so common in this part of the country. Lower plain is crossed by numerous drainage channels.

Plains support extensive tracts of mulga. Wildflowers may be seen after winter rains.

Booylgoo Range rises above the road; the prominent peak is Mt Anderson.

Breakaway country lies to the north of the road; lower plain to the east crossed by numerous drainage channels.

Plains support mulga shrublands.

MAP 36 MT MAGNET-LEINSTER-MT MAGNET
via Sandstone

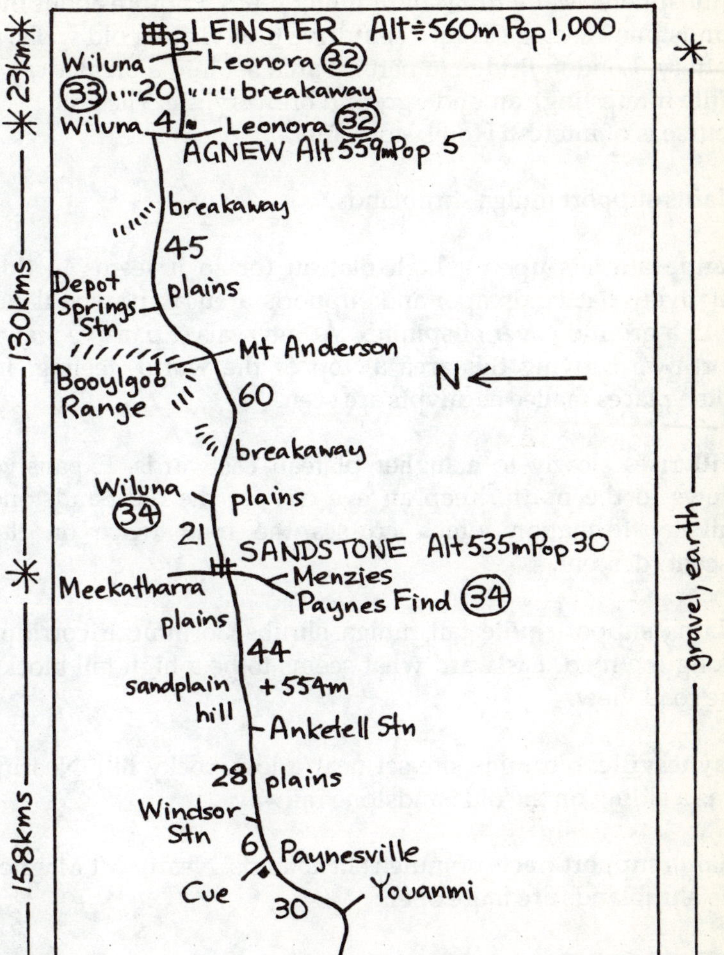

SANDSTONE: interesting old mining township; photogenic buildings. Worth stopping for a while to absorb the relaxed atmosphere. Many ruins and mining relics. Enquire about the Sandstone Heritage Trail, a self-drive tour visiting old wells, a battery, London Bridge (a natural arch set into a breakaway - quite interesting), an underground brewery, etc. The golf course is of interest. Hotel, store, fuel.

Plains support mulga shrublands.

Sandplain sits upon a high plateau (or so it seems in this relatively flat landscape) and supports a eucalypt woodland with a ground cover of spinifex. At intervals expansive views northward giving this area a 'top of the world' feeling. In some places mallee eucalypts are seen.

Hill rises slowly to a higher plateau eastwards. Expansive views to the north. Keep an eye out for the old Sandstone railway formation which crosses the road twice on the ascent/descent.

Plains support quite tall mulga shrubs, forming a corridor along the road. Eastward what seems to be a high hill blocks the road view.

Paynesville: old mine site set near a low, rocky hill. Nearby was a siding on the old Sandstone railway.

Plains support tracts of mulga shrublands. Nearer Mt Magnet the shrublands are more open.

MT MAGNET: interesting old mining town with photogenic buildings. Worth spending some time here to absorb the atmosphere. Hotels, motel, stores, fuel.

NOTES

NORTH-WEST COASTAL HIGHWAY

Virtually parallel to the west coast, the North-West Coastal Highway is the main outback route running north of Geraldton. It is a moderately trafficked highway supplying the north-west coastal towns, the Murchison, Gascoyne and Pilbara hinterlands (including the iron ore mines), and is the main western access to northern Australia. Those are its good points. Its bad points are that it is rarely in sight of the coast and that for much of its length it passes through what many people consider to be very boring country indeed! It does, though, provide access to some very interesting coastal areas west of the highway (Shark Bay, Point Quobba, Ningaloo Marine Park, Exmouth and Onslow) as well as some of the most scenic arid mountain country in Australia: the Hamersley Ranges.

For these reasons the North-West Coastal Highway should be considered as a travel option and, given time (by slowing down), even the long 'boring' stretches will be of interest. It is worth noting that north of Northampton there are no towns on the highway till Roebourne (Carnarvon is just off the route), but the highway is serviced by roadhouses at regular intervals.

Warnings: beware of stock and kangaroos at night. Be careful when passing or overtaking roadtrains. Extreme summer temperatures will be experienced; if travelling at this time carry plenty of water in the vehicle. Road may be subjected to minor local flooding.

MAP 37 GERALDTON-OVERLANDER ROADHOUSE-GERALDTON via Northampton

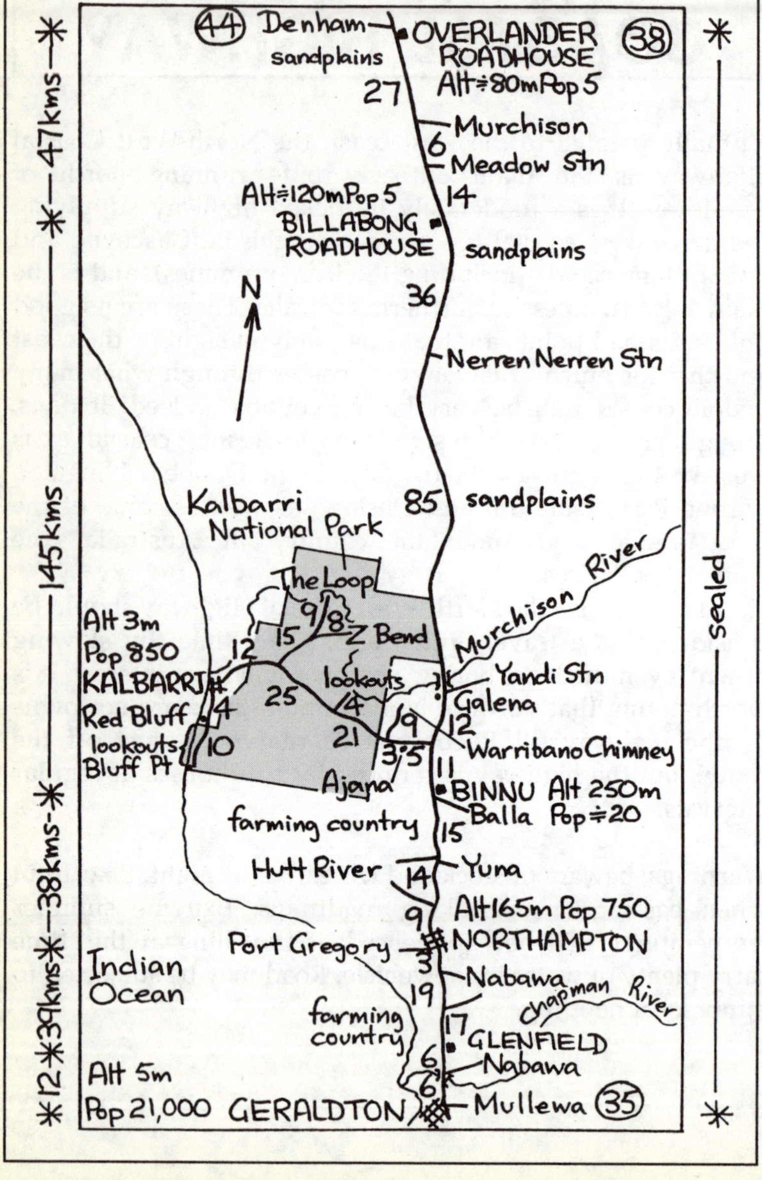

MAP 37 GERALDTON-OVERLANDER ROADHOUSE-GERALDTON

via Northampton

Grade 1

Total Distance: 280km
Average Vehicles per day: 920 north of Geraldton/600 south of Overlander Roadhouse
Regions Traversed: Wheatbelt, Murchison

OVERLANDER ROADHOUSE: roadhouse facility with little character. Notable for being centrally situated on a hundred kilometre or so stretch of straight road. Motel, fuel.

Sand plains support a relatively dense acacia shrubland with a shrubby understorey. From the tops of low rises the dead-straight highway can be seen vanishing near the horizon; these rises are very low limestone ridges.

BILLABONG ROADHOUSE: (occasionally referred to as Wannoo) roadhouse facility with some character. Motel, fuel.

Sand plains support acacia shrublands with a shrubby understorey.

Sand plains, though looking dreary from a fast moving car, support a diversity of plant life, including mallee eucalypts and numerous shrubs and heaths. Worth stopping the car (well off the road) for a quick look at least.
Murchison River: pleasant crossing worth stopping at for a rest break, picnic, etc. Farming country hereabouts.
Galena: locality only; no facilities. Old mining area.
BINNU: small roadhouse settlement situated within farming country. Store, fuel.

Farming country occupies extensively cleared land given over to cropping and grazing. Landscape usually a lush green after winter rains; brown and dried after the summer drought. Fair views from the tops of rises.

NORTHAMPTON: old mining town, nowadays a farming settlement, with plenty of character. Many photogenic old buildings including miners' cottages constructed in the 1860s. Interesting main street. One old mine site (the Gwalla) clearly visible east of the highway, south of the town. Museum. Hotel, motel, stores, fuel.

Farming country occupies cleared land given over to cropping and grazing. Good views from hilltops across the rolling paddocks. Closer to Geraldton the flat-topped Moresby Range can be seen to the east; the Indian Ocean to the west.

GLENFIELD: outlying suburb of Geraldton. Store, fuel.

GERALDTON: large regional centre with many tourist features, especially the Gregory Street historic buildings precinct, cathedral, various lookouts and museums. Enquire locally for more details. Full town facilities; stock up here if heading north.

Kalbarri Road

Lookouts extend to Bluff Point on an unmade road; those in conventional cars should seek local advice before proceeding. Numerous vantage points just off the main track. Sights include colourful plunging clifflines (best in the afternoon light), gorges, gullies, coves, arches and rock formations. Take care if walking.
Red Bluff: coastal tourist facility set at the northern end of the cliffed coastline. Excellent lookout nearby.

KALBARRI: low key seaside resort settlement set by the mouth of the Murchison River. Very attractive and popular area; a nice place to relax for a few days. Nearby are many scenic lookouts, including Meenarra Hill Lookout (not shown on map; 6km east then 2km south - good views over the Murchison River mouth and Kalbarri). Good fishing hereabouts. Hotel, motels, stores, fuel.

The Loop: excellent views overlooking the Murchison River Gorge. Area exhibits colourful cliffs, waterholes and wildlife.
Z-Bend: tall cliffs and colourful rocks line the 150m deep Murchison River Gorge. Very scenic area.

Lookouts provide excellent views over the Murchison River Gorge. Interesting rock formations.

Kalbarri National Park: large national park preserving vast tracts of wilderness country. Landscape dominated by heathlands; species include various banksias, grevilleas, grass trees, cypress pines, eucalypts, acacias, etc, which produce impressive wildflower displays. The heathlands are clearly visible from the main road. Elsewhere the Murchison River has cut a deep and scenic gorge, whilst on the coast the underlying rocks have produced a fantastic cliffline. No car camping allowed in the park. Enquire locally about bushwalks etc.

Warribano Chimney: remains of an old lead smelter; photogenic ruins. Access road unsealed.
Ajana: locality only; no facilities. Old mining area.

NOTES

MAP 38 OVERLANDER ROADHOUSE-MINILYA ROADHOUSE-OVERLANDER ROADHOUSE

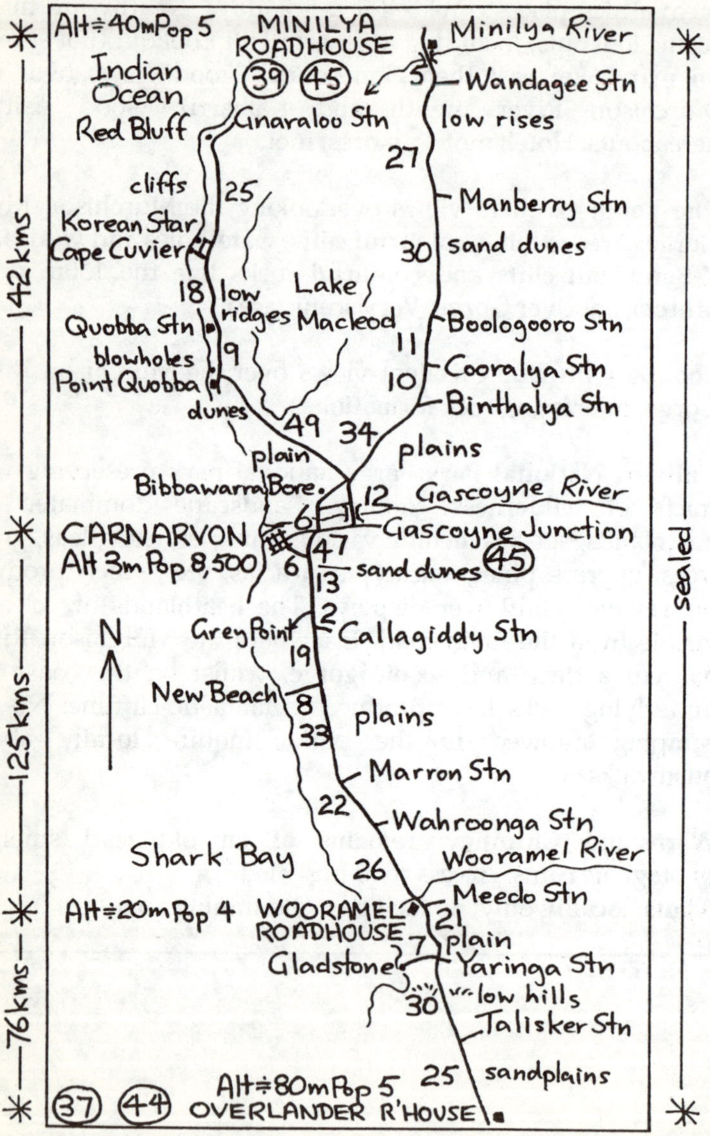

MAP 38 OVERLANDER ROADHOUSE-MINILYA ROADHOUSE-

OVERLANDER ROADHOUSE via CARNARVON

Grade 1 (Carnarvon-Point Quobba Grade 2) (Point Quobba-Red Bluff Grade 3)

Total Distance: 343km
Average Vehicles per day: 490 south of Carnarvon/400 north of Carnarvon
Regions Traversed: Gascoyne, North-West

MINILYA ROADHOUSE: roadhouse settlement with some character. Attractive river red gum-lined watercourse nearby. Fuel.

Low rises provide limited views of nothing in particular. Shrublands common.

Sand dunes form part of the Carnarvon Dunefield; acacia shrublands common. Dunes with their bare red crests are quite photogenic in the right light.

Plains support vast tracts of shrublands; saltbush common in the understorey. Some open saltbush areas provide expansive views.

Gascoyne River: wide, normally dry, sandy river bed lined with river red gums. Plains either side of the river support irrigated farms, typically fruit plantations. This attractive countryside contrasts vividly with the dry semi-arid plains beyond. Scattered development including motels, caravan parks and roadhouses, lines the road into Carnarvon.

CARNARVON: sizeable coastal town servicing fishing,

pastoral and tourist industries. Town itself has limited character (some scenes of the old Carnarvon may be glimpsed in the side streets) but surrounding area worth a few days exploration. Tourist features include the 'Long' Jetty, the Fascine, Dwyers Leap, etc; make local enquiries. Numerous fishing spots including 'Long' Jetty, Dwyers Leap, Small Boat Harbour, Oyster Creek, Miaboolya Beach, etc. Full town facilities. Stock up here if heading in any direction.

Sand dunes with saltbush flats line the road. The long dune east of the highway is called the Baxter Range; upon it sits the remains of the OTC Satellite Earth Station.

New Beach (unsealed access) is quite attractive at high tide; worth a quick look. Good beach fishing.

Plains support extensive tracts of acacia shrublands. Whilst not scenic, the vivid red soils of the plains are impressive in the late afternoon sunlight.

WOORAMEL ROADHOUSE: small, modern roadhouse. Enquire here about the short-cut to Gascoyne Junction (dry weather only). Fuel.

Plain supports an open treeless area of saltbush, one of the few such areas south of the Pilbara. Low hills and rises can be seen in the distance. Westward are distant views across Shark Bay.

Gladstone: former port for trans-shipping sheep and sandalwood. Degraded area is unattractive, but old jetty ruins and good views of Shark Bay make a detour worthwhile. No facilities; unsealed access track.

Low hills (would be called jump-ups in the Eastern States) line the road and provide good views overlooking the saltbush plains and Shark Bay beyond.

Sand plains support extensive tracts of acacia shrublands. Occasional long views down the dead-straight road.

OVERLANDER ROADHOUSE: roadhouse facility. Motel, fuel.

Point Quobba-Red Bluff road

Red Bluff: remote and isolated headland standing over 100m above the Indian Ocean. Occasional surfing area. Access road is usually rough; make local enquiries if heading north of Cape Cuvier.

Cliffs line the coast for some distance, though barely visible from the road.

Korean Star wreck: remains of ship which has broken into two. Well worth seeing; the swell washing through the wreck, and its situation at the base of high cliffs, is awesome, spooky and dangerous. Take extreme care if walking down to the wreck - people have died here being pulled off the jagged limestone rock platform by king waves. Good views can be had of the wreck from the Cape Cuvier viewpoint.

Cape Cuvier: port for a nearby salt mine; no public access but the loading facilities can be seen from a nearby viewpoint (look for tracks heading towards the cliffs north of the salt mine's haul road). Cliffs provide excellent views of the Cape and the wreck of the Korean Star - well worth visiting for the spectacular scenery. Warning: viewpoint area unfenced and dangerous.

Low ridges of limestone rise above sand patches that support a thin covering of vegetation. Occasional good views across this arid coastal landscape, especially in the late afternoon light.
Quobba Station: working station. Camping facilities may be

available; make local enquiries. A couple of kilometres south is a memorial to the sinking of the HMAS *Sydney* during World War II, a sinking that raises many unanswered questions. Worth visiting just to experience the strange aura of the place.

Blowholes: eerily set upon a jagged limestone platform edged by a low seaward cliff. The ocean's swells bubble and seethe through narrow fissures within the rock occasionally erupting through holes in the surface, blowing water to great heights (up to 20m). Only closely inspect during calm seas; even then there is the ever-present danger of king waves washing the platform. This is a dangerous place, but very impressive. Nearby, set upon a limestone ridge, is the Point Quobba Lighthouse; excellent views can be obtained from here.

Point Quobba: locality only; no facilities. Numerous rustic fishing shacks give this area an interesting if somewhat rundown character. Popular spot with the locals on weekends; good fishing. Attractive beach protected by a coral reef. A low hill gives good views across a coral lagoon to a small island. Good views from the high dunes behind the beach.

Dunes line the coast, often in conjunction with limestone ridges. Dunes and ridges clearly visible to the west.

Lake Macleod: large saltlake visible from the road; smaller outlying saltlakes are crossed by causeways. Open country provides expansive views.

Plain supports a sparse covering of vegetation. Occasional views towards saltlakes, limestone ridges, etc.
Bibbawarra Bore (located on an unsealed back road); deep flowing bore (over 900m deep) and pool of very hot water (be very careful). Interesting for those who have not seen flowing bores before.

MAP 39 MINILYA ROADHOUSE-FORTESCUE ROADHOUSE-MINILYA ROADHOUSE
via Nanutarra Roadhouse

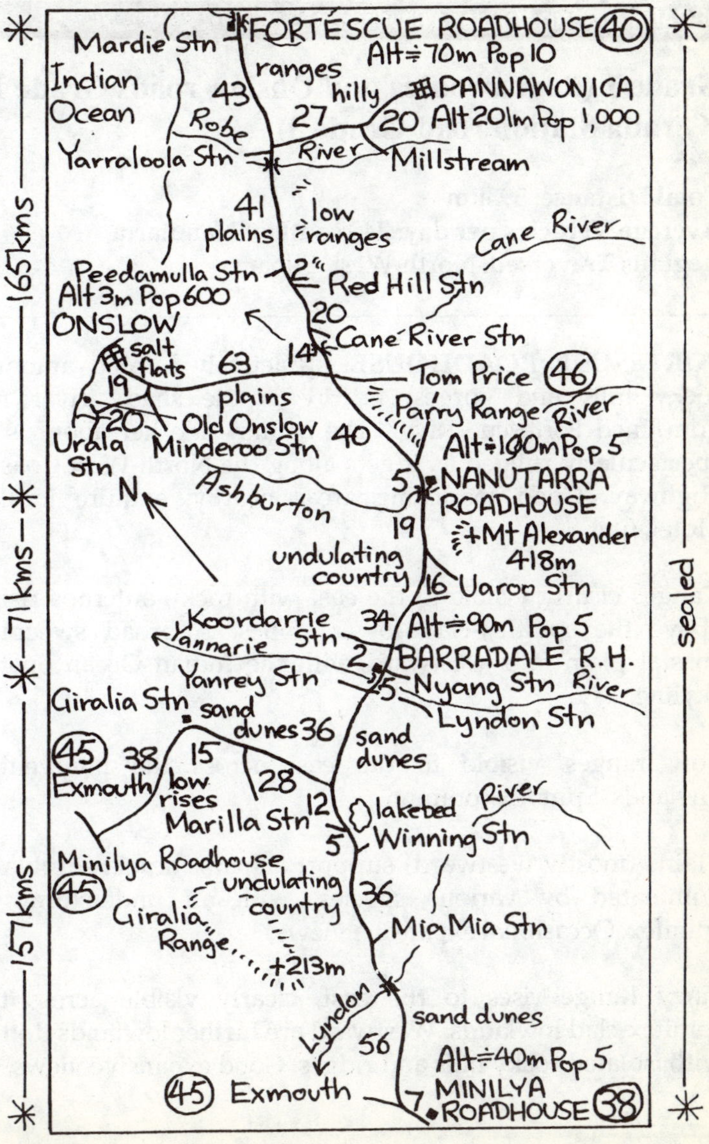

MAP 39 MINILYA ROADHOUSE-FORTESCUE ROADHOUSE-MINILYA ROADHOUSE via Nanutarra Roadhouse

Grade 1 (Pannawonica and Onslow roads Grade 1) (Giralia Station road Grade 3)

Total Distance: 393km
Average Vehicles per day: 240 south of Nanutarra
Regions Traversed: North-West, Pilbara.

FORTESCUE ROADHOUSE: attractively located amongst rocky hills and gorges; nearby is the shady river red gum-lined Fortescue River. The countryside hereabout is as spectacularly rugged as it gets along the North-West Coastal Highway. Good fossicking areas nearby; enquire locally. Motel, fuel.

Ranges clearly visible to the east with rocky outcrops rising above the spinifex-clad lower slopes. A broad sweeping coastal plain falls westward with the Indian Ocean on the skyline.

Low ranges visible to the east across the intervening lowlands. Spinifex common.

Plains (mostly westward) support a sparse acacia shrubland dominated by various species, with an understorey of spinifex. Occasional expansive views.

Parry Range rises to the east, clearly visible across the spinifex-clad lowlands. Westward are further lowlands dotted with isolated rocky hills and ridges. Good expansive views.

NANUTARRA ROADHOUSE: pleasant roadhouse settlement situated near the banks of the shady Ashburton River. Good walks along bush tracks and in the river bed during the dry season; note the bent melaleucas and incredible pothole formations. Good waterholes. Motel, fuel.

Undulating country consisting of low rocky rises covered with spinifex (with expansive views from tops of rises) and occasional sand dunes also covered with spinifex, and a very sparse low tree and shrub overstorey (a variety of species are present).

BARRADALE ROADHOUSE: roadhouse facility with some character; nearby is the normally sandy bed of the Yannarie River. Motel, fuel.

Sand dunes cross the road at regular intervals, their vivid red crests being quite photogenic in the late afternoon light. Fair views from the tops of the dunes. Spinifex common on the sand dunes with a sparse covering of other shrubs.

Lake bed occupies a lowland east of the road. Desolate country hereabout with expansive views over the lake bed. Nearby are low hills and rises supporting a sparse shrub cover.

Undulating country includes plains, low rises and a distant range visible to the west (Giralia Range). Plains support tracts of acacia shrublands with a spinifex understorey, while the low rises support only stunted plant life. Anthills are common north of the Lyndon River.

Sand dunes form part of the Carnarvon Dunefield and support spinifex and various acacias.

MINILYA ROADHOUSE: roadhouse facility set by the Minilya River, an attractive shady river bed. Fuel.

Pannawonica road (Grade 1)

PANNAWONICA: modern iron mining settlement made famous by its examples of how not to conduct industrial relations. Surrounded by high flat-top hills and ranges. Limited tourist facilities, but the countryside is worth a visit.

Hilly country of flat-topped mesas and residual hillocks is very scenic in the right light. The cappings on the hills are iron ore formations; the hills themselves are sparsely covered with

NOTES

spinifex, while the lowlands support various acacias and eucalypts.

Onslow road

ONSLOW: interesting older style 'north-west' town with plenty of character and characters. Well worth visiting; a pleasant spot to relax for a while. Good fishing at Four Mile Creek and Beaden Creek. Hotel, motel, stores, fuel.

Salt flats line the road into Onslow, providing broad views. Near tidal creeks are mangrove formations, while on the edge of the flats there are low salt-tolerant shrubland communities.

Old Onslow: site of the former settlement, today marked by a number of stone buildings. Worth a brief visit at least, as is the nearby Ashburton River (good fishing). Grasslands common hereabout with a smattering of eucalypts. Unsealed access.

Plains support extensive tracts of spinifex and large anthills, some of which have formed into interesting shapes. Shrubs on the plains include various acacias, hakeas and stunted eucalypts. Eastward views to distant ranges near the highway.

Giralia Station road

Low rises support extensive tracts of acacia shrublands. Fair views from tops of rises.

Giralia Station: working sheep station; basic accommodation available.

Sand dunes and broad sand plains support a low woodland of eucalypts with a spinifex understorey. Sand dunes are quite photogenic in the afternoon light. Good views from the tops of some dune crests.

MAP 40 FORTESCUE ROADHOUSE-PORT HEDLAND-FORTESCUE ROADHOUSE via Roebourne

Grade 1 (Point Samson and Dampier roads Grade 1)

Total Distance: 342km
Average Vehicles per day: 1100 east of Karratha/350 east of Roebourne
Regions Traversed: Pilbara

PORT HEDLAND: unattractive regional and industrial centre set upon a vast coastal plain. Major iron ore port. Some features of interest including the nearby Pretty Pool. Some good fishing spots - make local enquiries. Museum. Full town facilities. Stock up here if heading north or south.

Salt flats and tidal estuaries provide expansive views; a variety of mangroves line the estuaries. Extensive industrial development south of the flats. A tourist lookout (4km north of the highway junction) overlooks some saltworks.

SOUTH HEDLAND: a charmless modern town development built to accommodate the overflow from Port Hedland. Full town facilities.

Plains provide expansive views across either grasslands or spinifex (in association with a sparse acacia-dominated shrubland). At intervals are low rocky knolls and hills. River red gums and melaleucas line the Yule River.

Low hills support spinifex, occasionally with a variety of shrubs. In some places are bare, black boulders that appear very striking in the landscape.

MAP 40 FORTESCUE ROADHOUSE-PORT HEDLAND-FORTESCUE ROADHOUSE via Roebourne

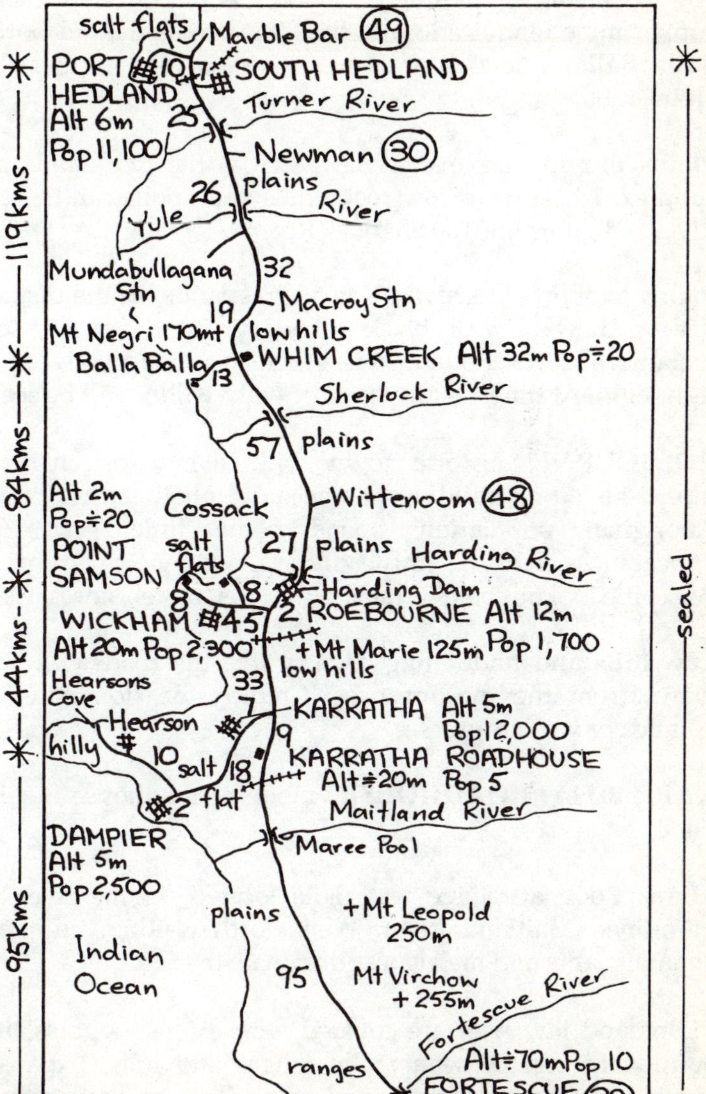

WHIM CREEK: old mining centre and bush pub with plenty of character. Worth stopping here to absorb the atmosphere and to do some exploring on foot, especially around the old copper mine (enquire locally first). Nearby is the old port of **Balla Balla;** a few ruins remain. Access road is unsealed. Hotel, fuel.

Plains provide expansive views across the grasslands and spinifex. At intervals low rocky hills and knolls can be seen. River red gums line the Sherlock River.

Plains support extensive tracts of grasslands; in the distance flat-top ranges with black bouldery faces can be seen. Expansive views abound, some of which are impressive in the right light. At times, whirlwinds or willy-willies will be seen.

ROEBOURNE: historic town with plenty of character; numerous stone buildings, some quite photogenic. Sizeable Aboriginal population; spend some time here, first appearances can be misleading. Good views from Mt Welcome lookout behind the town. Hotel, motel, stores, fuel.

Low hills and undulating country line the road with good views from the tops of rises. Countryside dominated by spinifex or various grasses.

KARRATHA ROADHOUSE: modern roadhouse facility. Fuel.

Maree Pool: attractive waterhole located on the river red gum-lined Maitland River. Well worth visiting; numerous aquatic plants and melaleucas dominate the area.

Plains and low rises are covered with extensive grasslands. Southward can be seen rocky ranges and hills. Expansive views from tops of rises, including one that encompasses the tidal flats and off-shore islands of the Indian Ocean coastline.

Elsewhere are distant views towards the Dampier Archipelago.

Ranges with impressive rocky outcrops can be seen to the north and south; these are rent with deep, rocky valleys and gorges. The hillsides support a sparse eucalpyt woodland with a spinifex understorey. This landscape is the most rugged through which the highway passes.

FORTESCUE ROADHOUSE: interesting roadhouse facility located within an attractive and rugged setting. Nearby is the river red gum-lined Fortescue River. Well worth stopping to take a short walk, explore, or to have a picnic. Motel, fuel.

Point Samson road

POINT SAMSON: old port with plenty of character; old ruins, etc. A pleasant spot to relax for a few days to go fishing, explore the reefs, go swimming, etc. Best fishing in the tidal creeks. Motel, store, fuel.

Salt flats and tidal estuaries can be seen from the road. The flats themselves are barren; the estuaries are lined with a variety of mangroves. In the distance are low, rocky hills and ranges.

WICKHAM: modern iron ore mining development town that looks a lot like a transplanted suburb. Nearby is the Cape Lambert wharf, one of the largest open ocean wharves in Australia. Full town facilities.

Cossack: an old ghost town and former port for the region. Numerous stone buildings; some quite photogenic. This old settlement is well worth visiting for an hour or two. Road to Cossack crosses salt flats and tidal estuaries.

Hearsons Cove/Dampier road

Hearsons Cove: locality only; no facilities. Very attractive cove set amongst rocky hills; a quiet area which is worth exploring on foot.

Hilly country dominated by rocky outcrops which have the appearance of loosely jumbled boulders. In places these boulders (which are characteristic of this land, the Burrup Peninsula) have Aboriginal engravings - enquire locally as to their location.

Hearson: industrial development and settlement connected with the North-West Shelf Project. Nearby (not shown on map) is a port also connected with the Project.

DAMPIER: modern iron ore port town which, though partly suburban-looking, has some character due to its location. It is set upon a low rocky ridge overlooking some of the islands of the Dampier Archipelago. Numerous photographic opportunities, especially across the tidal flats at dawn or dusk. Nearby lookouts are worth visiting. Full town facilities.

Salt flat provides expansive views to nearby rocky ranges.

KARRATHA: large regional centre with little character, its modern buildings looking like any city's suburbs. Nearby beach on Nickol Bay is interesting; reasonable views from TV Hill lookout. The Jaburara Heritage Trail is worth a look. Full town facilities.

NOTES

THE MURCHISON -GASCOYNE

The Murchison-Gascoyne is a vast area of country given over to large sheep stations, with cattle stations on its northern frontier. It is real backblocks country that receives few travellers, except for those making their way to its main tourist feature: Mt Augustus. This mountain has been considered the largest rock in the world, but it is better thought of as an upstanding and high mountain range. Whether it is worth travelling a long way to see is debatable, but on the way, especially in the northern region, the Gascoyne, there is some interesting country comparable to outback grazing country anywhere. The real attraction of the Murchison-Gascoyne, though, is its isolation and its untouched 'feel'.

A word of warning: the Murchison-Gascoyne country is a land of vast distances and very few services. Inexperienced outback travellers should give very serious thought before venturing here. Most roads are very lightly trafficked and a degree of self-reliance is required.

Warnings: avoid travelling at night. Roads subject to flooding and impassable in wet weather. Make local enquiries before proceeding; during adverse conditions or venturing off the routes described herein, inform a reliable person of your intentions. Due to high temperatures, stay out of this area in summer; if travelling at this time, either travel in convoy or inform a reliable person of your intentions. Note that there are very long distances between fuel supply points, especially Gascoyne Junction-Meekatharra (452km).

Note: no reliable habitation between Mt Sandiman and Gifford Creek Stations (138km, Map 42) or Landor and Glenburgh Stations (106km, Map 43).

Burrup Peninsula landscape, east of Dampier (Map 40)

MAP 41 MULLEWA-DAIRY CREEK STATION-MULLEWA via Murchison

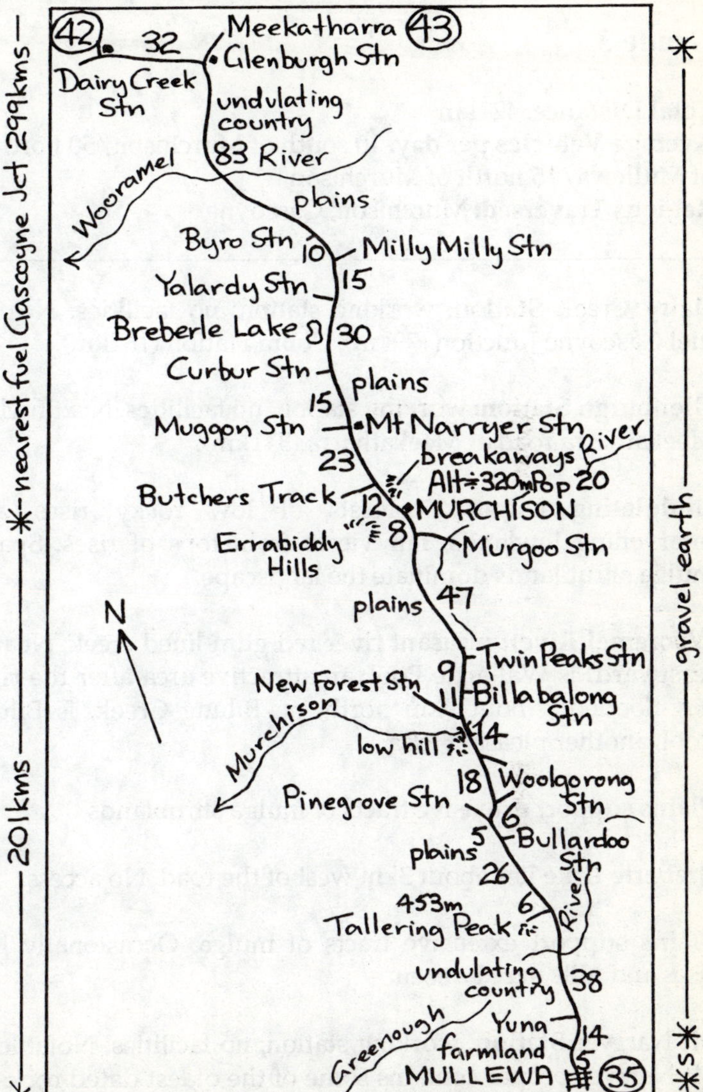

MAP 41 MULLEWA-DAIRY CREEK STATION-MULLEWA via Murchison

Grade 3

Total Distance: 421km
Average Vehicles per day: 10 south of Murchison/50 north of Mullewa/15 north of Murchison
Regions Traversed: Murchison, Gascoyne

Dairy Creek Station: working station; no facilities. Nearest fuel Gascoyne Junction (79km), Cobra Station (162km).

Glenburgh Station: working station, no facilities. Next fuel on Meekatharra road at Meekatharra (341km).

Undulating country consists of low rocky rises and intervening lowlands; fair views from tops of rises. Sparse mulga shrublands dominate the landscape.

Wooramel River: pleasant river red gum-lined creek. Nearby (eastward) is Wal-arrie Pool, an attractive area after the river has flooded. About 9km north, on Bilung Creek, is Bilung Pool, another pleasant area.

Plains support extensive tracts of mulga shrublands.

Breberle Lake lies about 3km west of the road. No access.

Plains support extensive tracts of mulga. Occasionally low rises and hills may be seen.

Mt Narryer Station: working station; no facilities. Notable as Mt Narryer proper contains some of the oldest dated rocks in the world.

Breakaways line the road to the east, providing a minor measure of verticality in this flat landscape. This attractive area is worth a quick look; quite photogenic in the afternoon light. The nearby Butchers Track (a well-formed road) leads to the North-West Coastal Highway. This lonely route carries only one vehicle every few days on average.

Errabiddy Hills can be seen rising above the mulga to the west, especially the prominent Errabiddy Bluff.

MURCHISON: business centre for the vast Murchison Shire, once known as the 'Shire without a town'. Today the settlement could be termed a township comprising as it does a roadhouse, a shire office, a shed and a few houses. Worth stopping here to soak up the atmosphere. Museum. Limited stores and accommodation, fuel.

Plains support extensive tracts of mulga shrublands.

Murchison River: pleasant river crossing with waterholes, shady trees, etc. Worth stopping to explore, take a short walk, etc.

Low hill can be seen rising above the mulga to the west.

Plains support extensive tracts of mulga. At intervals low isolated ridges are crossed (offering fair views) and the occasional breakaway can be seen.

Tallering Peak: moderately high rocky hills; definitely worth visiting for incredible vast views across a sea of mulga. Be careful walking on the steep, loose rocky hill slopes. Old iron ore mine shaft is worth investigating, as is the prominent breakaway passed on the access road. Breakaway area photogenic in the afternoon light.

Greenough River: interesting river crossing with rocky pools, etc. Worth a quick look.

Undulating country supports tracts of mulga and other shrubs, interspersed with occasional clearings used for grazing. Some fair views from tops of rises.

Farmland occupies land almost totally cleared and given over to cropping and grazing.

MULLEWA: interesting wheatbelt town with plenty of character. Definitely worth seeing is Our Lady of Mount Carmel Church, a photogenic building in the Romanesque style. A museum is attached. Hotel, motel, stores, fuel.

NOTES

MAP 42 CARNARVON-MT AUGUSTUS-CARNARVON via Gascoyne Junction

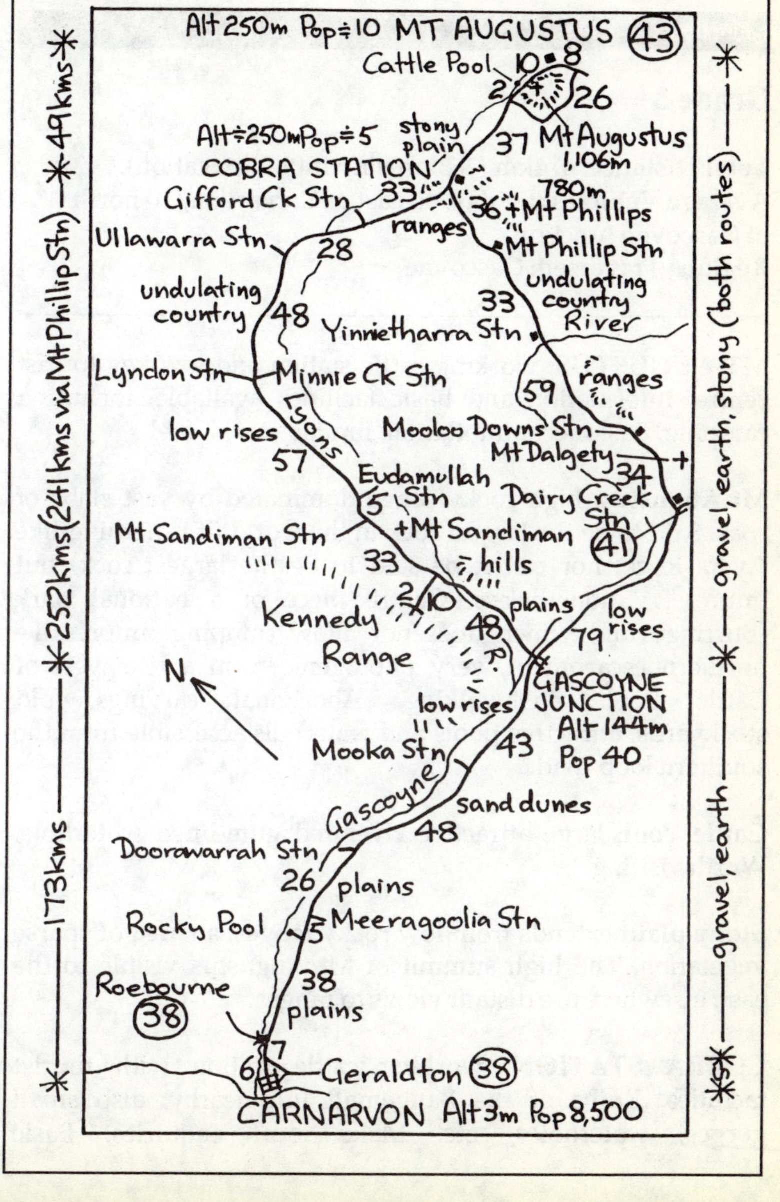

MAP 42 CARNARVON-MT AUGUSTUS-CARNARVON via Gascoyne Junction

Grade 3

Total Distance: 474km (463km via Mt Phillip Station)
Average Vehicles per day: 40 east of Carnarvon/10 north of Gascoyne Junction
Regions Traversed: Gascoyne

MT AUGUSTUS: working cattle station and low key tourist centre. Information and basic facilities available, including camping. Basic accommodation, limited stores, fuel.

Mt Augustus: high rocky range dominated by vast slabs of rock. Said to be the largest rock in the world (it is nothing like Ayers Rock, nor can it be said to be the largest rock) but impressive nonetheless. Centre piece of a national park (Burringurrah) which does not allow camping. Impressive northern escarpment, very photogenic from a rise west of Cattle Pool. Bushwalking, Aboriginal carvings, old stockyards, attractive pools and waterfalls accessible from the southern loop road.

Cattle Pool: large attractive river red gum-lined waterhole. Worth visiting.

Stony plain extends from low rocky ranges; an area of sparse vegetation. The high summit of Mt Augustus visible to the east; elsewhere are distant views to ranges.

COBRA STATION: working cattle station with tourist facilities. Ruins of the Bangemall Inn nearby; also small gorges, waterholes, etc. Make local enquiries. Basic accommodation, limited stores, fuel.

Ranges and low hills line the road, the intervening lowlands supporting a sparse mulga shrubland with little ground cover. At intervals, quartz blows may be seen. Occasional glimpses of the proud peak of Mt Phillips visible to the south-east.

Undulating country varies from stony plains with a mulga covering, to low rises also supporting mulga. At intervals are shady river red gum-lined stream beds and waterholes. Occasional views from tops of rises.

Low rises offer vast views towards other rises, isolated hills and distant ranges. Sparse mulga shrublands dominate the countryside. At intervals, sandy plains and low ridges are crossed. In the vicinity of Mt Sandiman are numerous dry, stony ridges. Distant westward views towards the Kennedy Range escarpment.

Kennedy Range: very impressive escarpment country; well worth visiting. Range rises about 120m above the plain and presents a bewildering display of smooth rock surfaces or intricately weathered sculptures (these are very photogenic). Elsewhere are deeply eroded valleys, water-worn rockholes, dry waterfalls, fossil beds, etc. Escarpment features are best photographed in the early morning light. This area has a wilderness quality (as well as an eerie feel); please leave no trace of your visit.

Hills rise to the east, reminiscent of the jump-ups in Eastern Australia. Mulga shrublands dominate the lowlands.

Plains support tracts of mulga.

GASCOYNE JUNCTION: small grazing township with plenty of character. Stop a while to absorb the atmosphere, especially at the bush pub. Hotel, store, fuel.

Low rises offer fair views northward towards the southern escarpment of the Kennedy Range. Rises fairly open and rocky; intervening lowlands support mulga shrublands.

Sand dunes form part of the Carnarvon Dunefield and support a variety of shrubs, often to such a density that bare red crests are rare. Intervening swales often contain claypans or tracts of mulga.

Plains support mulga shrublands.

Rocky Pool: pleasant waterhole on the Gascoyne River. Worth a quick look at least. Interesting rockholes, but shade is at a premium.

Plains support tracts of mulga. Near Carnarvon are irrigated tropical fruit farms, etc, which provide a vivid contrast to the dry mulga country beyond.

CARNARVON: large seaside centre catering for the pastoral industry and tourists. Town has come character (a few buildings from the 'old Carnarvon' can be seen in the side streets), but is otherwise just a service centre. Tourist features include the 'Long'Jetty, the Fascine, Dywers Leap, etc; make local enquiries. Full town facilities. Stock up here if heading east.

Mt Phillip Station road

Ranges line the road; numerous rocky outcrops and gibber surfaces. Good views eastward towards the proud peak of Mt Phillips. Low shrubby growth common.

Mt Phillip Station: working station; no facilities.

Undulating country exhibits stony hills, undulating plains and red soil plains supporting a sparse cover of mulga, as well as other acacias. Much of this country appears to be degraded due to stocking. Bare rock areas and granite tors can be seen.

Yinnietharra Station: working station; no facilities.
Ranges rise above the general level of the lowlands and support sparse shrublands dominated mostly by mulga. Fair views from tops of rises.

Dairy Creek Station: working station; no facilities. Turn-off for Meekatharra (next fuel 373km) and Murchison (next fuel 219km).

Low rises support extensive tracts of mulga shrublands.

NOTES

MAP 43 MEEKATHARRA-MT AUGUSTUS/ GLENBURGH STATION-MEEKATHARRA via Mt Gould

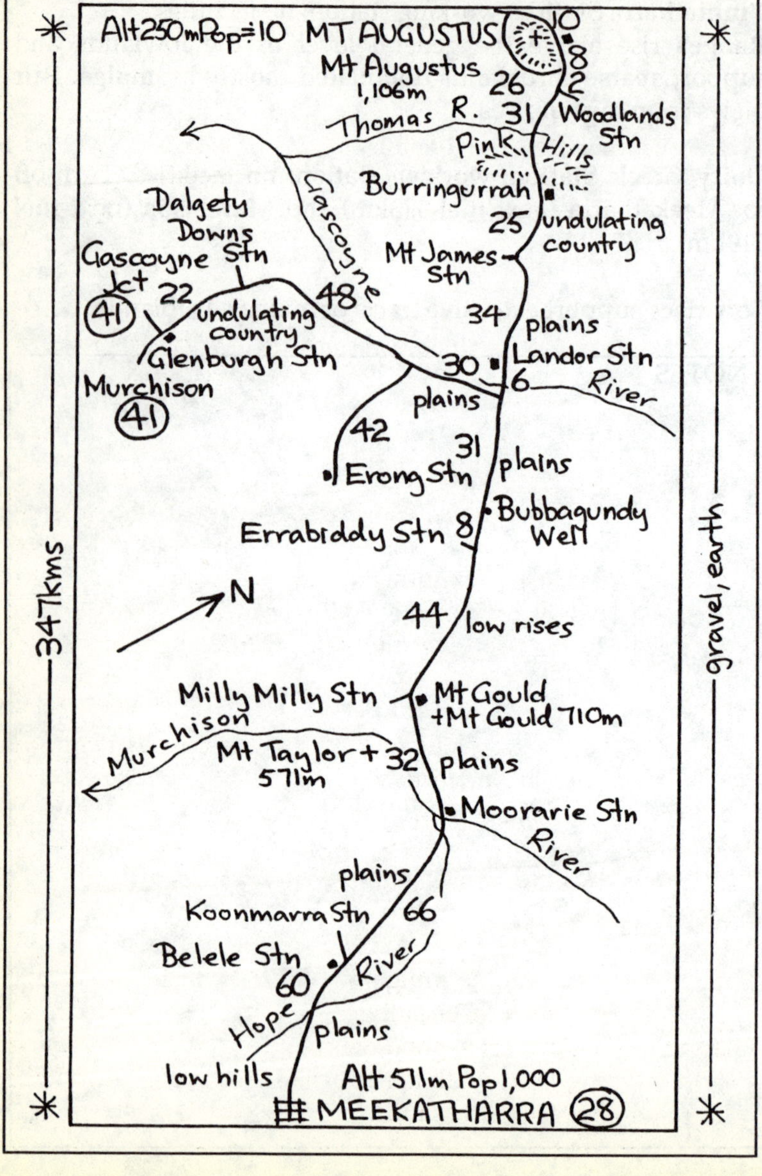

MAP 43 MEEKATHARRA-MT AUGUSTUS/GLENBURGH

STATION-MEEKATHARRA via Mt Gould

Grade 3

Total Distance: 347km (Glenburgh Station 341km)
Average Vehicles per day: 20 west of Meekatharra
Regions Traversed: Murchison, Gascoyne

MT AUGUSTUS: working cattle station and low key tourist facility. Information available about the nearby Mt Augustus (Burringurrah) National Park. Basic accommodation, limited stores, fuel.

Mt Augustus: high rocky range with a prominent northern cliff-face; very photogenic, especially from near the western end of the loop road intersection. Numerous features including Aboriginal paintings, dry waterfalls, rockholes, bushwalks, station ruins, etc. Enquire locally. Area now a national park; no camping allowed. Worth spending a few days in this area.

Pink Hills: dry, barren hills which look quite attractive in the right light. Good views northward towards Mt Augustus and the distant purple peak of Mt Phillips.

Burringurrah: Aboriginal settlement; no facilities, but help given if required.

Undulating country of mulga-clad plains and sparse, dry, rocky hills and rises; especially hilly about 9km north of Mt James Station turn-off - good views to the west and north. Worth taking a short walk here to find crystals. Hills covered with a sparse acacia shrubland.

Plains support extensive tracts of mulga shrublands.

Landor Station: working station; no facilities, except for a public telephone.

Plains support extensive tracts of mulga shrublands.

Bubbagundy Well: numerous ruins - shearing sheds, shearers' quarters, old windmills and station yards, etc. Some ruins very photogenic. This is private property, do not disturb anything.

Low rises and hills form the divide between the Gascoyne and Murchison River Basins. Though not high, there is a feeling of being on top of the world due to the stunted vegetation. Numerous rocky outcrops and gibbers. Good expansive views to the south across the mulga, to isolated peaks.

Mt Gould: former police station and lock-up, a degraded reconstructed building that would have been better left as a ruin. Surroundings are pleasant, especially the nearby Gould Creek. A short distance away is Mt Gould, a prominent peak scarred by mining activity.

Plains support extensive tracts of mulga.

Moorarie Station: working station; no facilities. Nearby is the Murchison River.

Plains support extensive tracts of mulga.

Belele Station: working station; no facilities.

Hope River: no obvious channel, but watercourse marked by numerous shady trees. Quite a pleasant area; worth a quick look at least.

Plains support extensive tracts of mulga.

Low hills and rises given fair views eastward towards Meekatharra.

MEEKATHARRA: mining and grazing town with some character and characters. Worth spending some time here to soak up the atmosphere. Hotels, motels, stores, fuel. Stock up here if heading north.

Glenburgh Road (Carnarvon-Meekatharra road)

Glenburgh Station: working station; no facilities. Next fuel Gascoyne Junction (111km); Murchison (187km).

Undulating country provides fair views from tops of rises towards distant ranges. Country hereabouts can be attractive in the right light. Sparse mulga shrublands common.

Erong Station: working station and low key tourist facility. Waterholes, wildflowers in season, rocky outcrops, etc. Basic accommodation, limited stores, fuel. Make enquiries before proceeding.

Plains support extensive tracts of mulga. Locally known as the Macadam Plains.

NOTES

WEST COAST COUNTRY

The West Coast Country includes some of the finest coastal areas of Western Australia, and probably the best of Australia's arid coastlines. In the south the Shark Bay area offers travellers some very scenic coastal and water views, as well as the friendly semi-wild dolphins of Monkey Mia, the sub-tropical settlement of Denham and access (4WD only) to the westernmost point of mainland Australia: Steep Point. This region has other interesting features as well, including some of the richest marine environments of coastal Australia. Travellers should contemplate spending at least a few days in this area.

Further north, on the north-western tip of the continent, is the Exmouth Peninsula, which houses the very arid Cape Range National Park, and the lengthy Ningaloo Marine Park that preserves a series of coral reefs comparable to the Great Barrier Reef. The advantage of the Ningaloo Reefs is that they lie very close to the coast (often only a few hundred metres off-shore), making them accessible to anyone with a small boat. Other areas of interest in the Exmouth region make this a region worthy of an extended break from travelling.

Warnings: beware of stock and kangaroos at night. Roads may be subject to flooding. Though coastal districts, these areas are subject to high summer temperatures along their inland access roads; carry water in the vehicle.

MAP 44 OVERLANDER ROADHOUSE-MONKEY MIA/ STEEP POINT-OVERLANDER ROADHOUSE

via Denham

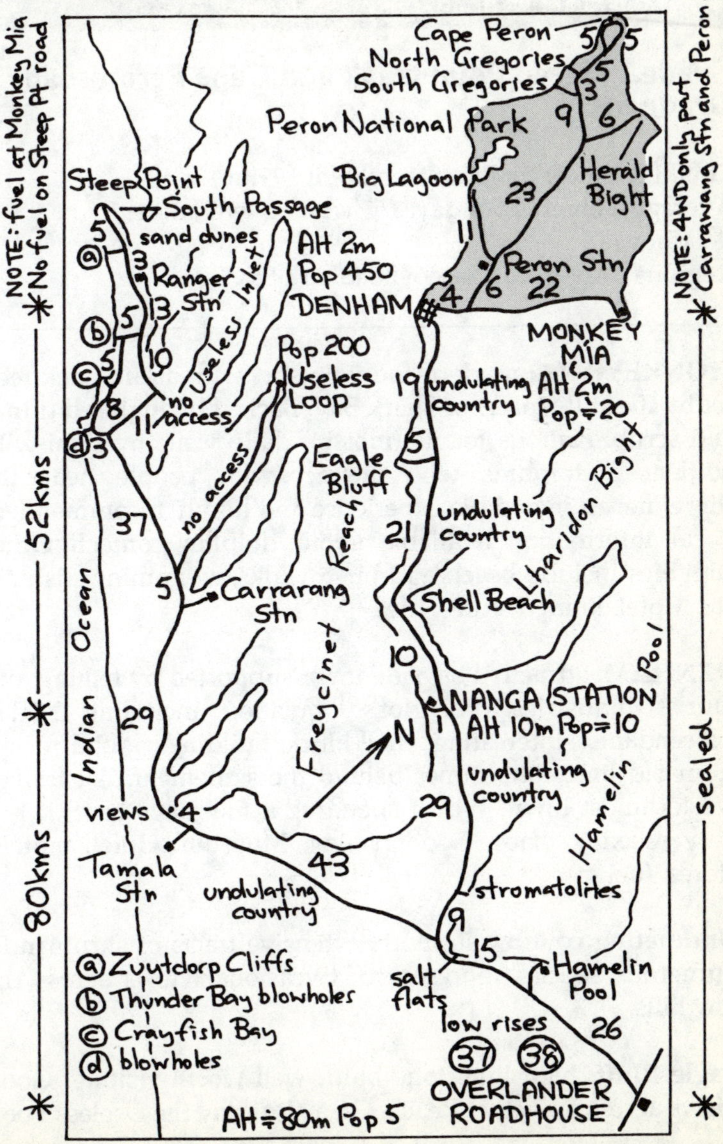

MAP 44 OVERLANDER ROADHOUSE-MONKEY MIA/STEEP POINT-OVERLANDER ROADHOUSE via Denham

Grade 1 (Steep Point track and Cape Peron road Grade 5)

Total Distance: 156km (Steep Point 191km)
Average Vehicles per day: 155 west of Overlander Roadhouse
Regions Traversed: Gascoyne (Shark Bay)

MONKEY MIA: modern tourist resort with a laid-back feel, set by the still waters of Shark Bay. Backed by high red dunes and scrub. Famous for its (mostly) daily visits by semi-wild bottlenose dolphins who interact with people near the shoreline; an incredible experience and highly recommended. Local information available about dolphin contact. Other activities include beach and bush walks, swimming, fishing, etc. Motel, limited stores, fuel.

DENHAM: attractive bayside town supported by fishing and tourist industries. Polyglot population including Malay descendants. Interesting shell-block buildings; good views from old limestone dunes behind the settlement. Australia's westernmost town. Worth spending a few days here; it is a very relaxing place. Good fishing. Museum. Hotel, motels, stores, fuel.

Undulating country supports extensive tracts of shrublands; numerous species represented. Occasional views across the low hills.

Eagle Bluff: high limestone bluff; well worth visiting. Good views across Freycinet Reach. On a clear day the Useless Loop saltworks can be seen. Patient watching of the waters will exhibit numerous marine life including turtles. Eagles common. Short walks (be careful on the loose slopes) recommended. Unsealed access road.

Undulating country provides good views across the low hills and towards Freycinet Reach. Low shrublands and spinifex dominate the landscape, giving this area an open feel.

Shell Beach: a beach composed entirely of countless tiny shells up to 10m deep and 110km long! Well worth seeing; take your sunglasses (very glary). Just north of the beach there is a good view overlooking Shell Beach and Lharidon Bight beyond.

NANGA STATION: working sheep station and low key tourist facility. Some shell-block buildings. Interesting place. Tours available. Motel, fuel.

Undulating country supports extensive tracts of shrublands and deep red dunes.
Views overlooks a portion of Hamelin Pool.
Salt flats visible from the road; some halophytes present. Good views across the flats from a low rise to the east.

Hamelin Pool: do not confuse with Hamelin Station (working sheep station; no access) passed on the way in. Old telegraph station, nowadays a museum and tea shop. Well worth visiting. Good views from a nearby dune overlooking the telegraph station on one side, and the still waters of Hamelin Pool on the other. Nearby Hamelin Pool is incredibly salty. Stromatolites may be seen at low tide. Whilst not scenically grand, these green-coloured objects that look like soft rocks are the oldest surviving life forms known - they have existed for about 3,500 million years! Stromatolites are matted sheets of blue-green algae that trap sediment, thus forming mounds. Do not stray beyond broadwalk.

Low rises formed by old limestone ridges; westernmost rises give good views over the salt flats. Various shrubs dominate the landscape.

OVERLANDER ROADHOUSE: roadhouse facility. Motel, fuel.

Cape Peron road

Cape Peron: interesting area; a good place to stroll the shoreline. Nearby is the Cape Peron lighthouse.

North Gregories: coastal campsite and fishing area.

South Gregories: coastal campsite and fishing area.

Peron National Park: former sheep station. Park incorporates gently undulating country covered with quite dense coastal scrubs and heaths, and lined with white sandy beaches backed by red clifflines. Interspersed throughout the park are gypsum-covered saltpans called birridas.

Herald Bight: attractive waterside camping area, perhaps more sheltered from the wind than those on the western side of the park.

Big Lagoon: attractive camping area. The lagoon itself is popular for fishing and small boating activities.

Peron Station: former sheep station homestead nowadays a national park ranger station. Pay applicable park use fees here. Information available, including park road and track conditions. Note: 4WD only north of homestead.

Steep Point road

Steep Point: high cliffs mark this westernmost point of mainland Australia. Access limited to high clearance 4WDs.

Opposite lies Dirk Hartog Island. Good fishing from the cliffs. Numerous access tracks head eastward towards the beaches over the last few kilometres.

Sand dunes back the high seaward cliffs; blowouts may be seen.

Zuytdorp Cliffs: spectacular scenery with awe-inspiring ocean views can be seen from these high sea cliffs; cliffs themselves are over 150km long.

Ranger Station: country hereabout is held on pastoral leases. Pay applicable users' fees here. Telephone available.

Thunder Bay blowholes: impressive blowholes set within the cliffs; best seen when a big swell is running.

Crayfish Bay: pleasant area when not too windy.

Blowholes are quite spectacular when a big swell is running. Countryside fairly desolate; areas of barren rock and low shrublands.

Useless Loop: closed salt mining settlement; no access. Route here and southwards okay for conventional drive vehicles.

Carrarang Station: working sheep station; no facilities.

Views overlooking Baba Bight, an arm of Freycinet Reach.

Tamala Station: working sheep station; no facilities but bush camping may be available. Make local enquiries.

Undulating country consisting of dunes and old limestone ridges extends along most of this route. Vegetation dominated by mixed shrublands with areas of low open shrublands that provide occasional views.

MAP 45 MINILYA ROADHOUSE-EXMOUTH (Yardie Creek)-MINILYA ROADHOUSE via Coral Bay

Grade 1 (Yardie Creek road Grade 3)

Total Distance: 225km (Yardie Creek 313km)
Average Vehicles per day: 165 north of Minilya Roadhouse
Regions Traversed: North-West

Yardie Creek: spectacular gorge of deep blue water hemmed in by vertical cliffs; worth visiting. Walking trails along the cliff tops. Very scenic area.

Cape Range forms a prominent escarpment along the eastern skyline, rent at intervals by gorges and creeks. Escarpment rises over 100m above a narrow coastal plain. Range formed from limestone. Vegetation is sparse, predominantly low shrubs, including mallee forms of the eucalypt variable-barked bloodwood and spinifex.

Mandu Mandu Creek: attractive inlet. Nearby is the Mandu Mandu Creek Gorge with its scenic walking trail. Coral reefs are located just a few hundred metres off-shore.

Cape Range National Park preserves the arid plateau of the Cape Range. Many scenic areas and camping grounds. Obtain information on additional attractions (not included herein) from Milyering Information Centre.

Milyering: Visitors Centre for the Cape Range National Park and Ningaloo Marine Park. Stacks of information, displays, videos, etc. Highly recommended. No other facilities available. The **Ningaloo Marine Park** preserves an extensive coral reef system as rich as any within the Great Barrier Reef.

MAP 45 MINILYA ROADHOUSE-EXMOUTH (Yardie Creek)-MINILYA ROADHOUSE

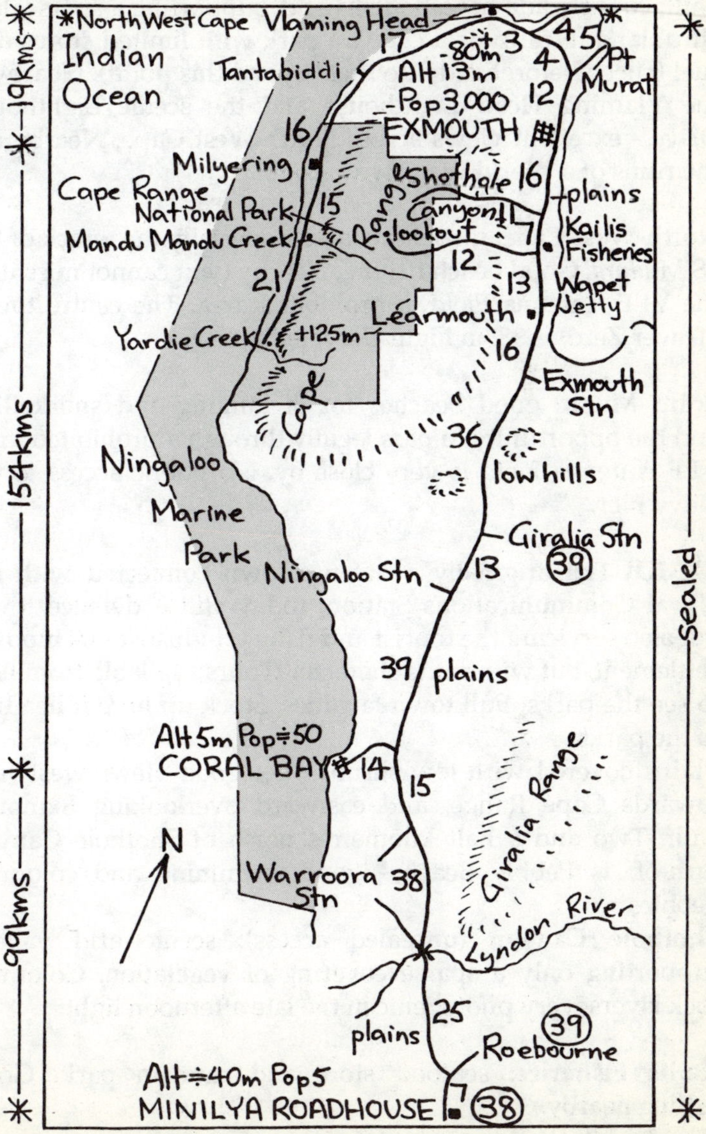

Tantabiddi: locality only. Good swimming and fishing.

Vlaming Head: a low promontory near the head of Exmouth Gulf; countryside hereabouts is arid, supporting a sparse, low shrubland. Nearby is a caravan park with limited stores and fuel (check beforehand - no fuel beyond this point). Nearby is the Vlaming Head Lighthouse and the scenic Lighthouse Drive - excellent views across North-West Cape. Nearby are the ruins of a World War Two radar site.

North-West Cape: interesting area, especially the wreck of the SS *Mildura*. Good beach fishing. Nearby (you cannot miss it) is the VLF Antenna Field, a prohibited area. The centre tower (Tower Zero) is 388m high! Unsealed access.

Point Murat: good beaches for swimming and snorkelling and the opportunity to pass legally through a prohibited area. VLF Antenna Field is very close by. No public access to the Navy Pier.

EXMOUTH: originally a defence town connected with the Naval Communications Station; today still a defence town, but also servicing the tourist and fishing industries. A modern settlement, but with some character. Tours available from here to see the parks. Full town facilities. Stock up here if heading to the parks.
Plains covered with low shrubs offer good views westward towards Cape Range, and eastward overlooking Exmouth Gulf. Two and a half kilometres north of Shothole Canyon turn-off is Pebbly Beach - good swimming and colourful pebbles.
Shothole Canyon (unsealed access): scenic arid valleys supporting only a sparse covering of vegetation. Colourful rock layers; very photogenic in the late afternoon light.

Kailis Fisheries: seafood store and caravan park. Good fishing nearby.

Lookout located at the end of Charles Knife Road. Road runs along a razorback ridge between two canyons. Walking tracks at end. Excellent place to watch sunrise over Exmouth Gulf. Unsealed access.

Learmouth: old World War Two base, but occasionally used by the Services. Nearby is the Learmouth Airport and **Wapet Jetty,** where trawlers can be seen. Visible from the road (no public access) is a solar observatory.

Wapet Creek (not shown on map - 2km south of Learmouth): semi-submerged World War Two wrecks make interesting photographic subjects. Beware of stonefish; wear heavy footwear if wading. Good fishing.

Low hills provide good views across the open undulating lowlands. Vegetation mostly sparse low shrublands and spinifex.

Plains support extensive tracts of acacia shrublands, dominated by dead finish. Giralia Range occasionally visible to the east.

CORAL BAY: small coastal tourist and holiday settlement with some character. Tours available to view the Ningaloo Coral Reef, one of the world's major reef systems. Reef located about 150m off-shore. Also worth seeing is the Mangrove Bay boardwalk and bird hide. Hotel, motels, stores, fuel.

Lyndon River: countryside hereabout is sparse and open, providing expansive views; saltbush common. Distant views to Giralia Ranges.
Plains support extensive tracts of acacia shrublands.

MINILYA ROADHOUSE: roadhouse facility set by the attractive, sandy bed of the Minilya River; a pleasant area for walks under the shady river red gums. Fuel.

THE PILBARA

Incorporating some of the grandest arid mountain country in Australia, the Pilbara is a region of vivid contrasts: high mountains, deep gorges, vast stony plains, expansive grasslands, huge tracts of spinifex, gently sloping coastal plains, huge tidal variations, gigantic iron ore mines, some of the longest trains in the world, modern suburban-looking towns, old mining townships, and some of the fiercest summer temperatures in Australia. The Pilbara is a region definitely worth visiting, and, if time allows, for exploring in detail. It is a microcosm of the arid Australia outback. Its biggest shame is that it is so far away, not just from the settled country of south-eastern Australia, but from the populated southern corner of Western Australia itself. Another shame is that in driving to the Pilbara one travels through some very mediocre country indeed.

Nonetheless the Pilbara should be on every traveller's itinerary for its huge size and relative isolation gives this a region a grandeur that might otherwise be swamped if it were more visited or more populated. Be warned though that there are long distances and many lonely roads in this sparsely settled area; only the coastal route provides services at regular intervals.

Warnings: Avoid travelling at night; if on the sealed roads beware of stock and kangaroos at this time. Unsealed roads are impassable in wet weather and are subject to flooding. In summer monsoonal rains and resulting floods can isolate sections of roads for considerable periods. Make local enquiries before proceeding. Off the bitumen avoid travelling during the summer months - high temperatures and humidity can prove dangerous. If travelling at this time always inform a reliable person of your intentions; convoy travel recommended. Note: no fuel between Nanutarra Roadhouse and Wittenoom except at Tom Price (21km off the through road); no habitation between Wyloo and Rocklea Stations (138km, Map 46), between Tom Price and Wittenoom (130km, Map 47), and between Camp Curlewis and Hamersley Station (129km, Map 48).

MAP 46 NANUTARRA ROADHOUSE-TOM PRICE/

PARABURDOO-NANUTARRA ROADHOUSE

Grade 3 (Nanutarra-Tom Price via Paraburdoo Grade 1)

Total Distance: 294km (Paraburdoo 275km)
Average Vehicles per day: 70 east of Nanutarra
Regions Traversed: Pilbara

TOM PRICE: modern iron ore mining town which looks like an established, transplanted suburb. Prides itself on being Top Town in WA, being the highest town in the state. Attractively located amongst the high hills of the Hamersley Ranges. Excellent views from Mt Nameless lookout; access road highest in the state - 1128m. Full town facilities. Stock up here if heading east or west.
Ranges surround the road with high flat-top hills in the vicinity of Tom Price; some of these hills rise 300m above the lowlands. Elsewhere are isolated rocky hills and undulating lowlands. Hill sides support a covering of spinifex with small eucalypts (the white-barked ones are snappy gums) forming the overstorey. Elsewhere, in the more undulating country, mulga and other acacias are seen.

Beasley River: attractive area; stream bed lined with river red gums.

MAP 46 NANUTARRA ROADHOUSE-TOM PRICE/ PARABURDOO-NANUTARRA ROADHOUSE

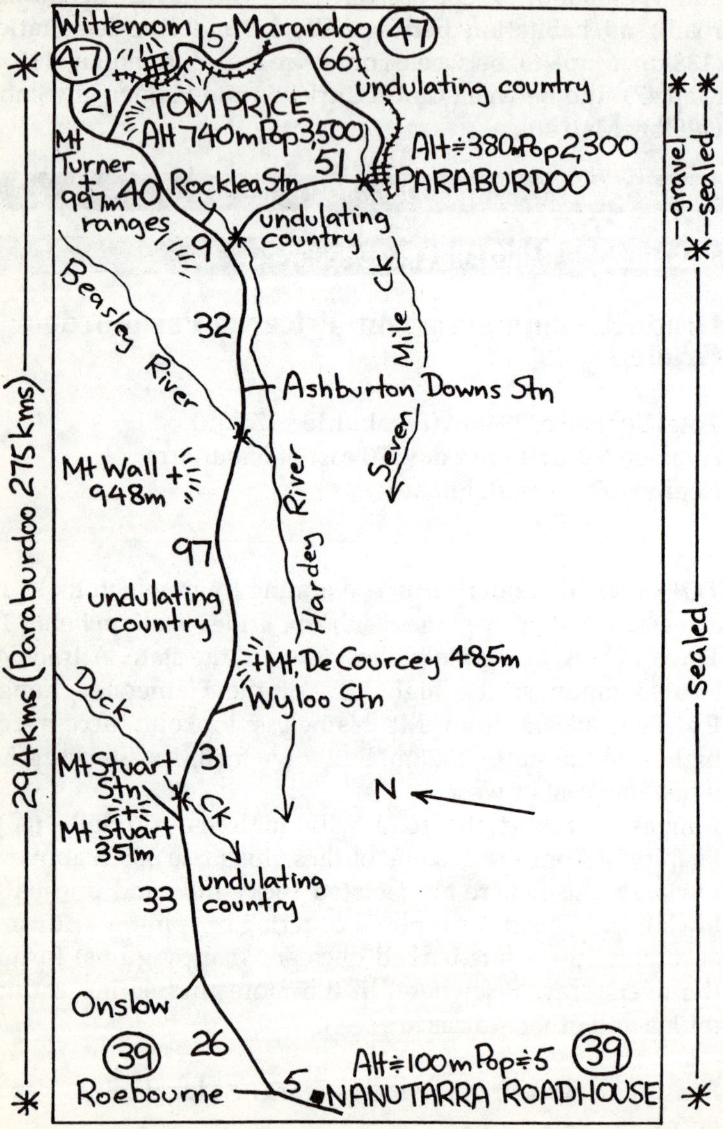

Undulating country provides good views across the lowlands to distant ranges - very attractive early or late in the day. Some far-flung purple peaks and ranges will be seen. Countryside ranges from low hills and rocky rises to gently undulating plains and riverine valleys. Vegetation is mostly spinifex with overstoreys of mulga and other acacias. In some places eucalypts are present, forming a sparse covering.

Mt De Coucey and its attendant range are visible to the south.

Undulating country provides vast views across the spinifex-clad lowlands; the typical shrubby overstorey is absent in many places - where present it may be mulga or other acacias. Keep an eye out for unusual rock formations: low bouldery hills rising like pyramids; near **Duck Creek,** tombstone rocks - flat, vertical sheets rising a metre or two above the ground. These interesting features are worth a quick look.

NANUTARRA ROADHOUSE: pleasant roadhouse attractively sited by the banks of the Ashburton River. River area worth exploring on foot - interesting rockholes, shady river red gums, flood-swept melaleucas. Motel, fuel.

Paraburdoo Road

Undulating country provides good views over the lowlands. Some high rocky hills are of interest. Spinifex ground cover is common with an overstorey of mulga and other acacias. In some areas, on low ground, variable-barked bloodwoods (a eucalypt) will be seen.

PARABURDOO: modern iron ore mining town set at the foot of the Paraburdoo Ridge. Interesting geological formations hereabout. Town itself is starting to look settled. Hotel, motel, stores, fuel.

Undulating country provides occasional good views, especially towards Paraburdoo Ridge; otherwise fair views from tops of rises. Spinifex ground cover along with a sparse acacia overstorey that includes mulga.

MAP 47 TOM PRICE-ROY HILL STATION/KARIJINI NATIONAL PARK-

TOM PRICE via Wittenoom

Grade 3 (Karijini National Park roads Grade 3)

Total Distance: 319km (Karijini National Park 182km)
Average Vehicles per day: 30 west of Wittenoom/3 west of Roy Hill Station
Regions Traversed: Pilbara (Hamersley Ranges)

Roy Hill Station: working cattle station; no facilities. Next fuel Newman (102km); Nullagine (92km).

Plains support extensive tracts of acacia shrublands with a spinifex understorey. In low lying areas are attractive low eucalypt woodlands.

Yandicoogina Creek: pleasant area, interesting railway bridge nearby.

Plains provide good views towards the Hamersley Range escarpment to the south. Acacia shrublands dominate the countryside; some areas of low growing eucalypts with an understorey of spinifex.
AUSKI ROADHOUSE: modern roadhouse facility set at the base of the Hamersley Range escarpment. Store, fuel.

WITTENOOM: old asbestos mining township with plenty of character. Interesting and photogenic buildings. Worth spending a short time here. Town is built upon asbestos fibres - do not disturb! Nearby is the attractive Wittenoom Gorge with shady river red gums, swimming holes and spectacular cliffs - old asbestos mine nearby (no access). Side gorges are free of asbestos fibres. Stores, fuel.

MAP 47 TOM PRICE-ROY HILL STATION/KARIJINI NATIONAL PARK-TOM PRICE via Wittenoom

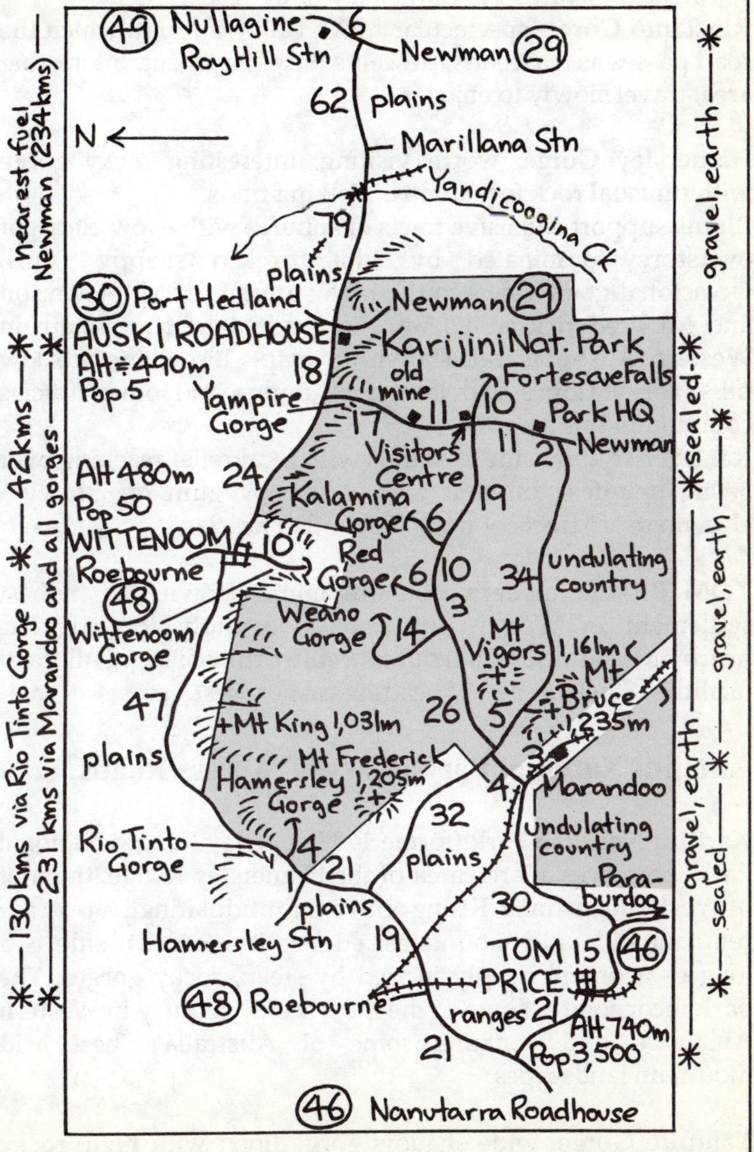

Plains support tracts of acacia shrublands and patches of low eucalypt woodlands; spinifex common. Good views southward towards the Hamersley Range escarpment.
Rio Tinto Gorge: spectacular rocky valley through which the road passes as it ascends/descents the escarpment. Interesting area; travel slowly to enjoy it.

Hamersley Gorge: worth visiting; interesting rocky gorge with unusual rock formations. Walking trails.
Plains support extensive tracts of spinifex with a low eucalypt overstorey dominated by white-trunked snappy gums. Occasional good views to the high summits of Mt Stevenson and Mt Frederick, at 1205m, the third highest mountain in Western Australia (not shown on map). Elsewhere are low hills, rocky ridges and low rises; mulga and other acacias common in this area.
Ranges rise above the lowlands with local relief reaching over 300m; spinifex common with a snappy gum overstorey - elsewhere are tracts of mulga and other acacias.

TOM PRICE: modern iron ore mining town, the highest settlement in Western Australia. Pleasantly located. The nearby Mt Nameless lookout is well worth visiting. Full town facilities. Stock up here if heading east or west.

Karijini National Park: Gorges' Access Roads

Karijini National Park (formerly Hamersley Ranges National Park) preserves a large area of the Hamersley Range, the roof of Western Australia. Rising above this undulating plateau are remnant hills and mountains; edging its northern side is a long escarpment deeply incised by steep, rocky gorges. The park incorporates some of the most scenic country in Western Australia, and contains some of Australia's best arid mountain landscapes.

Yampire Gorge: wide shallow gorge lined with high, rocky bluffs; very scenic. Keep an eye out for the Fig Tree Soak (12km from Wittenoom-Auski road turn-off); about 800m further on is a very photogenic terraced rock formation on the eastern side - mornings best for photography.

Old mine: numerous relics still visible around this old asbestos mine. Good place to see exposed minerals. Do not disturb asbestos fibres. A few kilometres further on is the northern exit of the Doug Francis Drive, a one-way route (heading north) that provides good views overlooking Yampire Gorge. Entrance to Drive a few kilometres further on. **Visitors Centre:** stops here for information on the national park.

Fortescue Falls: well worth visiting - attractive area of weeping waterfalls, ferns and deep pools (Circular Pool at base of falls). Walking tracks including easy access to Dales Gorge beyond. Camping available. At the Falls turn-off look for an old termite mound about 200m off the road - they do not come much larger than this one.

Kalamina Gorge: not as spectacular as the other gorges, but readily accessible and good for bushwalking. Springs, pools, ferns and river red gums all feature.

Red Gorge: spectacular gorge over 100m deep, linked with incredibly red cliffs. Good views. Nearby a walking track leads to Knox Gorge. On the way (about 2km in, not marked on map) is Joffre Falls, an attractive weeping fall at the head of Joffre Gorge. Attractive area. Camping available nearby.

Weano Gorge: spectacular gorge, really a chasm, that should not be missed. Above the gorge is the Three Gorge Junction Lookout, one of the most awe-inspiring lookouts to be seen anywhere. Here Weano, Joffre and Hancock Gorges all meet to become Red Gorge. Very scenic area. A steep track descends into Weano Gorge, a narrow chasm 100m deep and

a few metres wide, that leads to a large rock pool. Camping available. West of **Mt Vigors,** on a low, rocky ridge, are excellent views towards Mt Bruce. The road on this ridge is the highest through-road in Western Australia: 820m.
Plains support tracts of spinifex with a snappy gum overstorey; good views northward to Mt Stevenson rising 400m above. Elsewhere are tracts of acacia shrublands. Hills and rocky ridges will also be seen.

Karijini National Park: Mt Bruce-Marandoo-Tom Price Loop road

Park Headquarters: ranger station.

Undulating country supports extensive tracts of acacia shrublands, typically mulga with a spinifex understorey. Occasionally low, rocky hills rise above the lowlands. Dry weather only

Mt Bruce: second highest mountain in Western Australia; appears as a spectacular high bluff rising over 500m above the lowlands. Very photogenic from a distance in the afternoon light. Walking track to the summit.

Marandoo: Iron ore mine; no access or facilities at present.
Undulating country offers good views towards district ranges, especially southwards. Mulga shrublands and spinifex grasslands common.

NOTES

MAP 48 WITTENOOM/TOM PRICE-ROEBOURNE-WITTENOOM/TOM PRICE

via Millstream

Grade 3

Total Distance: 288km (Tom Price 304km)
Average Vehicles per day: 30 south of Roebourne
Regions traversed: Pilbara

ROEBOURNE: interesting historic town; many old photogenic buildings. If alarmed by the street-life, give the town some time - there is lots happening; much more than meets the eye. Good views from Mt Welcome Lookout behind the town. Hotel, motel, stores, fuel. Stock up here if heading south.
Plains support wide sweeping grasslands; expansive views abound. Horizon lined by distant flat-top hills and ranges. Willy-willies may be seen.

Pyramid Hill: interesting and photogenic conical hill west of the road.
Plains support vast tracts of grasslands; good views. Skyline delineated by numerous flat-top hills. Southward the Chichester Range escarpment can be seen; near the escarpment are low rocky hills and boulders.

Millstream-Chichester National Park preserves a large portion of the Chichester Range escarpment and the adjacent plains, as well as a portion of the Fortescue River. Much of the park is wilderness.

Python Pool: large rock pool set at the base of a high cliff and normally dry waterfall. A very pleasant spot, relatively cool

MAP 48 ROEBOURNE-WITTENOOM/TOMPRICE-WITTENOOM/TOM PRICE via Millstream

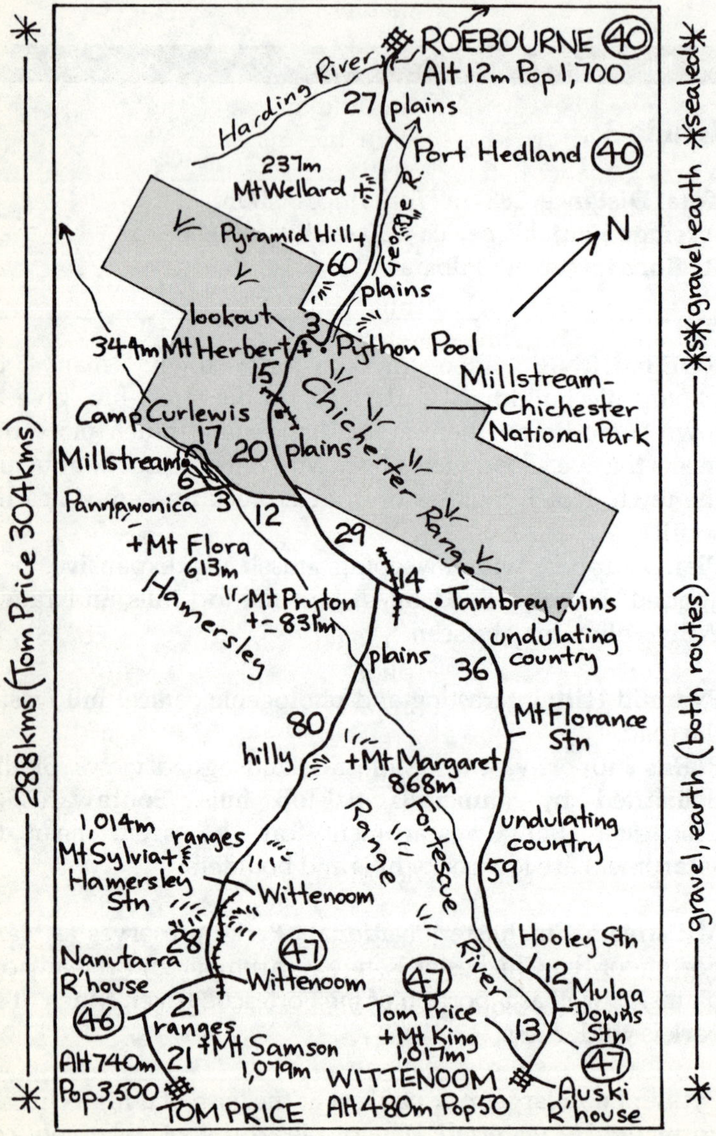

and shady. The countryside around is very dry and rocky, and covered with virtually nothing but spinifex. Nearby is Snake Creek (camping available).

Lookout on Mt Herbert offers wide sweeping views across the spinifex-clad escarpment and the distant George River plain. Pyramid Hill can be seen in the distance. The sparse low shrubs hereabout are a type of acacia. South of Mt Herbert, the far distant escarpment of the Hamersley Range can be seen to the south.

Camp Curlewis (Barowanna Hill): old railway camp. Basic accommodation, limited stores and caravan park may be available - check beforehand.

Plains offer fair views towards distant ranges. Vegetation comprised of a sparse eucalypt woodland with a ground cover of spinifex. Snappy gums dominate.

Millstream: definitely worth visiting - an oasis amid an expanse of aridity. Millstream itself is a former station homestead, nowadays a ranger station: camping, water, information and telephone available. Adjacent is Chinderwarriner Pool, a tropical waterhole lined with palms and paperbarks, and covered with lilies, etc. On the nearby Fortescue River are waterholes (Deep Reach and Crossing Pool) with camping facilities, etc. These river red gum and bullrush-lined waterholes are very attractive. The scenic Snappy Gum Drive encircles the waterholes. Walking tracks.

Tambrey ruins: old homestead ruins; very photogenic. Nearby are old station relics: wells, stock yards, old fence lines, etc. Worth a quick look; do not disturb anything.

Undulating country covered with snappy gum woodlands and spinifex. Occasional views from tops of rises.
Undulating country supports extensive tracts of mulga.

Occasional rocky outcrops. Excellent views of Hamersley Range at Mulga Downs Station turn-off.

Fortescue River: there is no obvious stream but rather a flat covered with grasses. Northward are low hills covered with spinifex; nearby are tracts of mulga shrublands. South of the grassy flats is a sparsely vegetated plain covered with spinifex; good southward views toward the high escarpment of the Hamersley Range.

WITTENOOM: old asbestos mining town, nowadays virtually a ghost town due to the health hazards of asbestos fibres; short-term visitors not kicking up dust will be pretty safe. Interesting settlement; many old buildings. The place is definitely worth a visit. Nearby is the attractive Wittenoom Gorge with pleasant river red gum-lined waterholes and narrow side gorges. Stores, fuel.

Tom Price road

Plains support snappy gum woodlands north of the Fortescue River. Occasional fair views southward towards the Hamersley Range. South of the Fortescue River (a pleasant area) are mulga shrublands; occasional good views towards nearby ranges.

Hilly country rises above the road where it enters/exits the main Hamersley Range escarpment. Good views towards distant hills and ranges. Some mulga shrublands grading into sparse eucalypt woodlands and spinifex.

Ranges and hills provide good views; very scenic in the afternoon light. Eucalypts and spinifex abound; note the moderately denser overstorey due to increased altitude and precipitation.

Ranges rise above the road near Tom Price; very scenic area. Spinifex clads the steep slopes with snappy gums on the lower hillsides, and mulga shrublands in the valley floors.

TOM PRICE: modern iron ore mining town attractively situated amongst hills and ranges. The nearby Mt Nameless Lookout is definitely worth visiting. Full town facilities. Stock up here if heading north.

MAP 49 ROY HILL STATION-PORT HEDLAND-ROY HILL STATION

via Marble Bar

Grade 3

Total Distance: 405km
Average Vehicles per day: 160 south of Great Northern Highway junction
Regions Traversed: Pilbara

PORT HEDLAND: large iron ore port and regional service centre with a heavy industry atmosphere; the old Port Hedland has some character. Some tourist features and good fishing spots - make local enquiries. Full town facilities. Stock up here if heading south.

Salt flats separate Port Hedland from the mainland. Good views across the flats and from a lookout (not shown on map) located 4km north of the highway junction. Mangroves line the estuaries; industrial landscapes south of the flats.

Plains slope gently towards the far distant Indian Ocean. The plains are sandy with a covering of spinifex and dwarf shrubs. Great views at night across the plains towards the lights of Port Hedland.

Plains north of Shaw River area provide wide, expansive views over its spinifex covering. Forming a sparse overstorey are various acacia shrubs. At intervals, low rocky hills and ridges can be seen. The river crossings are attractive areas with shady river red gums.

Gorge Range: low but steeply rising rocky range mostly seen at a distance across the spinifex plains. The steeper parts of the ranges support spinifex with white-trunked snappy gums. Near the Coongan River crossing is some interesting hilly country; very photogenic in the afternoon light. This area is worth exploring on foot.

Bamboo Creek: old gold mining area currently undergoing further exploitation. Many old mine workings, township ruins, cemeteries, etc, make this a good place to explore for a day or two. Nearby is the attractive Coppins Gap, a waterhole set amongst barren, rocky hills. Bamboo Creek today is a mining camp - no fuel or accommodation. Make local enquiries before proceeding.

Undulating country provides good views from tops of rises. Low red rocky hills contrast with the green spinifex and white-trunked snappy gums. Acacia shrublands occupy the lowlands.

MARBLE BAR: interesting historic town with many fine, old stone buildings; some very photogenic. Sizeable population of Njamal people (among others). Said to be Australia's hottest town but whether this is based on annual averages or summer maximums is debatable; it certainly has had 160 consecutive days of temperatures reaching 100F (37.8C). Many features worth seeing: Comet Gold Mine, Ironclad Hotel, Government buildings, One Mile Gorge and the Marble (really jasper) Bar. Other features nearby; make local enquiries. A few pleasant days could be spent in this area. Hotel, motel, stores, fuel.

Undulating country provides good views across the lowlands. Rocky outcrops and distant ranges rise above the

MAP 49 ROY HILL STATION-PORT HEDLAND-ROY HILL STATION via Marble Bar

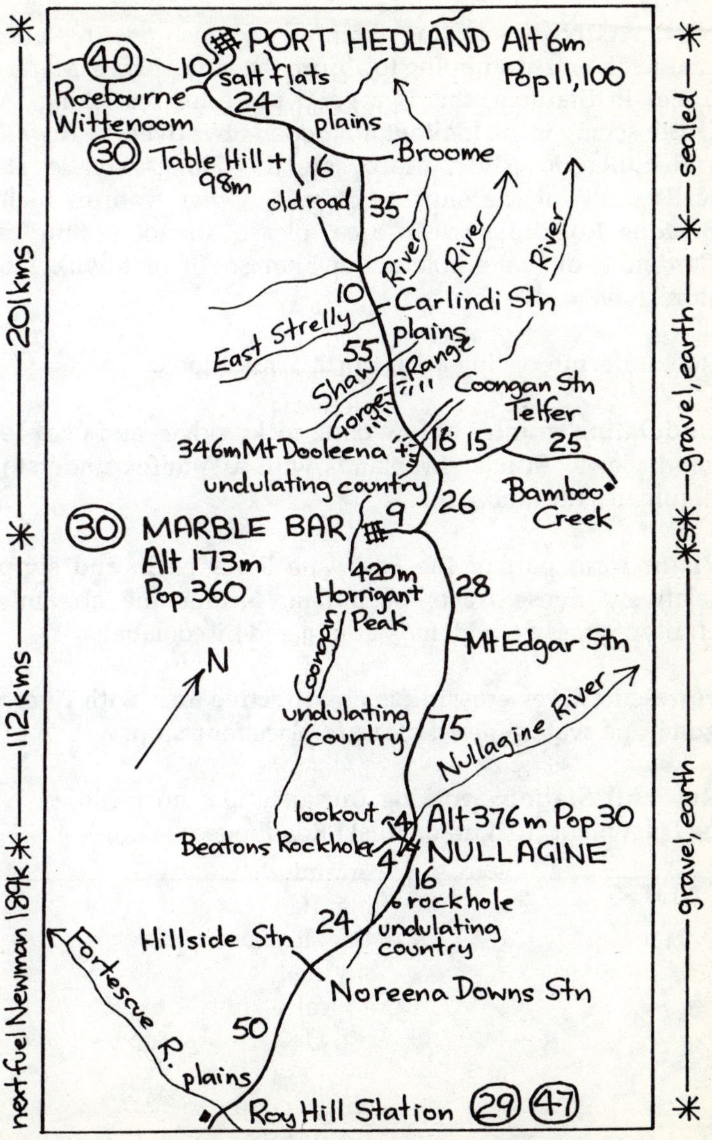

spinifex lowlands. Some areas of sparse eucalypt woodlands, otherwise tracts of acacia-dominated shrublands.

NULLAGINE: interesting old mining township with plenty of character; worth stopping to absorb the atmosphere. Many old mines in the area; this is a good place for fossicking. Also worth seeing is the **lookout,** for good views over the township and Nullagine River; nearby are the Chinese Walls, stone walls built for the sluicing of gold. Other features include **Beatons Rockhole** (clean area, please do not pollute) and Garden Pool (waterhole about 5km south of town). Hotel, store, fuel.

Rockhole: interesting area; worth a quick look.

Undulating country of low rises, rocky ridges and occasional good views. Acacia shrublands with a spinifex understorey dominates the landscape.

Plains form part of the Fortescue River basin and support relatively dense tracts of mulga. Nearer the stream are eucalypt grassy woodlands dominated by coolabahs.

Fortescue River crossing is an attractive area with river red gums and waterholes; a pleasant place for a stop.

Roy Hill Station: working cattle station; no facilities. Next fuel Newman (102km) or Auski Roadhouse (147km).

NOTES

THE WESTERN DESERTS

The two routes described herein - the Warburton road and its easterly extension, and the Gunbarrel Highway - cross some of the most remote country in the non-polar world. Reaching far beyond the last cattle station fence line, the Western Deserts were people by tribal Aborigines living traditionally until only two or three generations ago; their descendants still inhabit parts of these deserts today.

These routes could not be described as scenic, except for the area around Giles and Docker River; their main attraction is that they provide not only a short cut for West Australian travellers heading to or from Central Australia along the Warburton Road, but a chance to experience a wild Australia little altered by non-Aborigines (save for the depopulation of the Aborigines themselves and the impact that has had on the environment). This is wilderness country, especially away from the road. As a consequence, journeys along these routes should not be undertaken lightly, for the country is unsettled and help a long way off. Although both routes are passable to conventional vehicles when dry, neither should be undertaken in these vehicles by inexperienced travellers. In the case of the Gunbarrel Highway, conventional vehicles should travel in convoy with a 4WD. The advantages of travelling this country are that the traveller will have the opportunity to experience a relatively untouched wilderness and to certainly appreciate the vastness of the outback.

Warnings: avoid travelling at night. Roads are impassable when wet and subject to flooding. Always make local enquiries before proceeding and always inform a reliable person of your intentions. If using the Warburton road inform police at Laverton or Ayers Rock Resort. You will be given a form to fill out with instructions to hand in the bottom half at the other end-they will fax the other police station of your safe arrival. Stay out of this area during the summer months. Convoy travel is highly recommended (even if using 4WDs) on the Gunbarrel Highway. Experienced travellers using 4WDs could travel in convoy during summer along the Warburton road and further east. The routes themselves are not difficult, just incredibly remote. Do not stray off the described routes. Note that sufficient fuel must be carried as supply points are far apart. Permits are required for entry to Warburton Aboriginal Land; a separate permit is required to cross Petermann Aboriginal Land; permist no longer required to visit Giles Meteorological Station. No camping is allowed at Uluru National Park. Only legal camping available between Ayers Rock Resort and WA border is at Lasseters Cave.

Note: no reliable habitation between Laverton-Tjukayirla Roadhouse (320km,Map 50);Tjukayirla Roadhouse-Warburton (245km,Map 50 and Warburton (565km, Map 50); Warburton-Giles (339km, Map 51); Giles -Docker River (106km, Map 51); Docker River and Ayers Rock Resort (237km, Map 51); Millibillilie and Wongawol Stations (211km, Map 52); Wongawol-Carnegie Stations (127km, Map 52); and Carnegie Station-Warburton (493km, Map 53).

NOTES

MAP 50 LAVERTON-WARBURTON-LAVERTON via Warburton Road

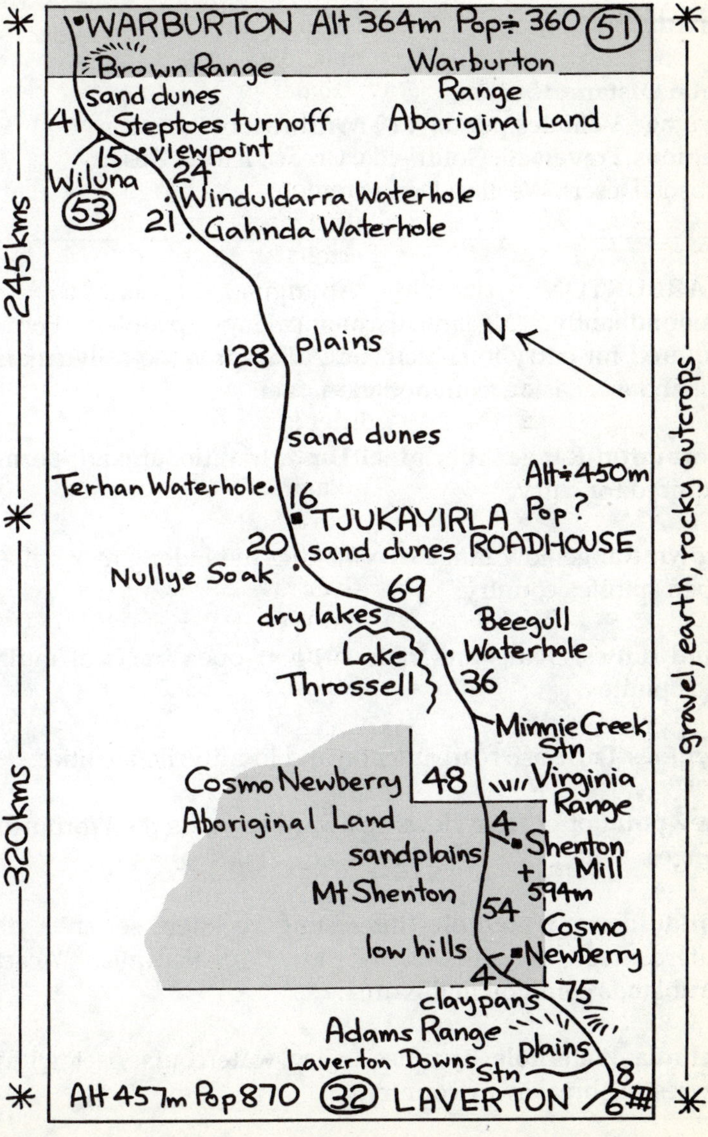

MAP 50 LAVERTON-WARBURTON-LAVERTON via Warburton Road

Grade 3

Total Distance: 565km
Average Vehicles per day: 10 north-east of Laverton
Regions Traversed: Goldfields, Great Victoria Desert, Gibson Desert, Western Desert

---

WARBURTON: sizeable Aboriginal community of predominantly Ngaanyatjarra-speaking people. Permit required for entry to settlement. Adjacent is the Milyirrtjarra Roadhouse. Basic accommodation, fuel.

Warburton Range Aboriginal Land: traditional land; permit required for entry.

Brown Range: low range overlooking the Elder Creek valley. Open spinifex country.

Sand dunes, plains and rises support open tracts of mulga and spinifex.

Steptoes Turn-off: road junction and locality; no facilities.

Viewpoint offers fair views eastward towards the Warburton Ranges.

Winduldarra Waterhole: interesting rockhole set in a dry watercourse beneath some low breakaways. Acacia shrublands common in this area.

Gahnda Waterhole occupies a dry watercourse, set within interesting breakaway country.

Plains covered with acacia shrublands with understoreys of either spinifex or grass. At intervals low rises are crossed and breakaways will be seen. These plains form the southern part of the Gibson Desert and exhibit sandy or stony surfaces.

Sand dunes form part of the Great Victoria Desert and run, somewhat discontinuously, east-west. Acacia shrublands with a grassy understorey dominate the countryside.

Terhan Waterhole: worth a quick look.

Tjukayirla Roadhouse: new roadhouse. Store, fuel.
Sand dunes line the road. Acacia shrublands with grassy understoreys dominate.

Nullye Soak: small soak just off the road; often difficult to locate.

Dry lakes form part of the Lake Throssell complex but are not readily visible from the road. Soils are lighter coloured hereabout, and there are limestone outcrops. Lake country can be identified by the presence of she-oaks with an understorey of low shrubs.

Beegull Waterhole: small waterhole set upon a low breakaway. Nearby are some small caves. Fair views from the breakaways.

Cosmo Newberry Aboriginal Land: traditional land.

Virginia Range: low range barely rising above the plain. Point Virginia can be seen just south of the road when heading west.

Shenton Mill: outstation. Water usually available.

Sand plains support extensive tracts of spinifex with a sparse eucalypt overstorey. Keep an eye out for patches of grasstrees

13 to 19km west of Shenton Mill turn-off.

Low hills line the road; interesting granite outcrops, etc.

Cosmo Newberry: former Aboriginal settlement, no abandoned. Traditional lands of the Tjalkaljara people.

Claypans visible to the north (63km from Laverton); worth investigating on foot when dry. Surrounding plains support tracts of spinifex with a sparse eucalypt overstorey.

Adams Range: low range offering reasonable views westward. Deeba Rockhole located on top of rise south of road.

Plains support tracts of mulga with a shrubby understorey. Occasional low hills and ridges rise above the plains. Just north of the Leonora turn-off, the Lancefield Mine can be seen. This area is known as Beria.

LAVERTON: a mostly reconstructed modern-looking mining town built around the original mining town's service centre; this older part of the town has some character. Numerous old mine sites nearby; make local enquiries. Fair views from Billy Goat Hill overlooking the town and surrounding plains. Hotel, motel, stores, fuel. Stock up here if heading east.

NOTES

MAP 51 WARBURTON-AYERS ROCK RESORT-WARBURTON via Docker River

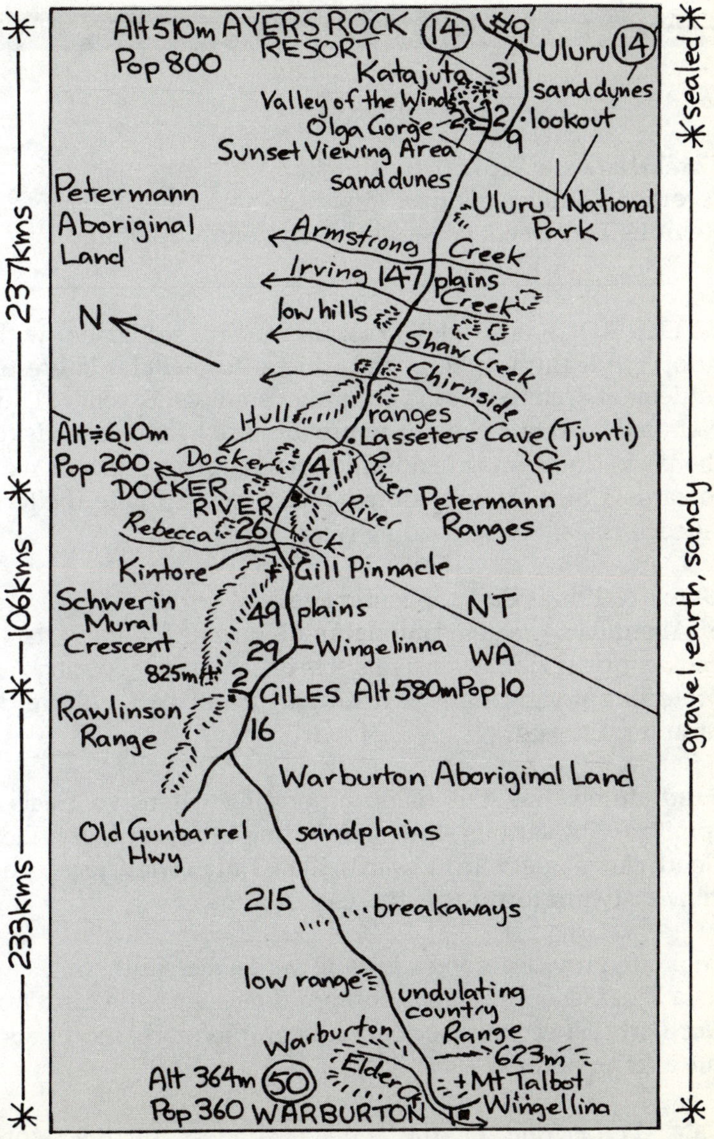

MAP 51 WARBURTON-AYERS ROCK RESORT-WARBURTON

via Docker River

Grade 3

Total Distance: 576km
Average Vehicles per day: 15 west of Kata Tjuta
Regions Traversed: Western Desert, Central Australia

AYERS ROCK RESORT (Yulara): modern settlement with a resort style atmosphere and prices to match. Interesting settlement architecturally, but rather soulless. Excellent Uluru National Park information centre (browse here before visiting the park); interesting sand-hill lookouts giving distant views towards Uluru. Hotels, stores, fuel. Stock up here (better in Alice Springs) before heading west.

Uluru National Park: splendid national park containing two of Australia's greatest landmarks - Uluru and Kata Tjuta - as well as preserving extensive tracts of sand dune country, and protecting a significant part of the Pitjantjatjara culture. No camping allowed.

Sand dunes line the road, supporting extensive tracts of spinifex with various shrubs, including mulga and grevilleas. Good views westward towards Kata Tjuta (The Olgas); good view eastward towards Uluru (Ayers Rock).

Lookout provides good views towards the southern face of Kata Tjuta, especially the southern domes and the Liru Wall. Northerly aspect not good for photography; early mornings or late afternoons best.

Kata Tjuta: one of the scenic wonders of the world.

Numerous domes of conglomerate rock rise vertically, some reaching over 500m above the ground. Access somewhat restricted nowadays due to the secret/sacred nature of the site. (Uninitiated Pitjantjatjara people would be speared in the leg or killed if they ventured to these places. Aboriginal law is still very strong in this part of the country.)

Sunset Viewing Area: well worth visiting, the sunset here is as good as at Uluru without the 'circus feel'.

Olga Gorge: spectacular chasm set between two giant domes. An easy walk that is awesome in its power (if no tourist buses are there) - try to experience it alone.

Valley of the Winds: also spectacular and well worth visiting. Numerous photographic opportunities. Good walking trails and lookouts.

Petermann Aboriginal Land: home of Pitjantjatjara-speaking people. Permit required for entry.

Sand dunes support extensive tracts of spinifex, with an overstorey of desert oaks, an attractive she-oak with a pendulous crown. These trees are very photogenic. Near Kata Tjuta there are excellent eastward views towards the domes.

Plains support tracts of spinifex with desert oaks. Occasional low hills are seen, especially to the south - this is the eastern end of the Petermann Range complex. Numerous, normally dry, streams with sandy beds and river red gum-lined banks cross the plains. In this country they tend to be known by their Pitjantjatjara names, viz: Armstrong Creek (Karu Pultanya) and Hull River (Karu Kali).

Low hills located near the road are significant in the wild plum dreaming; locally known as Arrnguli-arrnguli.
Chirnside Creek: nearby is Puta Puta, a country camp (no

access). Ridge south-east of crossing known as Ituntu as is a nearby soak.

Ranges line the road forming part of the Petermann Ranges; in places impressive bluffs and steep talus slopes can be seen. Country hereabout is dominated by mulga shrublands with spinifex on the hillslopes.

Lasseters Cave: (locally known as Tjunti) small cave set into sandstone rock; place where Harold Lasseter, of the famous gold reef, died. Cave and a plaque located south of road - worth visiting. Camping and water available. Range to the south called Curd Range; north-west runs Mananya Ridge. Distant northern range known as Piultarana. The nearby Hull River (Karu Kali) is tree-lined and pleasant.

DOCKER RIVER: locally known as Kaltukatjara, home to Pitjantjatjara and Ngaanyatjarra-speaking people. Settlement surrounded by ranges; gap in the southern range known as Livingstone Pass. A spread-out and unstructured township, it offers only limited facilities. Fuel.

Rebecca Creek area: very attractive range country in this vicinity. North, near the border crossing, lies Mt Taylor. East of Rebecca Creek lies the western end of the Petermann Ranges; westward lies the eastern end of the Schwerin Mural Crescent which lines the road for a short distance. Kuntuntari country camp is located nearby (no access).

Plains support tracts of mulga shrublands with a grassy understorey. Occasional good views eastward to the distant Petermann Ranges (Dean Range) and excellent views northward to the Schwerin Mural Crescent.

GILES: weather station settlement. Nearby is a roadhouse facility (just north of the intersection), while north of the station is Warakurna, a largish Aboriginal community (no access without a permit). These settlements are set at the foot of the Rawlinson Ranges. Basic accommodation, limited stores, fuel.

Warburton Aboriginal Land is home to a significant number of Ngaanyatjarra-speaking people whose occupation extends back for thousands of generations. This land, never having been occupied nor settled by non-Aborigines, still has strong cultural and sacred links for the people; Aboriginal Law is strong here. Permit required for entry.

Sand plains form an outlier of the Great Sandy Desert dunefield (herein considered part of the Western Desert). Extensive sandy flats and sand dunes common. Acacia shrublands dominate the landscape.

Breakaways line the road offering fair views from tops of rises.

Low range of rocks lies west of the road; of minor interest to the traveller.

Undulating country forms part of the northerly section of the nearby Warburton Ranges; low rocky hills and rises offering fair views. Towards the south the main Warburton Range can be seen. Area supports minor tracts of mulga woodlands.

Warburton Ranges: moderately high hills and ranges with intervening lowland valleys; quite scenic in the afternoon light. Acacia shrublands and woodlands dominate.

WARBURTON: locally known as Mirlirrtjarra, a sizeable community of predominantly Ngaanyatjarra-speaking people. Adjacent to the settlement is a roadhouse facility. Basic accommodation, limited stores, fuel.

MAP 52 WILUNA-CARNEGIE STATION-WILUNA
via Wongawol Station

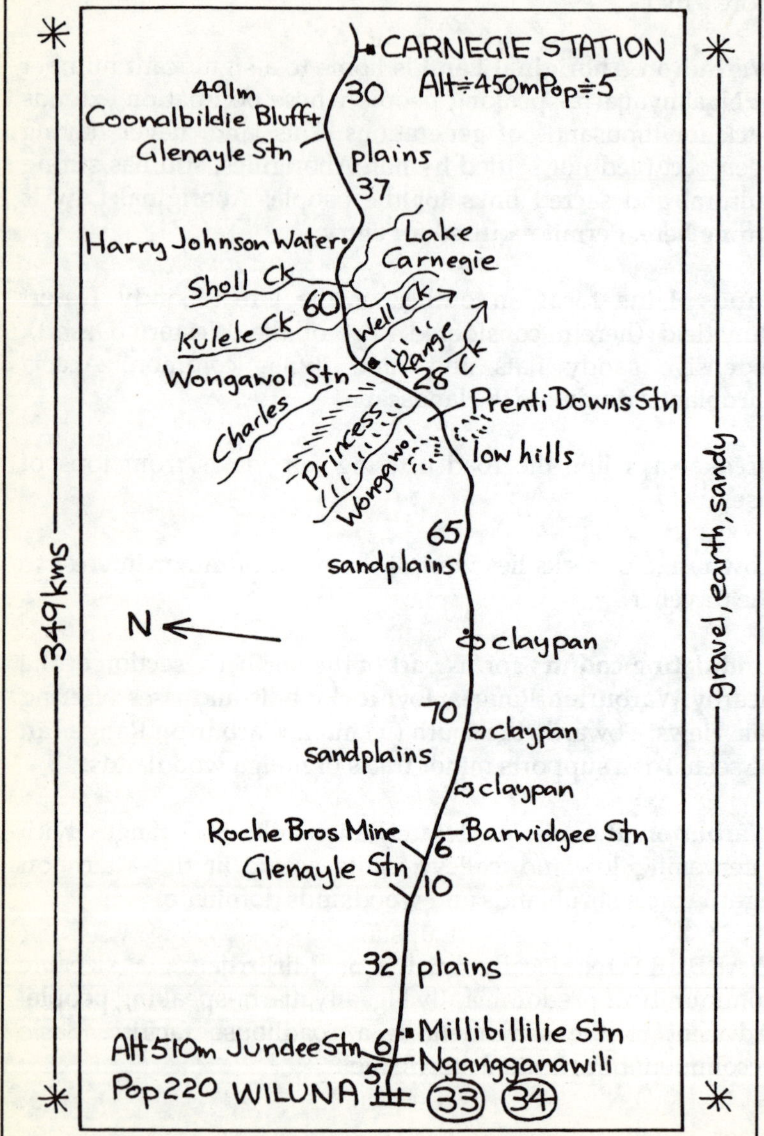

MAP 52 WILUNA-CARNEGIE STATION-WILUNA via Wongawol Station

Grade 3

Total Distance: 349km
Average Vehicles per day: 3-5 Carnegie Station (May to October)/1 every 3 to 5 days in summer!
Regions Traversed: Goldfields

CARNEGIE STATION: working cattle station located at the western end of the Gunbarrel Highway. Camping available. Limited stores, fuel.
Plains support extensive tracts of mulga shrublands with a grassy understorey. At intervals low sandstone bluffs and ranges can be seen. The hills stand 60 to 100m above the plains.

Harry Johnson Water (Mingle Pool): small waterhole; rustic picnic facilities; good camping.
Lake Carnegie, a large salt lake partially covered with saltbush, lies south of the road in the vicinity of Kulele Creek. Patches of stony plains hereabouts. Open mulga shrublands dominate the landscape.

Wongawol Station: working station; no facilities. Stone building is of interest, once used as a fort during early days of occupation.

Princess Range: low but upstanding rocky range with flat, stony valleys; quite scenic in the afternoon light. Sparse covering of mulga, etc.
Low hills (the ones near the Prenti Downs turn-off are known as the Wellington Range) appear at intervals near the road. Fair view from top of rise where road crosses small hill. Mulga shrublands with a grassy understorey are very

MAP 53 CARNEGIESTATION-WARBURTON-CARNEGIE STATION via Gunbarrel Highway

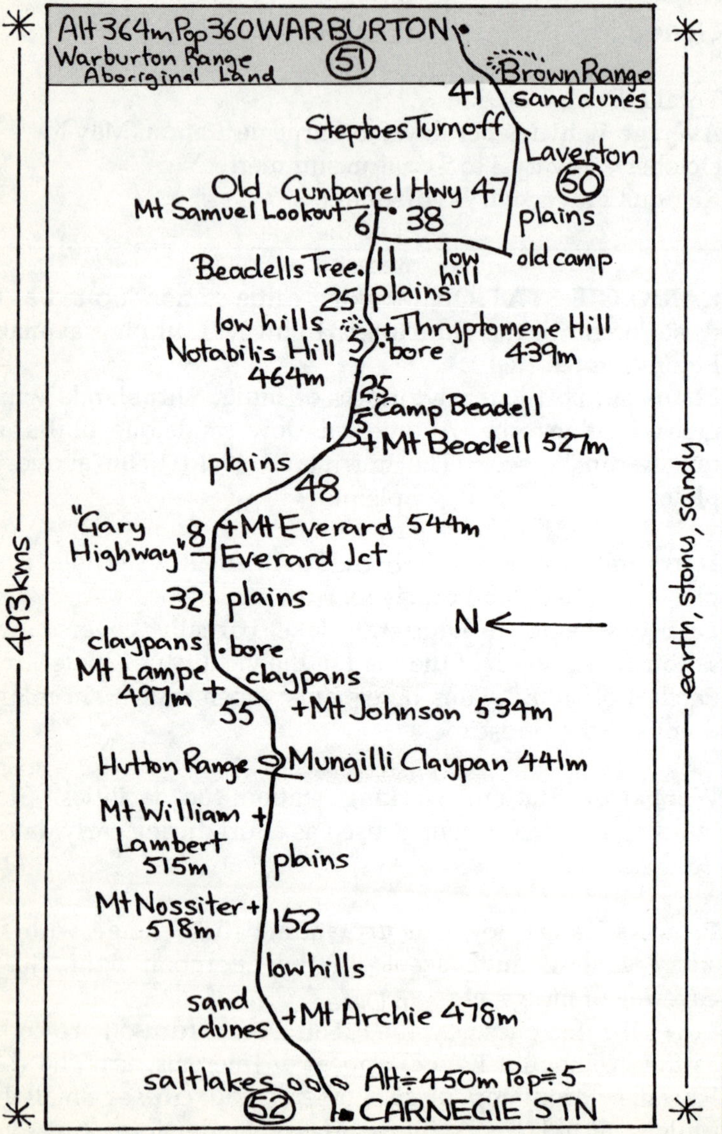

common.
Sand plains seem to stretch on forever. Mulga shrublands (some sparse) also seem endless; only the understorey changes from grassy, to saltbushes, to spinifex.
Claypan crosses the road providing a patch of open country. Worth stopping for a look.
Sand plains support tracts of mulga shrublands, often in conjunction with low eucalypt shrubs (Kingsmill mallees). Spinifex common in the understorey. At intervals, small claypans can be seen south of the road. Numerous grids and windmills provide some interest.
Plains and occasional low rises support vast tracts of mulga. Very fair views of nothing in particular from the tops of rises.

Millibillilie Station: working station; no facilities.

WILUNA: interesting old gold mining town which was once home to thousands of people; nowadays undergoing a small mining resurgance. Many interesting buildings; some photogenic. Nearby is the old Wiluna Mines with many photogenic ruins - definitely worth visiting. Hotel, store, fuel. Stock up here if heading east.

MAP 53 CARNEGIE STATION-WARBURTON-CARNEGIE STATION

via Gunbarrel Highway

Grade 4

Total Distance: 493km
Average Vehicles per day: 3-5 at Carnegie Station (May to October)/1 every 3 to 5 days in summer!
Regions Traversed: Gibson Desert, Western Desert

WARBURTON: sizeable Aboriginal community of predominantly Ngaanyatjarra-speaking people. Adjacent to the settlement is the Milyirrtjarra Roadhouse. Basic accommodation, limited stores, fuel.

Warburton Range Aboriginal Land: traditional homelands for Ngaanyatjarra people. Permit required for entry.

Brown Range: low range overlooking the Elder Creek valley. Open spinifex country.
Sand dunes, plains and rises support open tracts of mulga and spinifex.

Steptoes Turn-off: locality only; no facilities.
Plains support extensive tracts of mulga with a spinifex understorey.
Low hill offers fair views across the mulga. This is roughly the eastern edge of the Gibson Desert.

Mt Samuel Lookout: good views from atop a stony hill; worth visiting.

Beadells Tree: plaque placed by Len Beadell, the surveyor who constructed this and other Western Desert roads. Worth a quick look. Desert oaks common hereabouts.
Plains support extensive tracts of mulga shrublands with a grassy understorey.
Low hills offer fair views. Westward are some sand dunes.

Bore: water available after vigorous pumping. Country hereabout is quite attractive.

Notabilis Hill: reasonable views across the plains; other low hills are visible.

Camp Beadell: (500m off the road) shady camping area; water.

Mt Beadell: good views from the summit; interesting

clifflines. Good photographic opportunities for Gunbarrel Highway shots. Stony country around here.
Plains support extensive tracts of mulga with a spinifex understorey.
Mt Everard: interesting hill; well worth the climb.

Everard Junction: locality only; no facilities. Site of another Beadell plaque
Plains support tracts of mulga shrublands and spinifex.
Claypans line the road for a short distance, providing some open country. Interesting area in which to walk. Do not lose sight of the vehicle!
Bore (water). Nearby is Alexander Springs.
Claypans near the road make a change from looking at mulga.

Mungilli Claypan: interesting large claypan worth exploring on foot. Never lose sight of the vehicle or the road. Nearby is the Eagle Road intersection, a mining exploration road.
Plains support extensive tracts of mulga shrublands with a predominantly grassy understorey. Mt Nossiter roughly marks the western edge of the Gibson Desert.
Low hills line the road at intervals, with sand plains and dunes occupying the intervening plains. Vegetation somewhat sparser here than further east. Acacia shrubs and spinifex dominate.
Sand dunes line the road, an outlier of the Great Sandy Desert (it could just as easily be an outlier of the Great Victoria Desert). Spinifex common with a variety of shrubs, including acacias.
Saltlakes, with some low dunes, lie in an arc just beyond the road; various saltbushes dominate this area. Eastward are plains covered with mulga. The lakes country marks the edge of station properties.

CARNEGIE STATION: working cattle station with facilities for travellers. Camping available. Limited stores, fuel.

PART THREE: APPENDICES

APPENDIX ONE

GLOSSARY

Belah: a tree species of *Casuarina* exhibiting needle-like branchlets and a rather shaggy and untidy crown; found on some sand plains.

Bluebush: an attractive blue-tinged low shrub often found growing with saltbush; popular sheep fodder.

Breakaway: local Western Australian term describing a long, low escarpment that often separates a higher level plain or plateau from a lower level plain. Height rarely more than 30m.

Canegrass: a 'reed-like' grass that grows in semi-arid areas on inundated land.

Claypan: a clay-covered depression that holds water after rain.

Collapsed doline: a depression in the surface of the land whereby that surface has collapsed into a cave cavity beneath.

Coolabah: a species of eucalypt found on floodplain country.

Cypress pine: a species of *Callitris* with a Christmas tree appearance found growing on rocky arid hills (often with a gnarled appearance), or on sand dunes.

Desert oak: a tree species of *Casuarina*, often large, with a graceful rounded crown; common in the Amadeus Lowland and parts of the Western Desert.

Flat-iron: a roughly triangular-shaped hillside bounded by gorges and located on tilted rock strata. Common along the western side of the Flinders Ranges.

Gibber: small stone found scattered over plains.
Gidgee: a species of *Acacia* found on flood-plain country, drainage lines, etc.
Granite plain: plain exhibiting slabs, outcrops or domes of granite; elsewhere sandy.
Halophytes: salt tolerant shrubby plants.
Jump-ups: (referred to as breakaways in the Coober Pedy district) name given to low ranges, isolated hills or low tablelands exhibiting a flat-top or upper surface and bounded by steep sides. Would normally be called breakaways in Western Australia, but are different features to the 'breakaways' defined above.
Lake plain: plain, often of alluvium (flood-deposits) adjacent to a lake.
Lignum: a thicket of the species *Muehlenbeckia* which grows adjacent to outback waterholes and on flood-plain country
Local relief: difference in height between a hill top and adjacent valley, or between high and low points in undulating country.
Lunette: a crescent-shaped dune located on the downwind side of a lake bed.
Mallee: either a multi-stemmed shrub of a eucalypt species, or the name given to the countryside dominated by the same.
Mill: Western Australian term for windmill.
Mulga: a very widespread species of *Acacia* exhibiting either a shrubby or treed form found growing on all sorts of plains. Very common throughout the Central and Western Outback.
Pedimont plain: gently sloping plain found adjacent to high and thrusted ranges; common on the western side of the Flinders Ranges.
Pool: Western Australian term for waterhole.
Quartz blow: an area of stony plain or rises dominated by white quartz. Has the appearance of recently fallen hailstones.
River red gum: a species of eucalypt characterised by gum-like bark; often possesses a large trunk. Very common along river channels, sandy creek beds and waterholes.
Saltbush: common low-growing shrub with a bluish-grey

appearance found in the understorey of many woodlands and shrublands, or dominating the landscape in its own right, e.g. on the Nullarbor Plain. May grow in conjunction with bluebush.

Sand-hill canegrass: a species of *Zygochloa* characterised by a tangled mass of unattractive herbage, found growing upon sand dunes; e.g. Simpson Desert.

Saltlake: lake bed covered with a surface of salt. In some area, e.g. Western Australia, these lakes may support vegetation such as saltbush, halophytes, etc.

Sand plain: plain covered with a surface of sand, or exhibiting sand dunes and intervening interdunal areas of swales. In the south-west corner of the Western Outback is a typical Western Australian version of sand plains: light covered deep sands usually supporting a dense growth of shrubs and heaths.

Snappy gum: attractive small white-barked eucalypt common on the stony hills of the Pilbara and nearby districts.

Stony plain: flat to undulating plain covered with stone or gibbers; often found in jump-up country or adjacent to ranges.

Undulating country: plains country exhibiting low rises, ridges or undulations.

Western myall: attractive tree species of *Acacia* exhibiting a flattish crown somewhat reminiscent of the trees of the African savanna. Saltbush or bluebush very common in the understorey.

LIST OF TOOLS AND VEHICLE SPARES

Vehicle Spares

2/3 spare wheels with tyres
1/2 jacks
wooden base for jack
tow rope
fan belt
radiator/heater hoses
spare ignition key
set of fuses
2 spark plugs
light globes
headlamp
distributor points
condenser
distributor cap
rotor
coil
4 litres of engine oil
brake fluid
lubricating spray
tyre pump
fuel pump kit
insulating tape
plastic hand pump
silicone rubber gasket
radiator leak sealant
a few small corks (for holes)
carburettor kit
lengths of wire
air filter
oil filter
vulcanising clamp
patches
2 tyre levers
valve key
clutch cylinder kit
brake cylinder kit
air pressure gauge
spare nuts and bolts
workshop manual
bleeding spanner
2m plastic hose
2m low-tension wire
2m mid-tension wire
jerry can
jumper leads
fire extinguisher

Tools

hacksaw
soft hammer
set of ring/open spanners
feeler gauge
set of screwdrivers
pliers
pointy pliers
file
cold
chisel
lube gun
socket set and handle
wire brush
rag

A SUGGESTED LIST OF PERSONAL REQUIREMENTS, CAMPING EQUIPMENT, FOOD, ETC.

Camping Equipment

tent or bedrolls (swags)
spade
grate
toasting fork, griller
camping stove
gas bottle and fittings
gas lamp and spare mantles
camp oven
frying pan
billy
aluminium foil
matches
spare plastic bags
plastic bowls with lids
knives
forks
spoons and teaspoons
spatula
sharp knife
can opener
tongs
tea towel
oven mitts
chopping board
plates
bowls
tea mugs
bucket
detergent
pan scourers
washing line
pegs
scissors
folding chairs
table
hand broom
torches (one for everybody)
Esky
drinking water bottles
drinking water
needle and thread
old rug or tarpaulin

Toiletries

soap and container
hard-water soap
towel,hand towel
shampoo, deodorant
detergent, shaving gear
ladies requisites, nail clippers
tweezers, toothbrush and paste

Bedding

sleeping mat
thermal mat
sleeping bag or sheets,
blankets
pillow

Clothing

few shirts or T-shirts
lots of socks, undies
skivvies
woollen jumper
few pants, perhaps shorts
shady hat
boots and perhaps slippers
overalls
bathers

If wintertime:

down jacket or windcheater
scarf
beanie
flannelette singlet
long johns
gloves
raincoat

Personal items

money
cashcard, travellers cheques
wallet
licence and
registration papers
address book
pens and pencils, notebook
maps and guide books
necessary permits
camera and film
spare camera battery
binoculars
Medicare cards/
Health Care card

Medical Kit

tweezers
insect bite applicator
Insect repellent - RID
pain killers
antiseptic cream
band-aids and bandages
burn cream
small scissors
personal requirements
salt tablets
sunscreen 15+

Food

muesli or breakfast cereal
bread or dry biscuits
tea or tea bags, coffee
powdered milk, sugar
margarine, cheese
peanut butter, jam, spreads
sardines, tinned fish
baked beans, etc
dried tomatoes
dried beans, lentils/dried peas
self-raising flour, tinned meat
stock cubes, selection of herbs/
spices, baking powder
cooking oil, dried fruits
potatoes, onions, carrots,
pumpkin, parsley, garlic,
lemons, oranges, apples pears
bananas

include a few tins of cooked vegetables, meals, etc, for your emergency rations (these do not require water for cooking).

Stock up when possible on perishable items, bread and meat.

The above items will keep for a fair while, especially during cooler weather, saving on refrigeration. If wrapped in newspaper and stored in a cool place, cheese, margarine, etc, will keep for a week or so.

Keep camping items in a lidded box where possible, and store cooking implements in plastic bags to avoid soiling other items with charcoal, sand, etc.
Keep clothes in a heavy-duty plastic bag with a fold-over top; it makes it easy to find stray items without having to remove everything from a case.

Bedrolls (swags) means your bed can stay permanently made and also means you do not have to erect a tent each night. Save the tent for extended camps. A sleeping mat means you do not have to pump up air mattresses each night.

Before beginning the day's travels, cover the load with an old rug or tarpaulin to reduce the dust; this item can be used as a means of producing shade over the car (lay over roof and hold in place with the doors) at lunchtime stops, or when going for walks.

Store camera, film and binoculars in a cool place within plastic bags; this will reduce the likelihood of dust entering the equipment.

FURTHER READING

Absalom, J., *Safe Outback Travel,* Five Mile Press, 1987, Melbourne - highly recommended for its excellent hints to get you out of trouble.
Andrews, B., *Explore Australia's Great Inland,* Child and Henry, 1986, Sydney - useful for overall planning of your journey.
Blombery, A., *The Living Centre of Australia,* Kangaroo Press,

1985, Sydney - recommended for recognising plant and animal life.

Cowan, J. & Beard, C., *Starlight's Trail*, Doubleday, 1985, Sydney - interesting and colourful book about Cooper Creek, Strzelecki Track areas.

Gerritson, J., *Tibooburra-Corner Country*, Tibooburra Press - good local history.

Hardy, B., *Lament for the Barkindji*, Rigby, 1976, Adelaide - good Aboriginal history about western New South Wales.

Honeywill, B. & Plumb, T., *Wild Country*, Sunbird Publishing, 1990, Brisbane - a book to get you interested in travelling.

Idriess, I., *The Cattle King*, Angus and Robertson, 1951, Sydney - an interesting narrative about Kidman.

Learmouth, N. & A., *Regional Landscapes of Australia*, Angus and Robertson, 1971 - detailed descriptions of regional geography.

McKellar, H., *Matya-Mundi*, Cunnamulla Aust. Native Welfare Association, 1984 - excellent history of Aborigines in south-west Queensland.

Osterstock, A., *Andamooka Opal*, Roling Press, 1983 - a good local history.

Readers Digest, *Discover Australia*, 1991, Sydney - interesting and colourful details of Australia's regional landscapes.

Read, I., *The Bush: A Guide to the Vegetated Landscapes of Australia*, Reed Books, 1987, Sydney - detailed descriptions of Australia's vegetation and habitats.

Royal Automobile Association, *Touring the Flinders Ranges*, RAA, 1983, Adelaide - excellent detailed coverage of this region.

Sheedy, B., *Outback on a Budget*, Viking O'Neil, Melbourne - informative book on how to travel the outback cheaply.

Slatyer, R. & Perry, A., *Arid Lands of Australia*, ANU Press, 1969, Canberra - informative book about Australia's dry country.

Also refer to outback handbooks published by the motoring organisations: NRMA, RACQ, RAC. They also have booklets on opal mining, tours, etc, as well as many district maps.

SERVICES GRID AND SETTLEMENT INDEX

All listed settlements have fuel, (unless marked thus *), telephone and water. Note that stores, spares or other services may be limited in the smaller settlements, and that diesel fuel may not be available in small settlements or at homesteads servicing tourists - check beforehand.

SETTLEMENTS/TOWNS	Agnew	Alice Springs	Auski Roadhouse	Ayers Rock Resort	Balladonia	Barradale Roadhouse	Beltana Roadhouse	Billabong Roadhouse	Binnu	Border Village
BASIC REPAIRS/SERVICE		X	X	X	X	X	X	X	X	X
ROAD SERVICES		X		X						
HOTEL	X	X		X	X			X		
MOTEL		X		X	X					X
CARAVAN PARK/ CAMPING AREA		X	X	X	X	X		X		X
STORE		X		X	X	X	X	X	X	X
MEALS & SNACKS	X	X	X	X	X	X	X	X	X	X
POST OFFICE/AGENCY		X		X			X			
POLICE		X		X						X
CLINIC/HOSPITAL		X		X						
PUBLIC/TRANSPORT		X	X	X	X	X	X	X	X	X
BANK/AGENCY		X		X						
MAP NUMBER	32 33 36	4 10 12 16 17 18	29 30	14 51	22 23	39	5	37	37	21

SERVICES GRID AND SETTLEMENT INDEX

All listed settlements have fuel, (unless marked thus *), telephone and water. Note that stores, spares or other services may be limited in the smaller settlements, and that diesel fuel may not be available in small settlements or at homesteads servicing tourists - check beforehand.

SETTLEMENTS/TOWNS	Broad Arrow	Bullabulling	Cadney Park	Caiguna	Camp Curlewis*	Capricorn Roadhouse	Carnarvon	Carnegie Station	Ceduna	Cobra Station
BASIC REPAIRS/SERVICE			X	X		X	X	X	X	
ROAD SERVICES			X			X	X		X	
HOTEL	X	X				X	X		X	
MOTEL			X	X			X		X	
CARAVAN PARK/CAMPING AREA			X	X	X	X	X	X	X	X
STORE				X	X	X	X	X	X	X
MEALS & SNACKS			X	X		X	X		X	
POST OFFICE/AGENCY					CHECK BEFOREHAND				X	
POLICE										
CLINIC/HOSPITAL							X		X	
PUBLIC/TRANSPORT	X	X	X	X		X	X		X	
BANK/AGENCY							X		X	
MAP NUMBER	51	31	3, 8	22	48	29	38, 42	52, 53	20	42

SERVICES GRID AND SETTLEMENT INDEX

All listed settlements have fuel, (unless marked thus *), telephone and water. Note that stores, spares or other services may be limited in the smaller settlements, and that diesel fuel may not be available in small settlements or at homesteads servicing tourists - check beforehand.

SETTLEMENTS/TOWNS	Cocklebiddy	Coober Pedy	Coolgardie	Copley	Coral Bay	Cue	Curtin Springs	Dalwallinu	Dampier	Denham
BASIC REPAIRS/SERVICE	X	X	X	X		X		X	X	X
ROAD SERVICES		X	X	X				X		
HOTEL	X	X	X	X		X	X	X	X	X
MOTEL	X	X	X		X		X	X	X	X
CARAVAN PARK/ CAMPING AREA	X	X	X	X	X	X	X	X	X	X
STORE	X	X	X	X	X	X		X	X	X
MEALS & SNACKS	X	X	X	X	X	X	X	X	X	X
POST OFFICE/AGENCY		X	X	X		X		X	X	X
POLICE		X	X			X		X	X	X
CLINIC/HOSPITAL		X	X			X		X	X	X
PUBLIC/TRANSPORT	X	X	X	X	X	X	X	X	X	X
BANK/AGENCY		X	X			X		X	X	X
MAP NUMBER	22	2 3 8	23 31	5	45	27 28	13 14	27	40	44

SERVICES GRID AND SETTLEMENT INDEX

All listed settlements have fuel, (unless marked thus *), telephone and water. Note that stores, spares or other services may be limited in the smaller settlements, and that diesel fuel may not be available in small settlements or at homesteads servicing tourists - check beforehand.

SETTLEMENTS/TOWNS	Docker River	Erldunda	Esperance	Eucla	Exmouth	Finke	Fortescue Roadhouse	Fowlers Bay	Gascoyne Junction	Geraldton
BASIC REPAIRS/SERVICE		X	X	X	X		X		X	X
ROAD SERVICES			X		X					X
HOTEL			X	X	X		X		X	X
MOTEL		X	X	X	X					X
CARAVAN PARK/ CAMPING AREA		X	X	X	X		X	X		X
STORE		X	X	X	X	X	X	X	X	X
MEALS & SNACKS		X	X	X	X		X		X	X
POST OFFICE/AGENCY			X		X				X	X
POLICE			X	X	X				X	X
CLINIC/HOSPITAL			X	X	X				X	X
PUBLIC/TRANSPORT	X	X	X	X	X		X			X
BANK/AGENCY			X		X					X
MAP NUMBER	51	4 14		21	45	10 11	39 40	20	42	35 37

SERVICES GRID AND SETTLEMENT INDEX

All listed settlements have fuel, (unless marked thus *), telephone and water. Note that stores, spares or other services may be limited in the smaller settlements, and that diesel fuel may not be available in small settlements or at homesteads servicing tourists - check beforehand.

SETTLEMENTS/ TOWNS	Gibson	Giles	Glendambo	Glen Helen	Grass Patch	Hawker	Hermannsberg	Iron Knob	Ipolera	Kalbarri	Kalgoorlie
BASIC REPAIRS/SER.			X			X	X	X		X	X
ROAD SERVICES			X			X	X			X	X
HOTEL	X			X		X	X	X		X	X
MOTEL	X		X	X		X	X	X		X	X
CARAVAN PARK/ CAMPING AREA		X	X	X		X		X	X	X	X
STORE	X	X	X	X	X	X	X	X	X	X	X
MEALS & SNACKS	X	X	X	X		X		X		X	X
P.O./AGENCY			X			X		X		X	X
POLICE						X	X	X		X	X
CLINIC/HOSPITAL						X		X		X	X
PUBLIC/TRANSPORT	X	X	X		X	X		X		X	X
BANK/AGENCY						X		X		X	X
MAP NUMBER	24	51	1 2	16	24	5	17	19 25	17	37	23 31

SERVICES GRID AND SETTLEMENT INDEX

All listed settlements have fuel, (unless marked thus *), telephone and water. Note that stores, spares or other services may be limited in the smaller settlements, and that diesel fuel may not be available in small settlements or at homesteads servicing tourists - check beforehand.

SETTLEMENTS/TOWNS	Kambalda	Karratha	Karratha Roadhouse	Kimba	Kings Canyon	Kings Creek	Kookynie	Kulgera	Kumarina	Kyancutta
BASIC REPAIRS/SERVICE	X	X	X	X				X	X	
ROAD SERVICES	X	X		X					X	
HOTEL	X	X		X			X	X	X	X
MOTEL		X		X	X			X	X	
CARAVAN PARK/ CAMPING AREA	X	X		X	X	X		X	X	
STORE	X	X	X	X	X	X		X	X	
MEALS & SNACKS	X	X	X	X	X		X	X	X	X
POST OFFICE/AGENCY	X	X		X					X	
POLICE	X	X		X				X	X	
CLINIC/HOSPITAL	X	X		X					X	
PUBLIC/TRANSPORT	X	X	X	X	X	X		X	X	X
BANK/AGENCY	X	X		X					X	
MAP NUMBER	23	40	40	19 26	15	15	32	3 4 11 13	28 29	19

SERVICES GRID AND SETTLEMENT INDEX

All listed settlements have fuel, (unless marked thus *), telephone and water. Note that stores, spares or other services may be limited in the smaller settlements, and that diesel fuel may not be available in small settlements or at homesteads servicing tourists - check beforehand.

SETTLEMENTS/TOWNS	Lake King	Laverton	Leigh Creek	Leinster	Leonora	Lyndhurst	Madura	Marble Bar	Marla	Marree
BASIC REPAIRS/SERVICE	X	X	X	X	X	X	X	X	X	X
ROAD SERVICES		X	X		X				X	
HOTEL		X			X	X	X	X	X	X
MOTEL	X	X	X	X	X		X	X	X	
CARAVAN PARK/ CAMPING AREA		X		X	X		X	X	X	X
STORE	X	X	X	X	X	X		X	X	X
MEALS & SNACKS	X	X	X	X	X	X	X	X	X	X
POST OFFICE/AGENCY	X	X	X	X	X			X	X	X
POLICE		X	X	X	X			X	X	X
CLINIC/HOSPITAL		X	X	X	X			X	X	X
PUBLIC/TRANSPORT		X	X	X	X	X	X		X	X
BANK/AGENCY		X	X	X	X				X	
MAP NUMBER	24	32 50	5	32 33 36	32	5 6	21 22	30 49	3 7	6

SERVICES GRID AND SETTLEMENT INDEX

All listed settlements have fuel, (unless marked thus *), telephone and water. Note that stores, spares or other services may be limited in the smaller settlements, and that diesel fuel may not be available in small settlements or at homesteads servicing tourists - check beforehand.

SETTLEMENTS/TOWNS	Maryvale Station	Meekatharra	Menzies	Minilya Roadhouse	Minnipa	Mintabie	Monkey Mia	Mt Augustus	Mt Dare	Mt Ebenezer
BASIC REPAIRS/SERVICE	X	X	X	X	X					X
ROAD SERVICES					X					
HOTEL		X	X		X					
MOTEL		X					X	X		X
CARAVAN PARK/ CAMPING AREA		X	X	X	X		X	X	X	
STORE	X	X	X		X	X	X	X	X	X
MEALS & SNACKS		X	X		X	X	X	X	X	X
POST OFFICE/AGENCY		X	X		X					
POLICE		X	X							
CLINIC/HOSPITAL		X								
PUBLIC/TRANSPORT		X	X	X	X		X			X
BANK/AGENCY		X								
MAP NUMBER	10	28 33 43	31 32	38 39 45	19	3	44	42 43	9	14

SERVICES GRID AND SETTLEMENT INDEX

All listed settlements have fuel, (unless marked thus *), telephone and water. Note that stores, spares or other services may be limited in the smaller settlements, and that diesel fuel may not be available in small settlements or at homesteads servicing tourists - check beforehand.

SETTLEMENTS/TOWNS	Mt Ive	Mt Magnet	Mullewa	Mundrabilla	Murchison	Nanga Station	Nanutarra Roadhouse	New Crown Station	Newman	Norseman
BASIC REPAIRS/SERVICE		X	X	X			X		X	X
ROAD SERVICES			X						X	
HOTEL		X	X	X					X	X
MOTEL		X	X	X		X	X		X	X
CARAVAN PARK/ CAMPING AREA	X	X	X	X	X	X	X		X	X
STORE	X	X	X	X	X	X	X		X	X
MEALS & SNACKS		X	X	X	X	X	X		X	X
POST OFFICE/AGENCY		X	X						X	X
POLICE		X	X						X	X
CLINIC/HOSPITAL		X	X						X	X
PUBLIC/TRANSPORT		X	X	X		X	X		X	X
BANK/AGENCY		X	X						X	X
MAP NUMBER	25 26	27 35 36	35 41	21	41	44	39 46	10 11	29	23 24

SERVICES GRID AND SETTLEMENT INDEX

All listed settlements have fuel, (unless marked thus *), telephone and water. Note that stores, spares or other services may be limited in the smaller settlements, and that diesel fuel may not be available in small settlements or at homesteads servicing tourists - check beforehand.

SETTLEMENTS/TOWNS	Northampton	Nullagine	Nullarbor	Nundroo	Onslow	Oodnadatta	Ora Banda	Overlander Roadhouse	Pannawonica	Paraburdoo
BASIC REPAIRS/SERVICE	X		X	X	X	X		X	CLOSED MINING TOWN	X
ROAD SERVICES			X	X	X	X				X
HOTEL	X	X		X	X					X
MOTEL	X		X	X	X	X		X		
CARAVAN PARK/ CAMPING AREA	X	X	X	X	X	X	X	X		X
STORE	X	X		X	X	X	X	X		X
MEALS & SNACKS	X		X	X	X	X		X		X
POST OFFICE/AGENCY	X				X	X				X
POLICE	X				X	X				X
CLINIC/HOSPITAL	X		X		X	X				X
PUBLIC/TRANSPORT	X		X	X		X		X		X
BANK/AGENCY	X				X					X
MAP NUMBER	37	49	20 21	20	39	7 8 9	31	37 39		46

SERVICES GRID AND SETTLEMENT INDEX

All listed settlements have fuel, (unless marked thus *), telephone and water. Note that stores, spares or other services may be limited in the smaller settlements, and that diesel fuel may not be available in small settlements or at homesteads servicing tourists - check beforehand.

SETTLEMENTS/TOWNS	Parachilna	Paynes Find	Penong	Pimba	Point Samson	Poochera	Port Augusta	Port Hedland	Quorn	Roebourne
BASIC REPAIRS/SERVICE			X	X		X	X	X	X	X
ROAD SERVICES							X	X	X	X
HOTEL	X	X	X	X		X	X	X	X	X
MOTEL				X	X		X	X	X	X
CARAVAN PARK/ CAMPING AREA				X	X	X	X	X	X	X
STORE			X	X	X	X	X	X	X	X
MEALS & SNACKS	X	X	X	X	X	X	X	X	X	X
POST OFFICE/AGENCY			X			X	X	X	X	X
POLICE			X			X	X	X	X	X
CLINIC/HOSPITAL							X	X	X	X
PUBLIC/TRANSPORT	X	X	X	X		X	X	X	X	X
BANK/AGENCY							X	X	X	X
MAP NUMBBER	5	27 34	20	1	40	19	1 5 19	30 40 49	5	40 48

SERVICES GRID AND SETTLEMENT INDEX

All listed settlements have fuel, (unless marked thus *), telephone and water. Note that stores, spares or other services may be limited in the smaller settlements, and that diesel fuel may not be available in small settlements or at homesteads servicing tourists - check beforehand.

SETTLEMENTS/ TOWNS	Ross River	Salmon Gums	Sandstone	South Hedland	Southern Cross	Stuarts Well	Tarcoola	Tom Price	Tuckanurra*	Tjukayirla Roadhouse	Useless Loop
BASIC REPAIRS/SER.		X		X	X	X	X	X		X	
ROAD SERVICES		X		X				X			
HOTEL		X	X	X	X		X	X			
MOTEL	X			X	X	X		X			
CARAVAN PARK/ CAMPING AREA	X	X	X	X	X	X		X	X	X	
STORE		X	X	X	X	X	X	X	X		
MEALS & SNACKS	X	X	X	X	X	X	X	X		X	
POST OFFICE/AGENCY		X	X	X	X			X			CLOSED MINING TOWN
POLICE			X	X	X			X			
CLINIC/HOSPITAL				X	X		X	X			
PUBLIC/TRANSPORT		X		X	X	X	X	X	X		
BANK/AGENCY				X	X			X			
MAP NUMBER	18	24	34 36	40	31	4	2	46 47 48	28	50	

SERVICES GRID AND SETTLEMENT INDEX

All listed settlements have fuel, (unless marked thus *), telephone and water. Note that stores, spares or other services may be limited in the smaller settlements, and that diesel fuel may not be available in small settlements or at homesteads servicing tourists - check beforehand.

SETTLEMENTS/TOWNS	Wallace Rockhole	Warburton	Whim Creek	Whyalla	Wickham	Widgiemooltha	William Creek	Wiluna	Wirrulla
BASIC REPAIRS/SERVICE				X	X			X	X
ROAD SERVICES				X					X
HOTEL			X	X	X		X	X	X
MOTEL				X	X			X	
CARAVAN PARK/ CAMPING AREA	X		X		X			X	X
STORE	X	X		X	X	X	X	X	X
MEALS & SNACKS			X	X	X	X	X	X	X
POST OFFICE/AGENCY				X	X				X
POLICE				X	X			X	X
CLINIC/HOSPITAL				X	X			X	
PUBLIC/TRANSPORT		X	X	X	X	X	X		X
BANK/AGENCY				X	X				
MAP NUMBER	17	50 51 53	40	19	40	23	6 7	33 34 52	19 20 25

SERVICES GRID AND SETTLEMENT INDEX

All listed settlements have fuel, (unless marked thus *), telephone and water. Note that stores, spares or other services may be limited in the smaller settlements, and that diesel fuel may not be available in small settlements or at homesteads servicing tourists - check beforehand.

SETTLEMENTS/TOWNS	Wittenoom	Woomera	Wooramel Roadhouse	Wubin	Wudinna	Yalata Roadhouse	Yalgoo	Yellowdine
BASIC REPAIRS/SERVICE	X	X		X	X	X	X	
ROAD SERVICES		X			X			
HOTEL	X			X	X			
MOTEL	X	X		X	X			X
CARAVAN PARK/ CAMPING AREA	X	X	X		X		X	
STORE	X	X	X	X	X	X	X	
MEALS & SNACKS	X	X	X	X	X	X		X
POST OFFICE/AGENCY	X	X			X			
POLICE		X			X			
CLINIC/HOSPITAL		X			X			
PUBLIC/TRANSPORT	X	X	X	X	X	X	X	X
BANK/AGENCY		X			X			
MAP NUMBER	47 48	1	38	27	19	20	35	31

INDEX

Note: entries in italics denote regional descriptions and major routes.

Notes

Notes

Notes